PRAISE F

"*The Son and Heir* is a chronicle that reads like a compelling novel. It can measure itself with the greatest books in the world."
— Pieter Waterdrinker, *De Telegraaf* (5 stars)

"This is an astonishing book! Once you start reading, you can't put it down."
— Maarten 't Hart, bestselling author of *A Flight of Curlews* and *Bearers of Bad Tidings*

"This is *One Hundred Years of Solitude* from the Low Countries; this is Europe's grief. This is Turgenev."
— David van Reybrouck, *De Correspondent*

"A book to make every writer envious and every reader grateful."
— Chris van der Heijden, *De Groene Amsterdammer*

The Son and Heir

The
Son
and
Heir

A Memoir

Alexander Münninghoff
Translated by Kristen Gehrman

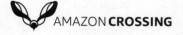

Previously published as *De Stamhouder* by Prometheus Amsterdam in the Netherlands in 2014. Translated from Dutch by Kristen Gehrman. First published in English by Amazon Crossing in 2020.

Published by Amazon Crossing, Seattle

www.apub.com

Amazon, the Amazon logo, and Amazon Crossing are trademarks of Amazon.com, Inc., or its affiliates.

ISBN-13: 9781542004558 (hardcover)
ISBN-10: 1542004551 (hardcover)

ISBN-13: 9781542004541 (paperback)
ISBN-10: 1542004543 (paperback)

Cover design by Jarrod Taylor

Cover photography courtesy of the author's archives

Printed in the United States of America

First edition

For Ellen and Wera

The Münninghoffs: A Twentieth-Century Family

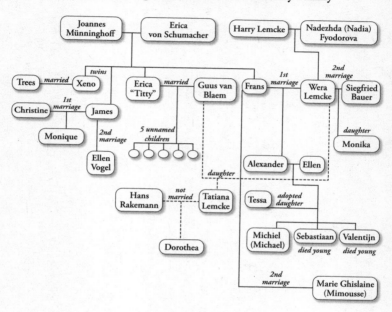

AUTHOR'S NOTE

While writing this memoir, I've changed many of the figures' names, though the events and occurrences are as I recall them.

I was born on April 13, 1944, in Posen, an old Polish city that for centuries had been called Poznań. But when I was born, during a bombardment that seemed to herald the end of time, Posen was a German city, a logistical junction from which Hitler had sent his Nazi troops into the Soviet Union in three waves of attack just one year before. It was a miserable adventure, and Posen paid dearly: gruesome mutilations, the wounded crying out in agony in the barbaric field hospitals, piles of dead loaded onto carts and dumped into trenches. And the endless lines of refugees who only wanted one thing: to get out.

My family was part of that drama. And that is what this book is about. It's about the consequences of the war. It's about a sly grandfather who became—in the most remarkable ways—one of the richest people in Latvia, but who, two days before the war broke out, was forced to leave everything behind and flee to the Netherlands with his Russian wife and four children. It's about a naive father who, out of idealism against the Soviets, went to the eastern front wearing the uniform of the SS, only to be destroyed when he returned to the Netherlands. It's about a mother who, after getting divorced, fled to Germany and was no longer allowed to be my mother. And it's about me, the grandson, the son, and heir.

The Hague, January 2014
Alexander Münninghoff

PART 1

THE SMOKING ROOM

ONE

My first encounter with the secrets that would dominate my life was a discovery I made one lost afternoon in the attic of our house in Voorburg. Behind a few tightly sealed boxes, tucked away beneath a thick hedge of heavy winter coats hung up in mothballs, I found another box way in the back that—strangely enough in hindsight—turned out to be openable. Inside, along with some shirts, pants, and other odds and ends, was a helmet. Jet black and menacingly shiny, it had a black-white-and-red emblem on one side and two bright white lightning bolts on the other. Instinctively, I knew the thing represented a secret. I put it on and skipped downstairs to the smoking room, where the whole family was having drinks before dinner and waiting for the Old Boss to start the daily canasta ritual.

It was 1948, and I was four years old. The helmet came down over my eyes, but if I tipped my head back, as if peeping out of the slit of a bunker, I could just make out what was going on in front of me.

The first person to see me was my mother, Wera. She didn't say a word, but I could tell by the look on her face that I had done something bad. She seemed about to jump up and grab me, but then was overcome with an air of resignation and slouched into the corner of the sofa. The rest of the family, gathered around the table sipping drinks, reacted more strongly. Almost in unison, Omi and Aunt Trees threw their hands over their mouths, and Xeno, my uncle, pointed his finger at me. Guus and Aunt Titty looked at each other and then glared at me, their eyes round as saucers. The only one to let out a chuckle was Dr. Van Tilburg, family physician and friend.

The Old Boss broke the silence. "Frans! Didn't I tell you to throw that junk away?" he barked at my father in that raspy, whispery voice that scared everyone to death. My father had been sitting with his back to the doorway and only saw me after standing up and turning around.

"Bully, take that thing off right now. Where in the world have you been playing? Give it to me!" my father commanded loudly. "Damn it, Wera, can't you keep a better eye on him? Sorry, Father, I hadn't gotten around to it yet. I'll get rid of it right now." And true to his word, he snatched the helmet from my head and bolted out of the room and up the stairs. A few seconds later, we heard the attic door slam shut.

"Come here, boy," Grandpa said. When my father left the room, it was as if a weight had been lifted from the family's shoulders. Everyone became immersed in acting as if nothing had happened—everyone except my mother, that is, who stared silently into space. Naturally, Dr. Van Tilburg was ready with a joke, at which Omi, Aunt Trees, and Aunt Titty laughed long and hard. They shuffled the cards loudly for canasta, the Catholic version of bridge. Frau Kochmann, our fantastic family cook, whom we'd brought with us from *das Baltikum*, was informed over the in-house telephone that dinner could be served at six thirty and that Dr. Van Tilburg would be joining us. That gave them enough time for another drink and a few practice rounds before the real game after dinner, when there'd be money on the table.

I went over and sat on Grandpa's knee like I always did. Oftentimes, he'd open the big *Andrees Handatlas* in front of me, and together we would study the map of Europe. Never the Americas, though he did have some good business contacts there, or Africa or Asia, but always Europe. The atlas, which had been printed in Leipzig in 1926, only showed the borders from before the Second World War. These were

Grandpa's borders, the borders in which he had built up his tremendous wealth in humble Latvia, where, through blind luck or fate, he had found his wife and fortune.

I loved the Old Boss, and I was the only one in the house who wasn't afraid of him. The fondness was mutual: Grandpa's strict face would soften at the sight of me. His dark eyes, always scrutinizing the world around him with mild suspicion, would drop their guard and take on a merry twinkle whenever I was around, and that made me feel better. Usually, he would stand up from his massive oak desk in the smoking room where he had been working, pick me up, twirl me around a couple of times, and set me on his knee. I would reach for the gold watch hanging from his breast pocket on a little gold chain, open it, wind it, and ask him what time it was. He would always report it down to the exact second. After, we'd head over to the big oak bookcase, slide open the glass doors, and start our atlas ritual.

Those moments always gave me the feeling that I played an important role in Grandpa's life, that I offered him distraction from his countless business troubles. And I think that was true. In any case, I was an object worthy of constant attention in Grandpa's eyes. He took every opportunity to explain to me how important I was, not only to the family, but to him personally. I was the heir to the family name. I didn't really understand what that meant at the time, but I had already realized that being the only grandchild of a rich grandfather wasn't entirely unpleasant.

"No more nosing around in the attic, you naughty boy," Grandpa said. He raised his voice in a way that made everyone fall quiet and listen. "We're going to get that mess up there cleaned up. I've had enough of it. Who knows what Bully will bring downstairs next time, when we might have guests over who don't know us so well?"

By now my father was back from the attic and leaning against the doorframe. "There's nothing else up there," he said flatly, "or at least nothing that any of you need to be worried about."

Sitting on Grandpa's knee like a Christ child, I felt a chill come over him at his eldest son's words. But before he could react, Omi— who was crazy about canasta—shrieked in a booming voice distorted by deafness, "Come, children, let's play!" Without another word, my father pulled up a chair to the card table where Omi, Aunt Trees, Guus, and Aunt Titty had already taken their seats. Grandpa set me down, excused himself, and went upstairs. Mother remained on the sofa, staring out the window. I couldn't help but notice that I had been at the center of something important and went off in search of Freddy, my dog. I would tell him the whole story down to the very last detail, just like we'd agreed.

TWO

I grew up in a large villa in Voorburg, a small town in the suburbs of The Hague. The house is still there, but over the years it's relinquished most of its vast, mysterious backyard to an encroaching apartment block. But back in 1948, I could spend whole days roaming the yard. Before venturing out, I would survey the estate from the back balcony, one of my grandmother's colorful Russian shawls wrapped around my shoulders like a count's cape. A false sense of calm would hang in the air, but I could feel the eyes of the enemy upon me. After a few secret ground-reconnaissance missions, I knew their exact position. I had scouted out places to spy on them, locations from which I could carefully select the best means to defeat them in the imminent battle. But I needed an ally. There was Freddy, of course, but he was often nowhere to be found. When I think back on all the times my grandfather had to put an ad in the paper because he'd run away!

"Why did you let him run off?" my family would ask in dismay.

"Because he asked me to," I'd answer, and that was the truth. Freddy was thus an unreliable choice, but I didn't have any other friends yet.

The family landed in Voorburg in 1940 after a hasty flight from Riga, the city Grandpa had gone to twenty-five years before, after leaving his Dutch hometown of Laren at the beginning of the First World War.

His motives for this expedition have always been somewhat unclear. According to Xeno, who knew him best of all his children, it was Grandpa's deeply pacifist nature that led him eastward. "He was afraid the Netherlands would be dragged into the war, and he would have to fight, which he was fundamentally against." I was still too young to ask the logical question, *why*. Why, of all places, had he gone to Latvia, a disputed territory right on the border with Russia, a country on the brink of revolution? I never brought it up later because I think, subconsciously, I wanted to preserve the mystery, and because over time, I'd pieced together a story that was as bizarre as it was romantic.

Grandpa initially went to Denmark to start a fruit-and-vegetable export company. Although I was deeply ashamed of the middle-class nature of such an activity, I understood why he did it. During the war, produce was scarce, which made apples and legumes desirable commodities. Once business took off, Grandpa expanded his products to cater to the tastes of the armies. With the profits, he bought a trawler that he sailed into Baltic Sea ports carrying less legitimate but no less intriguing cargo, items procured from equally dubious middlemen in Antwerp.

On one journey in 1917, he arrived in the old Hanseatic town of Riga. When he had left Copenhagen, a Danish acquaintance, the young doctor Arnold Berg, gave him a letter for the Russian countess Erica von Schumacher. Berg had met her the year before in Astrakhan on the Caspian Sea, where she'd nursed Russian soldiers wounded on the front. Berg, who led a Red Cross international response unit, fell head over heels in love with the sturdy suffragette. Erica von Schumacher fit the northern definition of an ideal woman in every way: she was independent, bold, witty, and original. Though she wasn't particularly beautiful, she was grounded and warm.

There was another reason she'd landed in Astrakhan, deep in the Russian hinterland. Because she was a young woman of Russian nobility—her father was on the State Council under Nicholas II—her parents intended her to attend the Smolny Institute in St. Petersburg, very much against her will. When the day arrived for her to leave for school, her aversion to Romanov pomposity exploded into outrage. She hid in a closet and refused to go. Fortunately, her parents didn't press further (the tsar had other things to worry about at the time); instead, they found her a position in a backcountry field hospital in Astrakhan, which is where she met Dr. Berg.

"He wasn't a very interesting man," she confessed to me fifty years later. "He was a good doctor, but kind of a *prostak*, an oaf. You know what I mean? A dolt."

When the Dutch merchant Joan Münninghoff delivered Berg's letter to Countess Von Schumacher in Riga—a letter that, among other things, declared that preparations for their wedding were underway—three lives were changed forever. My grandfather met the woman of his dreams and knew that he couldn't go on without her. The young countess couldn't resist his persuasions, and Dr. Berg was forgotten without a word. Joan Münninghoff and Erica von Schumacher married on October 19, 1919, in Riga Cathedral.

My grandfather was already quite well-to-do by then. Not as fabulously wealthy as he would later become through a bizarre twist of fate, but he was already among the upper echelons of Latvian expat society, which was largely ruled by German, Scandinavian, and Dutch merchants. How he managed to work his way up in such a short period of time has never been entirely clear.

At twelve, when my antennas were finally properly attuned to family gossip, I'd catch bits of arguments about my grandfather's past activities. The Old Boss had been dead for a few years by then.

"Of course he was in arms trading," said Uncle Jimmy, Uncle Xeno's twin brother, and by far the most intelligent of the siblings. "What did you think? That he was carrying tomatoes and cucumbers in his ships? The war was a once-in-a-lifetime opportunity for him, and he made the most of it. That's just the kind of person he was." That was something everyone had to admit, even Xeno, the only one who'd gotten along with Grandpa, and who still held him in high regard.

"An opportunity, yes. But who says it had to be weapons?" Xeno interrupted. "It could have been blankets or canteens, right?"

Everyone laughed at that, especially Aunt Trees, Xeno's red-haired wife, who excelled in sarcasm. "Yeah, or maybe it was caps or condoms," she added, which made Xeno even angrier. "The way you're ridiculing my father is disgraceful!" he shouted, lower lip trembling.

His father. Looking back, I'm surprised that in the melee of laughter no one scoffed at these words, just as I'm surprised that no one really knew the Old Boss for who he was.

The story in our family was always that things got out of hand in the Münninghoff house on New Year's Eve 1924, and the party degenerated into a bacchanal in which the hosts and a collection of thirty-some guests ended up in the house's many bedrooms. This wasn't unusual for the times, when the melancholic aftermath of the Great War gave way to unbridled sexual freedom and a lust for experimentation. In our family, the consequences of this materialized in September 1925, when Omi gave birth to twins, Xeno and James.

People gasped in surprise when they saw them: never before had anyone seen twins who looked so unalike. That the children had different blood types only fueled the rumors. James, nicknamed Jimmy almost immediately, a name that stuck for his entire life, had dark hair and obvious family traits, but Xeno was light blonde and looked more like—well, who actually? Mischievous innuendoes were stifled in my grandfather's presence, but everyone who could recall the guest list came to the conclusion that in addition to making love to her husband, the countess had succumbed to the charms of one of their friends, the businessman Hermann Sänger.

Sänger was a marine officer who'd built an empire of lumberyards and flour mills. Of Baltic origin himself, he'd helped my young Dutch grandfather on numerous occasions during the early years of his business adventures in Latvia. Though their business relationship was motivated by mutual profit, a genuine friendship developed between them. Moreover, it was a well-known secret that best friends Erica Münninghoff and Lotte Sänger occasionally went out hunting for men together. Most of the time, their escapades were nothing more than intense flirting sprees—with a few exceptions.

THREE

In the early 1930s, my grandfather went from being a minor huckster to a well-respected oligarch. Latvia was then, as it is today, an inward-focused, agrarian society. The country, strategically bordering the giant USSR, gained independence after the First World War. Riga, the capital, and a prominent city on the Hanseatic trade routes, was an ideal outpost for spies, correspondents, and diplomats. As a result, the small country's national politics were more important than they deserved to be: the international community was keeping an eye on all kinds of political plots unfolding in Latvia around that time.

This was particularly the case in 1934, as the elections approached. One of the candidates, Karlis Ulmanis, had famously tried to free his country from the tsar's grip in 1905. When he failed, Ulmanis fled to America, where he became a professor of agricultural science at the University of Nebraska. But in 1913, after Tsar Nicholas II granted a broad amnesty in honor of the three hundredth anniversary of the Romanov house, he returned home immediately. "I am married to Latvia," he would say dramatically whenever anyone would ask him why he didn't have a wife or children.

Ulmanis was very popular, and this earned him enemies among both Latvian industrialists and the German-speaking establishment of Courland barons. My grandfather stayed out of Latvian politics—as a foreigner, he didn't have the right to vote—but he did follow business affairs closely. As a businessman, he understood how important it was for him to align himself with the future president. And shortly before the elections, fate offered him a tremendous opportunity.

One day while he was waiting for his flight to Berlin to board in the first-class lounge at Spilve Airport in Riga, two men sat down at the table next to him. They must have assumed my grandfather was just another German on his way home: he was impeccably groomed and reading a German newspaper and had no reaction to the conversation they were having in Latvian. But my grandfather spoke Latvian fluently, and listened with interest from behind his newspaper.

Ulmanis, they said, had taken out immense debt to fund his campaign, and wasn't able to pay it back. The two men were extremely well informed; they mentioned exact amounts and discussed going public soon with the intention of openly discrediting Ulmanis and destroying his chance for the presidency.

My grandfather didn't need to think long. He let the plane for Berlin take off without him and made his way to Riga, where he managed to track down Ulmanis. As soon as the presidential hopeful recovered from the shock—none of this was ever meant to get out, of course—my grandfather offered to repay all his debts in the form of an interest-free loan. When Ulmanis's opponents triumphantly came forth with their story, Ulmanis's campaign would be able to dismiss their accusations as ridiculous rumors and condemn those who tried to spread them. My grandfather had one condition: he was never to be named as Ulmanis's financial backer. After all, he had good connections among the Baltic German elite, even if they were through marriage, and he didn't want his support for a populist candidate getting in the way of that. This is an example of the duplicity that marked my grandfather's life: he never wanted to openly commit himself fully to anything. Whatever he did, there was always another side to it, the back of the mirror that he held up to the world. And sometimes the image there was dark.

My grandfather made a good bet on Ulmanis. Indeed, the opposition published their story, but were immediately discredited by financial experts, and Ulmanis won the election by a landslide. The Old Boss was in the regime's good graces, and from then on everything he touched turned to gold.

Whatever facilities, licenses, or state-funded loans he wanted, the grateful president—who soon turned into a first-class dictator, abolishing the parliament and all political parties without hesitation—gave his approval, no questions asked. So my grandfather managed to build a number of factories and develop not only as a merchant but as an industrialist as well. Naturally, this called for management and finance skills, which it turned out my grandfather inherently possessed. He managed, within a few years, to build a massive business empire that included a bread factory (of strategic importance for any government), several sawmills, and concrete and textile factories, as well as a small fleet of three ships, his own bank, and a mercantile house. It would have been unfathomable without the active support of the Latvian government, which was ruled, at least in principle, by nationalism and had no real interest in foreigners.

By 1939, when the country's nationalistic dream was blown to smithereens, my grandfather had become one of the wealthiest, most highly regarded people in Latvia. By that time, he had exchanged his stately residence on Reimerstrasse in the center of Riga (where President Ulmanis also owned a house) for Von Lomani, a small estate in Ilguciems, an area on the other side of the Daugava River within walking distance of most of his factories. At the estate, he built a massive villa complete with a swimming pool and a tennis court. On the edge of the vast gardens were private stables for his three horses: Egli, Nora, and Jurka.

Von Lomani was the center of Riga's high society in the 1930s. The dining room could seat twenty-four, and the three housekeepers often needed extra help when the table was at maximum capacity. The parties at Von Lomani weren't limited to adults; my father and Aunt Titty, their friends, and other teenagers of elite Baltic German stock were equally welcome, and the estate hosted legendary parties for these jeunesse dorée. The happy youth came dressed to the nines in tuxedos and cocktail dresses, and after dining in the company of their powerful fathers and dazzling mothers, they'd gather on the terrace by the pool, or be driven by their chauffeurs to Hotel Otto Schwarz or Hotel Rom, the most exclusive nightclubs in Riga. Susternich, the Münninghoff's chauffeur, would wait with the Cadillac for Frans and his friends until the small hours of the morning to ensure that everyone made it home safely. It was clear that the Old Boss intended to provide the next generation of Münninghoffs with a smooth entry into the world of the Baltic's elite. At some point, my grandfather was offered the position of minister of economic affairs, but he declined; the role would have required him to obtain Latvian nationality, which he didn't want. That the Latvian government, who—in theory—didn't want any foreigners corrupting their national power base, would even offer him such a position speaks volumes.

FOUR

To the outside world, the Old Boss seemed exceptionally charming and worldly, the kind of man who inspired confidence. But at home, he was distant, even to his family, and especially to his wife. Still, he was crazy about Omi and couldn't refuse her anything. He preferred to leave all matters of the household and child-rearing to her, and when that proved ineffective, he hired a governess. Omi—who had always been extremely independent and averse to authority—had become the wife of a tycoon, after all. And when they were out in public, she enjoyed showing herself to be the very model of an ultra-emancipated woman.

She would leave on spontaneous trips to her friends' estates in Courland, where the ladies would host intimate gatherings and let Omi do most of the talking. Or she'd suddenly take off with her two best friends in her Hanomag convertible for a week or six to some exotic destination like Venice or Nice (*Nizza* as she called it in her stories, which always sounded so glamorous to me). She'd be suddenly struck by an insuppressible desire for excitement, but eventually one of her friends would remind her that she had twins still in the cradle back in Riga.

Exactly what the ladies did in the Côte d'Azur was a bit of a mystery, but their stay at the Hotel Negresco on the Promenade des Anglais, a hotspot for members of the old Russian elite, certainly cost a lot of money, money that the Old Boss promptly wired to his wife whenever she requested. Reading his letters to her, one gets the impression that though he loved her, he also enjoyed her absence. He traveled frequently himself and was a master at mixing business with pleasure. Money was no object, and nobody asked questions. It seems inevitable that this lack of cohesion within the family was bound to become a problem.

When the twins were around seven, the Old Boss noticed with alarm that they were speaking some kind of Russian-German thieves' slang. Since early childhood, they'd had a Russian *nyanya* named Anna and a Baltic-Russian governess named Eulanka (which was what Xeno and Jimmy called her because they couldn't say *Fräulein*). Left largely to her own devices, Eulanka had the impossible task of overseeing the two toddlers' linguistic development.

In theory, Jimmy and Xeno's mother tongue was supposed to be German, but instead the children learned to pronounce *h* as a guttural "kh," to drop articles entirely, their *ü* became "yoo," and their *o* sank an octave and became more of an "owa." On top of that, their daily speech was littered with Russian interjections like *nu* and *davai*, and the boys were known to suddenly switch between German and Russian and fill the gaps with bits of Latvian picked up from the servants.

And it wasn't just the twins. Frans and Titty both attended the Riga State German Grammar School, where they were supposed to be learning High German, but at home, they would make fun of all the German grammar rules. Despite all that, there was no Dutch of any kind in the Münninghoff children's Tower of Babel. Dutch was the Old Boss's language, the language of a distant country that had once been his, but the children had no connection to it whatsoever.

This was a real thorn in my grandfather's side. He decided to send Frans and Titty to the Netherlands at twelve in hopes that eight years of Dutch education would cleanse them of their linguistic cacophony. A bitterness must have crept into my grandfather's heart by then. Maybe he felt that in the chaos of his tremendous success, his history was slipping away, and his children might dismiss it as altogether irrelevant.

Maybe it was an act of revenge against his licentious Baltic German wife. Or maybe it was his devout Catholicism, which he'd had trouble maintaining in overwhelmingly Lutheran Latvia. Whatever my grandfather's reasons were, the decision was—at least in Frans's case—disastrous.

While Titty was sent to Our Lady of Lourdes in Voorschoten, my father found himself in the early summer of 1932, at the age of eleven, in the care of the Brothers of Tilburg at the Saint Nicholas Institute in Oss. The place was a monastery; the postcards he sent home to Riga showed the somber refectory where students ate at long wooden tables on hard benches without backrests, watched over by a crucifix hung between statues of Mary and Saint Peter, and surrounded by paintings showing serious religious scenes. The brothers wore long black habits and ran a tight ship; there was little time for sport or leisure, but plenty for prayer. Mass was held in the monastery chapel three times a day, and the boys were required to attend.

For Frans, the transition from a wealthy, fairly unsupervised life with his Baltic friends in Riga to the strictures of a rural Catholic boarding school was too much from the start. His Dutch classmates brushed him off as a foreigner, and when the brothers weren't watching, the other boys bullied him mercilessly. It didn't help that the Old Boss had told the director that his son's most recent report card in Riga stated that he "often disrupted class with his chatting and restlessness."

The brothers in Oss were instructed to take creative action. Their solution was to have Fransie, as they called him in their letters to Joan, recite catechism. And to make sure he did, Brother Ildefonso was specifically assigned to his case. At first, this seemed to work. Brought to his knees by the radical changes he'd been through, Frans gave in without a protest. He wrote a letter to his parents requesting a new hassock because, apparently, he'd been forced to kneel on a threadbare castoff.

After a few weeks, he started to complain that he was the only one who hadn't had his first communion yet.

During his first six months alone at school, he'd spent most of his free time in the library writing letters home. He wrote, on average, six letters a week—desperate messages from a hopeless boy in exile. After a month and a half, he wrote to his mother: "I've only gotten two letters from you. And I wrote you five!" Most of the time he wrote to her in German, and for obvious reasons he wrote to his father in Dutch, a language he never quite mastered. Throughout the eight years he was in school in Holland, even after he started attending Huize Katwijk, a renowned boarding school in The Hague, his letters contained spelling and grammar mistakes. He never achieved a satisfactory level of expression, either in Dutch or in German, a predictable consequence of his situation. That he continued to write separate letters to his father and mother says a lot about their relationship.

On top of it all, he missed his friends in Riga terribly. He sent desperate postcards to his three best friends, Manfred Dolgoi, Hans Erich Seuberlich, and Wolf Metzkeris: "Write to me at least twice a week! Even if you've got nothing to say!" But naturally the preteens weren't interested in writing letters, and the boys' worlds slowly drifted apart.

Frans was allowed to go home for the first time, for Christmas in 1932, and he was overjoyed. Even though he had to have a painful tonsillectomy in Breda that November, he knew he could bear it because "soon it will be Christmas, and we will see each other again." Just before he left for Riga, he was allowed to take his first communion in Oss, much to the Old Boss's delight. But though the brothers referred to him as "joyful Frans" that day, Frans didn't seem to long for the experience quite as much as he had a few months prior.

Back home in Riga over the holidays, still reeling, he sought comfort from his German elementary school friends. On their long horseback rides across the snowy fields outside the city, the boys took stock of the situation. They unanimously agreed the Old Boss had played a cruel trick on Frans by sending him abroad—and to the Netherlands of all places, a tiny country that rightfully belonged to the German *Reich*, just like the Baltics. "What's that they speak there?" the boys asked. Frans recited a few strange sentences with plenty of Dutch *je*'s and guttural *g*'s, tossing in a few curse words for good measure—*Godverdomme! Klootzak!* The boys roared with laughter. "Is that really Dutch?"

Manfred, Hans Erich, and Wolfi were already familiar with some Dutch idiosyncrasies: endless griping about everything being too expensive and the single cookie with their tea. Then there was the famous cheese slicer, apparently the ultimate symbol of Dutch stinginess. But his friends were surprised that most people traveled by bicycle. "Bicycle?! Isn't that for the countryside?" the boys exclaimed.

Shaking their heads, they lit some cigarettes Frans had brought. In his loneliness he'd started "smoking like a chimney," as he'd confessed to Omi in a letter. Oddly enough, the brothers in Oss had done nothing to stop him. One even asked the melancholy twelve-year-old to bring back some Latvian cigarettes.

Between Christmas and New Year's, the family visited the Rusgie Estate, where Omi's sister Litty lived with her husband, the surgeon Walter Lehmann. A mild-mannered intellectual by nature, the doctor had recently become an ardent supporter of Adolf Hitler. "We need to be annexed back into the German Empire," he would say with conviction, "otherwise, we Baltic Germans are doomed." Latvia and Estonia wouldn't be able to maintain independence against the Bolshevik monster to the east, claimed *Onkel* Walter beside the Christmas tree—and the same went for Lithuania, under threat from Poland. The Baltic German community in Livonia and Courland desperately needed protection, and no one was more suitable than Adolf Hitler, who'd been increasingly powerful in recent months.

"What do you think, Joan?" Walter asked the Old Boss amiably.

The Old Boss dissembled but said attacking Jews in the streets had become an alarming trend.

Lehmann answered, "You're Dutch. You don't know the Jews like we do. We've had them here for centuries. They're arrogant and think they can profit from the Bolsheviks. Just look at the people around Lenin in 1917: they were practically all Jews. Pretty soon, those same Jews are going to sell us out to the Bolsheviks, mark my words. They have to be dealt with—that's what's happening in Berlin. They need to learn their place."

You're Dutch. The words triggered a decisive mechanism in Frans. Uncle Walter's words—at least to Frans's ears—were dripping with contempt. Frans began to resist his father's Dutch identity with every fiber of his being. He wanted nothing to do with the Netherlands or its boring people. Frans belonged in the Baltics, with his friends and family! From that moment, something inside Frans changed, and the prepubescent boy began transforming into a frustrated and insecure young man. He categorically rejected the Dutch life the Old Boss had condemned him to, idealizing the Baltic of his youth. The fact that he would have to return to Oss the next week felt like a punishment, and he wondered what he'd done to deserve it.

Back in Oss, he made no effort to hide his disdain for the Netherlands. He was picked on for his German accent, but he never said a word about Latvia or his family. That was his domain, and he wasn't going to let anyone from the Netherlands inside.

None of this changed when he was transferred to the exclusive Catholic institution Huize Katwijk on Raamweg in The Hague in the summer of 1933. Huize Katwijk had the air of an English boarding school, with manicured fields for sports, but students were still required to spend nearly three hours a day in Mass. The boys in Frans's class were mostly from wealthy Catholic families, with high-society family names like Smits van Waesberghe, Van Nispen tot Sevenaer, and Van Hövell tot Westerflier. It was an elite group that Frans Münninghoff didn't belong to, or so he felt, but his father was determined to push him into it with all his might.

The priests at Huize Katwijk soon picked up on Frans's resistance, as did his classmates. He was often absent and depressed. He hung a portrait of Tsar Nicholas II on the wall in his bedroom, and if anyone asked him about it, he'd say he was the rightful heir to the Russian throne—so all you Dutch cheeseheads better watch what you say! He navigated the strange, inaccessible world of Katwijk with arrogance and aggression. He was a good fighter, but he didn't make any friends. Frans Münninghoff was a loner.

Only at Christmas, Easter, or summer vacation did he brighten. With a smile on his face, he'd take a taxi to the station, where he'd board a train for the two-day journey back to Riga. The trip included an early-morning transfer in Berlin, where a local business partner of the Old Boss would look after him for a few hours until he could board the direct train to the Baltics.

On his first trip home from Huize Katwijk, the Old Boss's partner treated Frans to breakfast at Berlin's famous Café Kranzler. For Frans, who'd never been to the German capital before, this was a major event. The flawless service, the chic crowds of stylish people, the endless stream of cars; Riga, let alone The Hague, couldn't compare to the grandeur of Berlin. He was enchanted by the dynamic city, and when they went to see Hitler's guards at the Reich Chancellery palace on Wilhelmstrasse, he was sold. The confidence and power of the helmeted soldiers ignited a fascination that bordered on obsession. That afternoon, as he boarded the train that took him via Posen, Radziwiliszki, Saulen, and Mitau on to Riga, it was all he could think of, and by the time he got home, he could talk of nothing else. His friends, who'd all been to Berlin, nodded in agreement: *"Berlin ist unsere Hauptstadt,"* they said. Berlin is our capital.

These schoolboy stories worried the Old Boss, but the boys' minds were made up. That summer, Frans spent a few weeks at his mother's cousin's estate near the seaside town of Jurmala. Aunt Maggi's husband was the police chief of Riga, and once Frans met Uncle Arno, there was no turning back. Arno, an excellent horseman, taught Frans all the secrets of riding. He was also an excellent host. It was no secret that the young people were already drinking *Dzidrais*, the local vodka, at their parties, so when drinks were served on his veranda before dinner, he had no qualms about serving alcohol to minors. Arno believed that drinking facilitated conversation, and Frans couldn't have agreed more. Frans also agreed with Arno's politics, which were in line with what he'd heard from Uncle Walter. "Hitler might be a middle-class crank," said Uncle Arno, "but he certainly managed to turn things around in Germany. His behavior might be inappropriate and his speech excruciating to listen to, but that's not the point. What's important is that the man isn't going to let us down. He's going to bring us together."

Frans took these words to heart. And once he did, the Old Boss's plans to properly Dutchify his firstborn son fully backfired. There was no love for the Netherlands left in Frans's heart. However, he did make an effort to keep up appearances for his father's sake and used the church as his smokescreen: "Every day I pray the rosary for you. I see it as my duty—otherwise, your business might be bad, right?" he wrote to his father, as though he were a pious Dutch Catholic schoolboy. He was anything but. During his layovers in Berlin, he'd buy postcards with pictures of Hitler and swastikas on them for his friends in Riga, where Latvian nationalism was on the rise. Everything Nazi related was outlawed in Latvia; swastikas and all other Germanic paraphernalia were forbidden. The same went for German newspapers; when Frans asked his mother to send him a copy of *Die Wehrmacht* and learned that there were no longer any German newspapers available in Latvia, he wrote back to her in outrage. Frans, sixteen years old, signed the letter in angry, scratched handwriting: "With German greetings, your son Franz," signing his name with a German *z*—something his father had explicitly forbidden him to do.

But the Old Boss never saw the letters between his wife and his son. In those years, the two developed a dark secret bond that would be significant in the radical steps Frans later took. Not only did Frans turn to his mother for all his material needs—and she made sure he got whatever he asked for and that the Old Boss paid for it—he also shared his newfound German ideology with her. Omi shared her son's opinions and hoped the Baltics would fall under Berlin's rule soon. A few times she even picked him up for the holidays in her Hanomag convertible. She'd step out of the car draped in her sable fur stole and long colorful shawls, and they'd greet each other with a dramatic display of affection. She'd drive off honking the horn and laughing with joy, sending gravel flying up behind them. This was very different from the one time Frans's father picked him up; that departure began with a long talk in the headmaster's office and the Old Boss storming out with a grim look on his face.

Frans wasn't exactly thriving at Katwijk. The Dutch language remained a struggle—he still spoke a shaky mix of Dutch and German: *"Du kaanst dir voorstellen," "Wir wurden allen gevragt ein Antwoort zu geben," "Ich habe bijna keen Zeit."* One of the priests who'd managed to get the stubborn teenager to open up about the situation tried to explain it to the Old Boss: while Dutch was Frans's father tongue, his mother tongue was—like it or not—German. The byproduct of Frans's language struggles was low grades in almost every subject. But Frans's linguistic skills weren't the only problem. His behavior left much to be desired: he was sullen, refused to participate in group activities, and— perhaps worst of all—he refused to participate in Mass. The headmaster gave him until the end of the fall term, 1936, to shape up. "Only for your sake," Frans wrote to his mother, "I'll put on a good show, otherwise they'll kick me out."

This all points to Frans having already developed his own agenda by then. His priorities appeared to be his study of Nazi ideology, riding horses, and participating in a fascist mounted-guard unit led by

Baron Degenhardt, a distant relative. With his horse, Egli, Frans spent every school vacation training with this underground brigade of Baltic Cossacks. The unit even had its own uniforms inscribed with runes and its own anthem.

After the training sessions, which always included a charge with the Caucasian sword, the Engelhärdtsche Riders, as they called themselves, gathered at one of Omi's relative's country houses for drinks and a thorough evaluation of their progress. Uncle Arno had put in a good word for Frans, and the group admitted him into its youth division. In one of the group's equestrian events, Frans proudly took second place, with his uncle in the audience. He was with the Engelhärdtsche Riders 100 percent; Katwijk meant nothing to him. The fact that he'd been held back three times and was still in his second year of high school didn't matter at all. As the boys around him seemed to get younger and younger, his contempt for the school only grew.

The Old Boss hardly noticed, and Omi never said a word about it. What Joan heard from Frans were repeated assurances that he was doing his best in school, and other inconsequential things, like that he had saved fourteen marks on his train ticket to Riga by forgoing the sleeping car. He flirted with Dutch frugality to get in his father's good graces and made sure to mention he'd used the extra money to buy a scientific book on horse breeding. "Egli is *my* horse," he declared from The Hague. "She may not, under any circumstances, be bred."

By then, it was the summer of 1936, and a crisis was unfolding at Von Lomani that stripped the family of its last remnants of cohesion.

FIVE

Jimmy and Xeno, the twins born in 1925, were destined for the same future in the Netherlands as Frans and Titty, but things didn't work out that way. In September 1935, they were playing cowboys at their tenth birthday party, and Jimmy fell off a pony and landed in a pile of manure. He seemed all right at first, but when he woke up the next morning unable to stand or walk, his parents called the doctor. After thoroughly examining the boy, the family physician called a doctor friend who happened to be attending an international conference on polio in Riga. The second doctor examined Jimmy, left, and returned the same day with several internationally renowned specialists.

The gentlemen came to the unanimous conclusion that Jimmy, by then in a coma, had polio—infantile paralysis, most likely from infected water from the Daugava River. "Your son will become crippled and eventually go mad. Pray that he dies soon," one of the physicians said, and Omi told him that there was no history of madness in her family and showed him the door. They found out that American president Franklin Delano Roosevelt was also a polio patient and at a medical center in the small town of Warm Springs, Georgia, specialists were attempting to fight the disease with warm baths and underwater massage therapy. Roosevelt claimed to have benefited from the therapy, though it hadn't been effective for everyone.

The Old Boss was planning a trip to America when he learned that the Roosevelt method was being used in Johannisbad, a small spa town in Czechoslovakia. Two weeks later, Omi and Jimmy moved into a suite at the Johannisbad spa. Xeno, who had traveled with them so as not to burden anyone else in the family, got his own room. Even under the circumstances, the Old Boss still considered the boys' Dutch education of primary importance, so he arranged for Temmy Kemper, a private Dutch tutor, to accompany them. She was the bright daughter of the municipal secretary of Voorburg, a small town in the suburbs of The Hague, where the Old Boss had purchased a villa on Prins Albertlaan. Although the purchase was viewed as an investment, his brother Wim and his sister, Marie, both of whom were unmarried, lived there as caretakers. Temmy came prepared to bring Xeno and Jimmy up to the Dutch level for their age group. The plan was to move the twins to the Netherlands in the next two years and enroll them in a Dutch high school.

In the end, the twins spent those two years in Johannisbad studying with Temmy. The first year, Omi was with them most of the time. She was quickly welcomed into the local salons but didn't find them particularly interesting. The village was located in the heart of the Sudetenland region of Czechoslovakia, and there was a strong Sudeten-German populist movement on the rise, with people calling for annexation to Hitler's Germany. Most of the conversations centered around this topic, which didn't help to lighten the mood. There was also the fact that the Czech government was using an iron fist, sending police to raid the homes of suspected conspirators. The prospect of having to remain in a state of semiquarantine was tremendously depressing, so it was an additional relief when, after ten months, the warm water treatments started to work. Jimmy's recovery was so miraculous that within a few weeks, in the summer of 1936, Omi was told her presence was no longer necessary. There was no reason she couldn't return to her husband in Riga.

Jimmy's recovery and Omi's well-being weren't the only reasons this announcement was fortuitous. The Old Boss had been diagnosed with throat cancer, and he'd informed his wife of his condition in a short, stoic letter. As a heavy cigar smoker, he had no one to blame but himself, he wrote, but that didn't make the situation any less difficult. At first, the Old Boss felt hopeless: his family was falling apart, and he was no longer well enough to hold it together. Once again, however, he was saved by his own decisiveness. He immediately began treatment under the leading cancer expert at the time, the Lebanese doctor Hamid Chaoul from King Fuad I Hospital in Alexandria, who also ran a clinic in Berlin. In mid-1936, the Old Boss began a six-month treatment program that required him to spend one week a month at Dr. Chaoul's clinic.

Between treatments, he made a pilgrimage to Lourdes, where he promised the Blessed Virgin to build a church if he recovered. When it became evident that the tumor was under control and recovery was within reach, the Old Boss was ecstatic; he made good on his promise and built the Christ the King Church in Riga. The project was extravagantly expensive, and a Dutch Jesuit in Riga who taught theology at the university made sure that Pope Pius XI in the Vatican knew about it. The promise of pontifical distinction hung loftily in the air. After all, it had long been the Holy Father's intention to bring "a garland of Christian establishments" to the borders of the Soviet Union so that, when the time was ripe, they might be "ready to win Russia for Christ," as stated in an internal Jesuit report from the time. The Old Boss's new church in the predominantly Lutheran city of Riga served as a kind of Roman Catholic outpost.

The Old Boss was most likely aware of this fact, but he wasn't interested in recognition at all. He told everyone that his recovery was the most wonderful blessing from heaven he could hope for, that he was fortunate to be a man of such deep faith, and that it was he—and not the pope—who should be grateful. He'd promised the Holy Mother to build the church, simple as that. To hear him tell it, you'd think he and Mary had a private little chat—one that the earthly representative of Christ had been explicitly left out of.

Around Christmas 1936, the Old Boss was swept away by a flood of frivolous ideas. He took Omi on a Mediterranean cruise on the *Milwaukee*, a luxury ship in the Hamburg-America Line fleet, and Frans and Titty went with them. Jimmy was on doctor's orders not to leave the sanatorium, and Xeno was attached to him at the hip, so the boys stayed with Temmy in Johannisbad, where they celebrated the loneliest New Year's of their young lives. But the Old Boss wasn't concerned about the twins. He counted his blessings and even enjoyed the time with his obstinate older son. For Frans, the trip was like a dream come true—he and his father donned tuxedos every evening, and for the first time in Frans's memory, the Old Boss was in high spirits. Frans left all his complaints about school at home, Omi danced the Charleston and drank champagne, and they tossed money around in the casino like it was nothing. *This must be the high life,* Frans thought.

Then Jimmy's return to Riga—originally planned for spring—was postponed until late fall. *Nothing to worry about,* the doctors said, *things were just progressing a bit more slowly than expected.* For Xeno, however, frustration was mounting. Did he have to stay in boring Johannisbad too? He'd had enough of Temmy's annoying Dutch lessons. What was he supposed to do with Dutch? He blamed Jimmy for the whole situation. When Omi came to visit, he'd become sullen, because he knew she was only there to see Jimmy, the frail twin who was constantly being pampered. The only time Xeno cheered up was when the Old Boss came, which wasn't very often. But when he did, they'd go to Prague together, watch soccer matches, and eat out in fancy restaurants, having a wonderful time. Xeno was crazy about his father.

Gradually, a rift developed between the two brothers. After months wrapped in blankets and lying on a deck chair, Jimmy was finally starting to move normally again. He joined a gymnastics club called Frisch-Fromm-Fröhlich-Frei (FFFF). The club was strikingly similar to the Hitler Youth, with only Sudeten-German boys as members. Xeno didn't want any part of it; he'd turned out to be an introvert, preferring to spend the whole day reading alone in the library. Jimmy, however, seemed to overcompensate after everything he'd been through. He was embraced by the group of friends, and though he had little talent for gymnastics, he happily donned his uniform and went to the FFFF meetings, where they'd gather around a campfire and sing Nazi songs.

The FFFF boys had a taste for trouble: they liked to detonate home-made carbide bombs so the Czech forest rangers would think they were doing target practice and keep their distance. Hitler's annexation of Czechoslovakia was on the horizon, and Jimmy soon figured out that the club's agenda was more than doing flips on the horizontal bars. When the Old Boss and Omi came to visit that summer, Jimmy's new activities caused quite a commotion. When he proudly walked in wearing his FFFF uniform, the Old Boss was livid. "God damn it! Take that off right now," he shouted. Omi was quick to jump to her favorite son's defense. "I don't want to hear it," she said. "Jimmy is coming out with us for cake." Later they were sitting at a table on a terrace when an orchestra began to play the Nazi Party anthem. It was a risky move, because the Czech police were under strict orders to intervene, but there were no agents in sight.

Almost everyone on the terrace stood up and extended their arm to *heil* Hitler. When Omi and Jimmy stood, the Old Boss spoke with anger. "Erica, I forbid you to do that! And control your son!" he shouted, his voice still hoarse from the radiation. He sounded dangerous. Omi sat back down, but for Jimmy, the moment of truth had arrived. He lowered his arm but didn't sit. With a strained look, he turned to his father and said, "I won't be ordered around by you anymore." And with that, their father-son relationship was definitively broken. Xeno, on the other hand, had remained seated the entire time; he just watched, shaking his head.

From then on, the twins only got along in the presence of a mutual opponent. And Temmy was their primary victim. Xeno and Jimmy had caught her in the arms of a local boy, and despite being only eleven, they knew this was prime blackmail material against their indomitable teacher and all her difficult dictation exercises. If the Old Boss were to find out, he would most certainly fire her. So, in a cool, businesslike tone, the twins told their teacher everything they'd seen and heard, and in exchange for their silence the dumbstruck girl promised to hide their weaknesses in Dutch.

The Old Boss's euphoria about conquering cancer soon faded as the crisis with Frans came to a head. In early summer 1937, after yet another dismal report card, the boarding school in Katwijk finally decided to cut ties with the troublemaker from Riga.

"We cannot allow him to repeat his second year for a third time. You'll have to seek another path for Frans," read the letter from Father Albers, the school's director. "I have little hope that you'll succeed in changing your son's mind at this point," he added ominously. "He's overpowered by tempting ideas at a young, impressionable age and has become actively bound to a movement that hampers his freedom of judgment. In my opinion, he's developed a narrative in service of his agenda." He closed the letter by saying: "I assure you that I've done everything in my power to serve Frans to the best of my ability. He shall be especially remembered in my Holy Mass."

At the Old Boss's request, Frans's uncle Wim and aunt Marie visited the other suitable high schools in The Hague, but word had already spread among the local schools. No school would accept him, not only because of his poor grades, but because of his reputation as a burgeoning fascist. At the start of the year, he'd disrupted a special performance in honor of the marriage of Princess Juliana and Bernhard zur Lippe-Biesterfeld by flicking wads of paper at the back of the minister of education's neck. And once it became public knowledge that "The Horst Wessel" was played at the end of the royal wedding gala, he sang it unsolicited and without shame in class. Frans Münninghoff was, in short, a hopeless case. In a last-ditch effort, the Old Boss asked his friend Kolfschoten to pull a few strings in his Jesuit network and get Frans into the Stedelijk Gymnasium in Maastricht. Father Huf, a prominent figure in Limburg society, arranged for him to live with Baroness Van Hövell tot Westerflier, the governor of Limburg's widow, who lived with her nine children in a castle just outside of Maastricht. This unusually fortunate arrangement was facilitated by the Old Boss's church in Riga, which was by then legendary in the Roman Catholic world. Aunt Marie accompanied a sullen Frans to Maastricht and turned him over to the school's Father Huf at the station. The father in turn took Frans to the dowager's castle himself, where they were invited for dinner. At the table, Frans told stories about Riga, which saved him—at least temporarily. After dinner, the director of the Stedelijk Gymnasium school board dropped by (not by coincidence) for a game of cards. He chatted with Frans for a bit, sized him up, and said, "I'll make sure you get into our school, don't worry."

Nepotism left a bad taste in Frans's mouth, but he didn't let it show, and he was invited to spend the night at the castle. The next day, however, when his parade through Limburg's upper class continued with a tennis match at the home of the Regouts, the ceramics magnates, he'd had enough. "I don't want to be friends with anyone in Holland," he told Aunt Marie when she came to pick him up, a statement as sad as it was sincere. Nevertheless, he was registered at the Stedelijk Gymnasium in Maastricht.

But Frans's heart was still in Riga, and his longing for home only grew stronger when, in the summer of 1937, he fell madly in love with a girl who, seven years later, would become my mother: Wera Lemcke. First love usually is a beautiful thing, but Frans was so consumed by his Nazi pathos and homesickness for the Baltics that it only fueled his frustration. It was his first love, and he didn't know how to handle it. In his mind, there was some strange link between the girl of his dreams and all that Nazi blustering: in an angry world full of enemies, he would be Wera's uniformed, swastika-bearing knight in shining armor.

Wera's background was unusual. Her mother, Nadia, was from Moscow and held on to her Russian roots. She left the capital shortly after the turn of the century and moved to Riga to attend secretarial school. After she finished her studies, she worked at the Remington typewriter factory, where she met Harry Lemcke, a soft-spoken Baltic German engineer who was an inventor in his free time. They married in 1920 and had Wera almost immediately. Nadia, who was then thirty-two, didn't want more children; she was the only surviving child of eight, all of whom had died from tuberculosis. She'd hoped that by moving to Riga, living close to the sea, and immersing herself in a thriving international environment, she'd be able to put her sad past behind her. But she was haunted by the misery of her childhood. There was a brokenness about her that, along with her wavy chestnut hair, had melted Harry Lemcke's melancholic heart. But it pushed Nadia further and further away from other people. On top of being shy, she spoke German with a heavy Slavic accent peppered with Russian words, which kept her outside her husband's social circles.

When Harry died suddenly of a heart attack in 1929 (while trying to open a chest of drawers), Nadia was so overcome with despair that she sent Wera to London to live with Harry's mother, who ran a guesthouse near the Crystal Palace. Wera stayed with Grandma Anna in the British capital for eight years. She returned to Riga in 1937 an extraordinarily beautiful girl of sixteen, with her long dark-blonde locks and bright blue eyes, and she created quite a stir in Baltic high society. She spoke English and German perfectly, had an elegant figure—thanks to intensive ballet lessons—played piano beautifully, had impeccable manners, and was well read and gifted, with a keen sense of humor.

That she returned to Latvia at all was thanks to her mother's uncle, who'd managed to escape Russia with the family's jewels. Shortly before his death, he visited Nadia and confessed that he had them. The confession came partly from guilt—he'd known she was in Riga but hadn't contacted her from Berlin—and partly from the fact that she was his only living relative. He had the bag of jewels with him. He just burst into tears and asked for her forgiveness so he could die in peace. She forgave him, and he spent the last three days of his life on her couch and died with a serene smile on his face. With her newfound Russian fortune, Nadia bought a small house in a leafy suburb of Riga and brought her daughter home from London. Wera adjusted quickly and graduated from one of the most elite high schools in Riga at seventeen. From there, she danced from one magnificent debutante ball to the next, until she met Frans.

Half-drunk in his tuxedo, he tugged on her waistband as she twirled past him at a party at the Sport Union. Frans wasn't much of a dancer, but he was charming. He made up for his rude first impression by getting her a glass of champagne, and they talked all night, parting with a warm kiss on the cheek. Wera already had a boyfriend, her neighbor, who was as good a dancer as she was and an excellent pianist. But Frans soon won her heart with his rough charm and family wealth. They saw each other at parties and social events throughout the summer.

The parties of Riga's young, rich elite were—when they didn't degenerate into drunken debauchery—characterized by a kind of Prussian formality, aptly described as *Höflichkeit*. People addressed each other with the formal *Sie* until such a level of intimacy was reached that they felt inclined to suddenly switch to the friendlier *du*. A kiss on the hand was common, but any other form of kissing in public was seen as a sign of an impending engagement.

The evenings were filled with cultured activities; often parties split into two groups, each trying to outdo the other with poems and riddles. Still, in the dark, secluded corners, there was plenty of groping as well. As the summer went on, Frans and Wera separated themselves from the party increasingly often, making Wera's boyfriend extremely jealous. The neighbor boy could only hope that after a few agonizing months he'd have her to himself again after Frans went back to where he came from. That was the image that people had of the Münninghoffs: filthy rich foreigners from a strange country to the west.

SIX

By the time Frans had to go back to the Netherlands, he was obsessed with Wera. With no attachment to the Netherlands at all, he thought of nothing but his girlfriend in the Baltics and the other boys around her. His new host in Maastricht had recently lost his wife and was unable to provide any real supervision for his young houseguest. He hardly noticed that Frans was skipping classes. Every evening, Frans listened to Radio Riga. He hung the Von Schumachers' family crest in his room next to his portrait of the tsar and an icon of Our Lady of Kazan, the holy protectress of the Russian army. Rather than doing homework, he started studying Russian. He began signing his letters to Omi in Cyrillic and occasionally trying to write to her in Russian—though, like his Dutch and German, his Russian was full of mistakes. He was searching for a new identity, one that would set him apart from all things Dutch and allow him to distance himself from the Münninghoff family. Senseless and conceited, Frans started to see himself as some romantic tsarist Russian in exile. At Christmas, when Frans's grades provided evidence that he was either unable or unwilling to meet the standards of the Stedelijk Gymnasium, the Old Boss was outraged. He withdrew him from the elite high school and enrolled him in a three-year vocational high school in Maastricht.

The Old Boss also tried to talk to his son about the future. "If you graduate—which you are certainly capable of doing—I'll send you to a trade school. Then you'll be able to take over the family business, like the oldest son is to do."

Desperate, Frans flew into a rage, first in Russian, then in German: "Leave me alone! I wasn't meant to be a businessman. I'm not like you!"

The Old Boss looked at him contemptuously. "So, what do you want to be, then? And answer me in Dutch, boy."

"If you really want to know, I'm going into the military. Next year I'm off to the military guard school in Zagreb."

The Old Boss was shocked. Suddenly, he realized he'd had no idea about his son's plans and cut the conversation short. He looked into it and confirmed that the military school wasn't just another strange fabrication; it really existed. It was run by former members of the Austro-Hungarian Imperial and Royal Military, who still referred to Zagreb as Agram. The school's leadership harbored pro-Nazi sentiments, and enrollment was open to foreigners. Frans had heard about the school from one of his relatives on Omi's side of the family. Once the Old Boss learned that all this had been going on behind his back, he was aghast, but knew that coming down hard on Frans wasn't going to help. In his next conversation with his son, he played his cards close to the chest. This time, Omi was at his side, seeming to realize that she and her family were partially to blame for the situation.

"If you think you can go to Zagreb without having graduated, you are mistaken," the Old Boss said. "You have my blessing, but they only want boys with a high school diploma, fully prepared to enroll in the officers' training program. So, first you must finish school. Like I said, you're perfectly capable of it, and it'll only take three years. Then we'll see."

The Old Boss seemed to have resigned himself to his son's decision, and Frans was naively pleased. The change in him was like night and day. With no Latin and Greek classes, the vocational school was no problem for him, and without his father on his back, he even seemed to thrive in his new environment. In Maastricht, he was fortunate to meet Alexander Poslavsky, the son of two Russian emigrants blown over from the United States. Like Frans, he, too, had plunged himself into a kind of mystic Russian messianism inspired by tsarist Russia. Neither of the boys wanted anything to do with the Netherlands, the country they'd been exiled to by their parents. They spoke Russian among themselves and even went so far as to set up a Russian Orthodox chapel in the attic of Alexander's mother's house, where they regularly prayed for the collapse of the Red Empire.

The biggest thing the two boys had in common, however, was their fascination with Adolf Hitler. In September 1938, Frans wrote to his mother that he had listened to one of the *Führer*'s radio addresses and was very impressed by what he'd heard. *"Haarig!"* he said, 1930s schoolboy slang for "totally cool." The Poslavskys, on the other hand, saw things quite differently. Alexander's mother was actually considering a return to the United States just to get away from all of Hitler's ranting and raving. Even Alexander, who would grow up to become a renowned psychologist, had to laugh pitifully at his friend; perhaps he had already picked up on the fact that Frans, who had just returned from his second long summer with Wera, was particularly sensitive to someone like Hitler, a leader with a clear goal and methods for achieving it. This undoubtedly appealed to Frans, because to him, life was one big mess.

That said, things were finally going well for him at school in the Netherlands. He began getting decent grades and was finally moved into the next grade. He also passed his driving exam on the first try, though no one could have known then that this would be the only exam he'd ever pass in his life. His relationship with Wera, however, was a mystery to him. He was head over heels in love with her, but she didn't seem to feel the same; for her, the fire might've been starting to go out.

This wasn't due to lack of effort on his part. Every day in the summer of 1938 Frans rode his horse to Wera's house on the outskirts of

Riga at the edge of the woods. There was a level of intimacy between them, but whenever Frans would say they were "destined for each other," Wera would just smile and kiss him. She couldn't help but feel that there was something lacking in him. He was exceedingly chivalrous, and committed to her, but this only made her long for someone softer, more poetic, less predictable. And she didn't really see how she fit into Frans's plans. Zagreb? Officer's school? No one in her family had ever married a solider, and she had no affection for uniforms or military pomp and circumstance. When Frans told her he wanted to marry her when he said goodbye in September, she laughed. She wasn't even eighteen yet! In the following weeks, Wera realized that she'd spent the last two summers with an irrational, pathetic rich kid. He was physically attractive—at eighteen, my father was nearly five-eleven and had beautiful dark eyes, thick blonde hair, and a pearly smile—and good for a laugh or a drink, but he left much to be desired. In November 1938, she wrote: "I can't imagine marrying you. I've got the world ahead of me. I'm not ready to be tied down yet. I've received an offer to work in Egypt as a hotel receptionist, and I'm going to accept. When you come home at Christmas, I won't be here. Farewell, sweet boy."

Alone in his rented room in Maastricht, Frans fell apart. He called in sick from school, stayed in bed for days, wandered the streets at night, took Sedobrol for insomnia, became terrified of going into cardiac arrest, and wrote home every day saying he had to come home, he needed to talk to Wera, he couldn't go on without her. On top of all that, his friend Poslavsky had moved to Utrecht with his mother after the start of large-scale military exercises in Maastricht, which were terrifying local residents. The bridges over the Meuse were barricaded for days, and groups of soldiers hid behind mortars or huddled in machine gun nests around every corner. Rumors were spreading like wildfire, and for many people living in Maastricht, this was their cue to leave. Hitler was implementing his annexation policy, and the Munich Agreement had turned out to be nothing more than a worthless piece of paper.

As the threat of war increased daily, many people concluded that living on the German border was just too risky. So, lonely and with no one to share his heartbreak with, Frans slowly came undone until early December, when he received another letter from Wera. She said everything was unchanged between them, that she wasn't going to Egypt after all, that she loved him, and that she would be waiting for him in Riga.

When he arrived home for Christmas, he learned that Omi had told Wera about her son's anguish and begged her to go easy on him until he came to his senses; Wera told him so herself. Frans accused Omi of meddling and ordered her never "to come between him and Wera again." As the situation escalated, the Old Boss made a decision that left Frans with a scar: he formally asked Wera to leave, as she was threatening to become "a permanent source of discord" in the family, and he wasn't sure she was the right wife for his eldest son, the son and heir to the Münninghoff family line. It was no secret that the Old Boss wanted a Dutch bride for his son.

"My son's future is in the Netherlands," he said stiffly. "I'm setting up a company for him there. It's of the utmost importance he marry someone who will fit into the Dutch business world. I hope you understand, *Fräulein Lemcke.*"

For Frans, this announcement was entirely unexpected; the scales fell from his eyes. "You deceived me!" he roared at his father in German. "Let me tell you something: I'm going into the military, and I'm going to marry Wera whether you like it or not!"

Although neither of these things seemed likely at that moment in time, that was exactly what happened, to the detriment of nearly everyone involved.

SEVEN

Having returned to Maastricht, Frans took measures to carry out his plans. He met with the director of his school to discuss the possibility of taking his final exams early, arguing that an eighteen-year-old in a class of mostly thirteen-year-olds was a distraction for everyone. The director developed a strict study schedule for Frans so he would be able to take his exams in early September 1939, just before the start of the next school year. "And then you'll work in your father's company?" asked the director, who'd been briefed by the Old Boss. "Of course," Frans replied. "I've wasted so much time—I can't wait."

Naturally, this was a lie. Frans's main objective was to be free from the Old Boss and his plans, but he also had to avoid conflicts. When he was called up for Dutch military service in January, he reported without complaint. He was confident he'd be wearing a German uniform in the end, so he did his best in the hopes of being declared fit for all arms. Such a recommendation would surely be in his favor when the real work started. He told the Dutch examiners that he aimed to join the cavalry, and when he learned that members of regional riding clubs received priority, he had his uncle Wim in Voorburg enroll him in a local club and reported it to the military examiner. However, Frans needed to finish school before he would be considered eligible for any kind of service.

Despite all this, the Old Boss still felt his son slipping through his fingers, so during Easter vacation he sent Frans to London to stay with a business associate, Sir James Charles Calder. Calder was also a devout Catholic, and in their fireside conversations at Von Lomani, the gentlemen had discovered that they were both ardently anti-Bolshevist, a sentiment that was mostly fueled by the Vatican's opinions on the matter. Their friendship was solidified when Sir James agreed to be Jimmy's godfather. Calder, a robust, energetic man in his seventies, received Frans at his impressive offices in London. He spoke good German for a Scotsman, which came as a relief to Frans—he'd been afraid he would have to put his high school English to the test. Sir James would take his guest for a week-long holiday at his enormous country house Lynford Hall in Norfolk. Calder invited another close friend to join them for the Easter holidays: Joseph Kennedy, US ambassador to Great Britain since 1937 and a man more Catholic than Calder and the Old Boss combined. Kennedy was also a good friend of the Old Boss, as was evident in his son Jimmy's middle name: Joseph.

Kennedy had brought some of his children with him. Although his daughter, Kathleen (who was called "Kick"), and Frans were about the same age, the two hardly exchanged a word. Frans was intimidated by women of her class, and being around the worldly, coquettish Kick only made him think, *When will I see my Wera again?* But Frans had even more trouble with the girl's brothers. Robert, the younger of the two who accompanied their father, was only thirteen and a little shy. But his big brother, John, who had just completed a European tour, explained everything that was wrong about Hitler and the Nazis. Since Frans was unable to translate his thoughts into English, he chose wisely not to contradict the confident John, who would, after all, be the president of the United States one day; on the inside, however, he had reached a boiling point. What an arrogant American! How dare he call the German occupation of Czechoslovakia an act of injustice! As if the millions of Sudeten Germans hadn't shown the world the truth: they wanted to be part of the German Reich, they longed for it, and Bohemia had no right to independence!

At the end of the week, Frans thanked Sir James for his hospitality. But at the same time Frans knew that, no matter what the Old Boss said or did, he would never belong to the upper class. His identity was anchored in the Baltics. Who cared about those Anglo-Saxon know-it-alls? When Germany finally rose to power, he knew he would be on the right side.

Summer 1939 brought a long heat wave to Latvia. The mood was languid and pastoral, perfect for the long, thoughtful conversations that Frans and Wera had under apple trees on their daily rides. Realizing his beloved had no interest in the military, Frans talked about his upcoming graduation and the studying he had to do to finish early. One day he'd brought *Uncle Tom's Cabin*, which he was reading for school, and when Wera took it and began reading it aloud with her beautiful English diction, it took on a whole new meaning. Lying on a blanket in the cool shade, Frans listened, enchanted. Off in the distance, their horses grazed peacefully in a field; he heard nothing but the chirp of crickets and the sound of her voice—his girl. Frans tingled with happiness.

On September 1, 1939, the Nazis blasted across the Polish border, and Hitler's war machine steamed east. The scythe of death thrashed across the battlefields. No life was left untouched; nothing was certain anymore. By then, the residents of Von Lomani had already fled. They'd gone to the Netherlands, this time as a family.

EIGHT

The Münninghoff family had been forced to leave Latvia in 1939 because of secret clauses in the Molotov-Ribbentrop Pact, negotiated between Nazi Germany and the USSR at the end of August. Hitler could have Poland, and Stalin was given the Baltic, including Livonia and Courland, which had both been governed by Germans for centuries. This secret agreement, part of the nonaggression treaty between the USSR and Germany, only became public after the war, but a small group of insiders had learned about it. My grandfather was one of those, and he was smart enough to understand the implications of the information he had been given. That the Soviets were poised to invade the Baltics was bad news for our family. Although we were by no means German royalty, we were *nouveau riche*, and the Bolsheviks had the same special treatment in store for their capitalist archenemies. Particularly on my grandmother's side of the family, there was no shortage of horror stories about the Bolsheviks.

Omi's older brother, Vladimir, had been a commander in General Denikin's White Army in the civil war that followed the Bolshevik's seizure of power. The White Army began wreaking havoc in Ukraine in 1919 and went on to carry out a total of approximately two hundred pogroms against the Jews, who were all Communists in the White Army's eyes. In reality, General Denikin's two hundred pogroms paled in comparison to the eight hundred carried out by Ukrainian general Symon Petliura and his gangs of local peasants in the same area the year before (the Ukrainian nationalists believed that the Jews were to blame for everything), but still, when the Reds captured Vladimir von Schumacher in 1920, they didn't hesitate to cut him open, gouge his eyes out, and hang him up by his ankles to bleed to death like an animal.

In the immeasurable chaos of the civil war, were the actions of individual members of enemy forces really so well documented that these types of executions could be justified? Or was Vladimir's execution just another one of the countless manifestations of the excessive, panicked cruelty that was so rampant in that part of the Russian Empire in those years? I suspect the latter, but I never found out for sure.

Whenever the story came up, my grandmother's eyes would well up with tears, and she'd sigh and shake her head. Vladimir, or Vova, as she called him, had been her favorite brother, and that fact alone was enough for me not to ask her any critical questions as I started learning more about the Russian civil war. I couldn't bear to see my dear old babushka weeping and wringing her hands at the thought of her beloved brother, and the last thing I wanted to do was cause her emotional despair in her old age.

Not that she couldn't handle it, of course. When the Red Army invaded Riga in January 1919 and established a Communist government with the support of the Latvian Social Democratic Workers Party, Omi marched in solidarity with the Bolsheviks, wearing a red scarf and waving a red flag. She didn't want anyone to think that just because she was a countess she didn't have her Red heart in the right place! Confident and cool under pressure, she used this cover to deceive the Reds.

A few months later, the predominantly Baltic German Iron Division had regained control, and Latvia was poised for internationally recognized independence. Everything going on confirmed what the Old Boss had said: the Germans were preparing for battle, and that would have direct consequences for Latvia, Estonia, and Lithuania. With such a large German community in the Baltics, that could have been expected. And how would the Latvians react? It was no secret that many Latvians harbored xenophobic sentiments, primarily against the German nobility, who were often referred to as "the cursed barons." One thing was certain, change was coming. The fact that Joan Münninghoff was actually Dutch and not German nobility wasn't readily apparent: his family surname was about as German-sounding as they come.

"I notice it in the factories," Joan said. "The workers look at me differently. It's as if they're thinking, *Just you wait, the Bolsheviks are coming, and then we'll be in charge.* I don't feel safe on my own property without the German shepherds anymore."

He'd heard what the workers were saying about the dogs behind his back: *He feels safer with two attack dogs at his side.* Their comments bothered the Old Boss. He'd just set up a social security net for his employees, and that had earned him the nickname "the Red capitalist," but none of that mattered anymore. Latvia was on the brink of a shift that threatened the entire Baltic upper class, regardless of where they were from.

Erica Münninghoff-Von Schumacher felt a change as well. She and her friends no longer spoke about their next trip to the Riviera and all the fun they were going to have in Nice. In the shadow of the looming war, the increasingly dominant topic of conversation was how to care for oneself and one's property. A few of the women were already packing their homes, but Erica wouldn't even consider it.

"My family has been living here for three centuries," she declared fiercely. "This is our country. No one will make me leave."

But her determination dissolved when one Sunday morning, while she was tending to the rose gardens, she was shot at by the longtime family gardener. The man hadn't shown up for work in a few days, and no one had heard from him. His absence aroused suspicion, especially

given the fact that he was a former fusilier in the Latvian Army and definitely pro-Bolshevik. Just the day before, her nephew had given her a
small revolver for protection, and she had it tucked in her apron pocket.

"I shot right back with my eyes closed," she told me decades later
in her flat in The Hague. Even then, she was still proud of the fact that
she'd hit him in the leg, and he was later arrested. "They shot at me in
1905, 1917, 1919, and in 1939, and they missed every time," she said.
"If you ask me, those Latvians are all bad shots!" With that, she let out
a hearty laugh and puffed out her chest, making a target that would be
hard to miss.

While the Soviet troops gathered on the Baltic borders in the fall
of 1939, my grandfather tried to save what could be saved. In the final
months of that year, the Dutch embassy in Riga estimated the value of
the Münninghoff family assets to be approximately seven million guilders, around sixty-five million euros by today's standards. In addition to
his ships, factories, houses, and land, my grandfather had accumulated
an astronomical amount of cash and assets. My family sees him now as
a kind of Scrooge McDuck with a swimming pool full of gold coins,
riches stashed away in Swiss bank vaults, and gold bars and jewels buried in the Courland countryside. Thanks to the seemingly unstoppable
rise of capitalism, these assets had multiplied exponentially in value
by the end of the twentieth century, resulting in an immeasurable fortune that we Münninghoffs all felt we had a right to. After all, hadn't
this wealth been confirmed with the signature, stamp, and seal of Her
Majesty's diplomatic representative in Riga? However, the Old Boss's
excessive caution prevented us from ever laying our hands on it.

Indeed, extreme discretion had long been Joan Münninghoff's trade-
mark. He had a widespread, influential network, which became apparent
in those final summer days before the Second World War. On August
28 he received a telegram with an announcement from Berlin from an

informant he would never identify: "The ball will begin in Warsaw in three days' time," code that an attack on Poland was imminent. He didn't waste a minute. The next day my entire family, suitcases in hand, boarded the last train to pass through the Polish Corridor unhindered.

"There was an armed Polish soldier at every train door," Xeno remembered. "I saw my father go gray overnight."

I took this to be metaphor, but when this critical episode in our history was discussed again many years later, Xeno stuck to his story: the Old Boss literally lost all his thick, dark hair in the twenty-four hours during which his business empire collapsed. The family albums confirm it: photos of the dynamic interwar tycoon are followed by images of a well-groomed fiftysomething with sad eyes and silvery-white hair.

No one in the family admitted that the Münninghoffs were leaving Latvia for good. Most adamant was my father; as soon as they arrived in Germany on their way to the Netherlands, Frans went into hiding with one of Omi's relatives in Hannover. Under no circumstances did he intend to move to the Netherlands permanently. In fact, he was planning to stay with Baltic friends who were in exile in East Prussia and Poland and had signed up en masse for the Wehrmacht, and especially for the SS, the elite forces. It was because he was still a minor—he was only nineteen and technically under his parents' authority until twenty-one—that the Old Boss was able to have him picked up by German police and brought to the Netherlands. Grandpa was the only one in the family who seemed prepared to accept their looming Dutch reality. They were so overwhelmed by longing for the luxurious lives they'd left behind that no one even tried to adapt. All eyes were on Riga, and German—or at least the Baltic variation of it—remained the household language, even in the Netherlands.

Still, most of our family wanted nothing to do with Hitler's sharp imperialist German, let alone all his shouting and barking. In Riga and Tallinn, members of the upper classes had nothing but contempt for that kind of speaking, and in the Netherlands, the attitude was no different. In our home, German was a language of courtesy and kindness, a language one could imagine being used for poetry, not militant propaganda. Personally, I will always remember the German language, which was my first, as a soft, loving whisper from my mother's lips.

But my mother wasn't in the Netherlands in 1940. Wera, along with hundreds of others, was stuck in Kolberg, a Prussian provincial outpost on the Baltic Sea, where she had ended up as part of the *Heim ins Reich* operation to return Baltic Germans to the "motherland." Her ship, the *Sierra Cordoba*, had fared better than the second one in the evacuation convoy, which one of her best friends had been on. It hit a sea mine and sank in less than two minutes before Wera's eyes.

In the fall and winter of 1939 leading up to *Fall Gelb*, which would terminate the Netherlands' precariously maintained neutrality in May, the Old Boss worked to save as much as he could. He made three short trips to Latvia to ensure that all of Von Lomani's household effects were stored safely in twenty-eight containers in the basement of Riga's city hall. He also had the brand-new machinery he'd bought for the textile factory packed into crates and stored in a nearby silo. These were dangerous trips because the Soviet troops could have invaded at any moment. Heim ins Reich had emptied the country of virtually all its Baltic Germans, and he didn't have enough friends left in Latvia—save for a few who'd worked for him and seen that his Dutch behavior was different—to guarantee his safety.

Once again, his special relationship with the president paid off; at first Ulmanis sent heavily armed guards to accompany him, and he was able to arrange his affairs without any trouble. This didn't last long, though. By December 1939, during Grandpa's third and final trip, Ulmanis notified him that tensions were high with Moscow and he should return to the Netherlands at once. The Old Boss's informants gave him a bit of extra time, but Ulmanis was unrelenting. As history would have it, my grandfather was right again: the Soviets didn't invade Latvia until June 1940. By then the Old Boss had moved his family to Voorburg, where his brother Wim lived.

Wim was a merchant with socialist sympathies who'd started an ammunition factory in Germany in the late 1920s, earned a fortune, and subsequently lost it all in the crash of 1929. The family story was that after the sale of his factory, Wim had just enough left to dine in a fancy restaurant one last time. At the end of the meal, he took a match to the deed of sale and used it to light a fat cigar. A hearty, jolly man with a sharp mind and a good head for business in fields like tropical crops, ballistics, and bookbinding, he, along with Aunt Marie—their eternally single and spiteful sister—always represented the Dutch side of the family for me. When Wim's marriage failed after twenty years, small, sickly Aunt Marie, a woman who wore lace collars and bore a strong resemblance to Princess Emma, had simply moved in with him. They saw it as a practical way to save money. The stately mansion they shared seemed straight out of a Couperus novel, with heavy curtains, chiming clocks, shiny dark brown parquet flooring, and tea served before the bright bay window on Sunday afternoons. When the family arrived from Riga, Wim was the primary tenant, and Marie had an entire wing at her disposal. Thea and Mietze, Wim's daughters, had already left home by then, in no small part due to their aunt's constant nitpicking.

Unsurprisingly, the sudden invasion from Riga was not entirely welcome at first—despite the fact that the Old Boss was, of course, the undisputed owner of the house. Marie's main target was Omi, her wild sister-in-law whom she criticized for what she considered an overly luxurious lifestyle. The women lasted three months under the same roof, and then our family moved to a nearby villa spacious enough to house all our displaced relatives. The first thing the Old Boss did after buying it was fill the entire basement with cans of corned beef and other nonperishables. "Enough for the next five years," he proclaimed, with what turned out to be an uncannily accurate vision of the future. He named the house Briva Latvija, Latvian for "Free Latvia," and painted the words over the balcony in Gothic script.

This inscription says a lot about how our family, and Grandpa in particular, viewed the war that broke out in the Netherlands a few weeks later. Although my grandfather was born in Laren and considered himself first and foremost a Dutchman, the Münninghoffs were foreigners to everyone there. And though we weren't German, the Gothic letters painted on our balcony certainly looked German. And if you really thought about it, you might come to the conclusion that the residents of the house were pro-Germany, since it was the Germans who "liberated" Latvia from the Soviets in 1941.

In the chaotic months between the departure from Riga at the end of August 1939 and the German attack on the Netherlands on May 10, 1940, the family was mostly in shock. Omi missed her friends and desperately tried to stay in touch with them. She wrote them countless letters, not knowing whether they'd reach their destinations. It was during this confusing period that she heard that her brother Stanislaw, who no one knew had even survived the Russian civil war, had been spotted in Shanghai. Omi became obsessed with the idea, and like any good Russian woman, she began consulting fortune-tellers and holding occult sessions. Meanwhile, the Old Boss was constantly out of town, not only in Latvia, but also in England, where a contact put him in touch with MI6. My grandfather was able to provide the agency with a significant amount of information about the Latvian border regions, and MI6 registered him as a reliable contact in the Netherlands. The twins were admitted to Huize Katwijk without any difficulties, and Titty was accepted at the art academy in The Hague, not far from the house in Voorburg, all of which came as a tremendous relief.

And Frans, the problem child? After relentless complaining, he managed to escape the family's grip and rent a room in the home of some friends in Utrecht. He promised to finish high school there, but the family had more important things to do than to keep tabs on his attendance. By the time the Germans invaded on May 10, Frans had made friends with a troubled group of boys with wealthy parents living in the Dutch East Indies. Left adrift and unsupervised, they saw war as an adventure and flirted with the idea of enlisting in the German military. Frans sent a postcard to his father, dated May 13, 1940, while battles were raging on Dutch soil, with an urgent request for money: "75 or 100 guilders. It'll be a long time before we see each other again. Frans." And his last communication arrived in mid-June, asking the Old Boss to send a telegram to Batavia to the parents of his friends, Albert and Jack, letting them know their sons were all right.

Then no one heard from Frans until September 1940. In those four months, he transformed into a military man, and when he returned to The Hague, he was his father's son no more. Still a minor in the eyes of the law, Frans knew exactly what he wanted and how he planned to get it. He arranged a meeting with the Old Boss at Huize Katwijk via Father Constant Kolfschoten, who was in the room when Frans laid out his plans for the future. The military school in Zagreb was no longer an option, but there was another route. The Old Boss reacted with horror when SS rolled off his son's lips, but Father Kolfschoten spoke to him. The fanatically anti-Communist clergyman was pleased with Frans's desire to fight the Red Army, and he put the Old Boss under such tremendous moral pressure that he finally surrendered. "Do what you want. I can't change your mind anyway," my grandfather said.

In October 1940, Frans reported for duty at the SS headquarters in The Hague with three goals in mind: to find his friends from Riga and join them, to drive the Bolsheviks out of his Latvia, and to marry Wera.

NINE

During Hitler's Heim ins Reich, most of the Baltic nobility were grudgingly regrouped in Nazi-occupied Poland. They'd been forced to leave their family estates and possessions, most of which had been in their families for centuries, but were given new estates across the border in what had been Poland, where the original population was being driven out. It was this so-called *Neuland*, or "new land," that would bring about the Germanization of the East, a key component of the *Lebensraum* philosophy—or that was the plan in Berlin. Contradictory feelings prevailed among the approximately 150,000 Baltic Germans who ended up in the Third Reich. On the one hand, they were aware that they'd escaped a Bolshevik invasion and Soviet occupation, exactly as the Nazi propaganda had predicted; in June 1940, the Red Army invaded the Baltic countries, and Communist puppet governments took power on behalf of Moscow. But had the hasty evacuation really been necessary? Trains full of bread, oil, salt, and other provisions for German troops were arriving from Russia every day, so it was clear that they were just pawns in a game between Stalin and Hitler, and no one knew who was cheating. But a new reality had manifested, and the residents of Neuland set to work building a new future. They were inspired by Berlin's charismatic totalitarian approach, and just as hypnotized by their Führer as their German compatriots.

One of the most important centers of the new Eastern territories was Posen, which served as the largest railway junction to the east, and the Luftwaffe had a major airport just outside the city. The majority of the Baltic Germans eventually settled here, including Wera and her mother, who spent their first few weeks in sleepy Kolberg until Wera got a job as a secretary to the chief dramaturg of Posen's Grand Theatre. Members of the younger Baltic generation gathered daily at Café Schwan, and in no time, three-quarters of Riga's handsome young men were marching around in SS uniforms. The Bolsheviks were coming one way or another, pact or no pact, they reasoned. It didn't take long for the Baltic German community to realize that they were on the brink of war with the USSR. Despite their initial doubts about Hitler, they eventually capitulated to his warmongering spirit—even though they still found the man himself pathetically bourgeois. With the girls looking on in silent adoration, the boys at Café Schwan made impassioned speeches and militant toasts. A confrontation with the Communists, their long-standing enemies, was inevitable. A feeling of inescapable threat was in the air, which, frightening as it was, gave way to a spirit of unbridled excitement.

My father had no idea just how quickly he needed to get to Café Schwan in Posen after reporting to the SS in October 1940. Luckily for him, the recruitment office in The Hague proved exceedingly helpful. They decided that, given his knowledge of Russian, he could best serve as an interpreter (further evidence that the Nazis were already planning an attack on the Soviet Union). Frans filled out the application forms for the interpreting school in Berlin on the spot and placed his signature at the bottom of the SS contract. He was given documents to travel to Posen and an advance payment, and three days later, he was sweeping a surprised Wera into his arms at Café Schwan as his friends from Riga cheered in the background. In his SS uniform with a red band around the left arm that read *Dolmetscher*, or "interpreter," he made a big show of signing the guestbook behind the bar at Café Schwan exclusively reserved for members of the young Baltic in-crowd. Wera—who hadn't seen him in over a year—immediately fell in love with him all over again, and from that moment on she, too, believed they were destined to be together.

The interpreters' training program fell through in the end, much to Frans's delight. He worked in Posen for three weeks as an interpreter with the Reich commissioner for the consolidation of German nationhood, but was so bored by the bureaucratic nature of the work he'd been assigned that he submitted a request to be transferred to Prague, where most of his friends were undergoing basic training with the first company of the SS regiment Deutschland. His request was granted, and his military passport was inscribed *usable as Russian interpreter*.

On one hand, the training in Prague was ruthless, but on the other, it built an indestructible sense of camaraderie and convinced the young soldiers that they were part of a mission to save Europe from the Bolsheviks. It was this fanaticism for a cause that enthralled the recruits. My father once told me, "I had to scrub the barrack toilets with a toothbrush, with my genitals hanging out!" The methods, the blows, and the booted kicks seemed perfectly normal to him, even effective.

"As far as I was concerned, our armies were already facing the Russians on Poland's eastern border, and pretty soon we'd be headed that way as well. We'd known this for a while and talked about it openly. The excitement of it all was indescribable! We were prepared to laugh off all the pain and punishment of training if it meant that we could continue with the glorious campaign," he said.

"We all believed that the harsh, sometimes even unjust treatment made us stronger mentally. We all received the same blows, heard the same stories, and sang the same songs, which created a sense of solidarity stronger than any I've ever experienced since. *Meine Ehre heißt Treue*—My honor is called loyalty—to us that meant loyal to each other. We were filled with the unshakable certainty that we would never let each other down. And that's how it was."

With this spirit, he was transferred to Munich and finally stepped onto the battlefield on June 22, 1941, Day One of Operation Barbarossa.

TEN

Meanwhile, the war was offering my grandfather opportunities to put his extraordinary talents for manipulation and opaque business deals to good use in the Netherlands. Thanks to his international reputation and good credit with former business partners, he managed to rebuild his commercial enterprise within a few months. He saw the war as a test of his business acumen, a game of Risk, in which the fundamental aspects of the war remained largely in the background. That his own firstborn son had chosen the other side was just a fact.

"He's dead to me," he said in the early days of the Occupation to Dutch Resistance fighter Bert Westenberg, a timber merchant from Riga. It was probably the worst thing he'd ever said about his son.

"I'd have done the same thing in his position," Westenberg replied, and the Old Boss learned his lesson. From then on, Frans was kept as a kind of trump card that, if necessary, could be played in conversations with German occupiers.

My grandfather used his trading company, N. V. Poortensdijk, which he'd founded in the 1920s, as a vehicle to build a new business empire. He'd have to work with the Germans—that much was clear—but he would also have to stay on good terms with the Allies. Apart from his dislike for all things Nazi, my grandfather never actually believed that Germany would win the war. Nevertheless, the Nazis had regained control of Riga shortly after the start of Barbarossa, so if he wanted to preserve his Latvian possessions, he needed to play both sides. While maintaining a good working relationship with the Germans, he needed to build enough credit with the Allies to ensure an immaculate moral reputation during peacetime and reconstruction. He had no way of knowing if returning to Latvia would ever be an option, but he sensed that re-emigration under German rule, which was possible, would've been a fatal error. Although much of the family returned to Riga after the German victory in the Baltic in 1941, most were from the fanatical Strandmann clan, my grandmother's side. My grandfather wanted absolutely nothing to do with them; still, he made plans to use their position to his fullest advantage. Beyond that, he couldn't imagine joining them. His strong sense of Dutch patriotism, despite all his opportunistic ideas, simply wouldn't allow it.

As always, the Old Boss held his cards close to the chest and said very little about his plans to anyone. But there it was, in black and white, in a letter he sent from Voorburg to Princess Juliana in Ottawa on January 8, 1942. I still have a copy of it:

> Due to rather unusual circumstances, I find myself presently in a position to send uncensored letters abroad. It is my pleasure to use this opportunity to carry out a long-cherished wish. I have commissioned the American Express Company Inc. in New York to transfer, after acquiring permission from the foreign exchange authorities, a sum of five thousand US $ to your Royal Highness in service of the war effort. While I am certain that countless Dutch compatriots would happily do the same given the opportunity, and that at least 98% of the Dutch—especially among the laborers and less fortunate—have proven themselves to be loyal patriots "through thick and thin," I remain the humble servant of Your Royal Highness, J. M. J. A. Münninghoff.

Five thousand dollars may not seem like such a staggering sum nowadays, but in 2019 values it's more than eighty thousand dollars. One could say that through his donation my grandfather brought himself into the House of Orange's field of vision. His estimate that 98 percent of Dutch people were loyal to the crown was optimistic, and I'm inclined to think it was an attempt to tug at Princess Juliana's heartstrings; my grandfather was simply too well informed to believe that was actually true.

Every time I read the letter, I wonder whether the Old Boss may have shepherded it through the war as a kind of insurance policy against any misfortune to come—and misfortune certainly came. How did he do it? The copy of the letter was kept in his safe, so if the Gestapo ever raided his house, they would find it. Perhaps he thought that if the Nazis came, he'd have time to destroy it. Or perhaps he assumed that since he'd already established good relationships among the high ranks of the occupying forces, his house wouldn't be raided.

It is not hard to imagine that the German occupiers, who were used to attracting the services of all kinds of opportunists, collaborators, and hotheaded Dutch Nazis, jumped at the chance to work with a man like my grandfather. After all, he had connections all over Europe, and in wartime being able to communicate via informal channels was incredibly important. The Nazis' impression that my grandfather was on their side was solidified when they learned that his eldest son, Frans, had been fighting with the Waffen-SS since October 1940. Any father who allows his son to put on the Nazi uniform and go to war has already made the greatest sacrifice a man can make, they reasoned.

That's what *Kriminalkommissar* Johann Munt, head of German police in The Hague, most likely thought when he paid the Old Boss a visit to discuss his history in Latvia. Munt was an intellectual who despised the authoritarianism the Nazis were displaying in the Netherlands, and certainly wasn't among the friends of *Reichskommisar* Arthur Seyss-Inquart or SS Leader Hanns Rauter. The Old Boss carefully built a relationship with Munt that could be described as a conscious effort between two polite, civilized people amid the misery of the war.

There was a story about a time when several German naval officers came for dinner at Briva Latvija. These were men with direct access to Admiral Wilhelm Canaris, head of the German military intelligence service. What these men discussed (the Old Boss never told anyone in our family their names) after dinner over cigars and cognac wasn't recorded. These meetings were extremely secret and dangerous; there were Gestapo agents and spies lurking around every corner. But through indirect remarks, gestures, meaningful silences, well-timed sighs, coughs, and the refilling of glasses, they managed to build an atmosphere of mutual trust, which later allowed them to discuss more significant activities, all the way to the July 20, 1944, attack on Hitler. Slowly but surely the Old Boss gained a foothold among those German authorities who realized that with Hitler they had bet their money on the wrong horse.

While thousands of soldiers in Berlin prepared for Operation Barbarossa—the fatal, decisive attack on the Soviet Union on June 22, 1941—the military apparatus was being steered by higher-ups who wanted a confrontation with the USSR but didn't want Germany to face the Soviets alone. Getting the Allies on their side seemed like a desirable solution. One of these high-ranking people was Admiral Canaris, who had the help of a number of his old navy buddies—though this wasn't confirmed until the end of the war when his diaries were found in a safe. They were stationed on bases all over Europe, and at his request they'd seek out important people in the business and public spheres who supported this plan. My grandfather was, or so the inhabitants of Briva Latvija believed, one of Admiral Canaris's interlocutors. After all, Admiral Canaris's scheme would have helped the Old Boss regain his Latvian estate. Someone inevitably, at some point or another, was going to try to sideline Hitler—but by internment or liquidation? That was the question. Rudolf Hess's mysterious flight to Scotland, where he reportedly aimed to negotiate peace with the Allies without Hitler's knowledge, in May 1941, seemed to be an indication of this.

If our family had been an average Dutch family, we would've been members of the Resistance. Uncle Wim was, in fact; the large house where he and Aunt Marie lived was the site of a clandestine Resistance operation making counterfeit passports, ration cards, and all kinds of other documents (Uncle Wim was, among other things, a trained calligrapher) and hiding people. The Old Boss certainly knew this, but he had other interests, and took a different approach to the realities of the war.

Briva Latvija served as a hiding place for a few people too: there was Peter Meyer Viol, a half-Jewish classmate of the twins' from Huize Katwijk who served as a courier for the Resistance, and Jan Boeder, a friend of Bert Westenberg, head of the Amsterdam Zuid Resistance group. Both men lived in the basement of Briva Latvija for several months, hidden among the extra provisions. There was also a friend of Uncle Wim's whom the family called "the Railroad Man." He lived in a maid's room that had a fake wall behind an opening in the back of a wardrobe filled with women's clothes, where he could comfortably hide if the house were ever searched. The rest of the room, down to the toiletries next to the washbasin, was decidedly feminine, to complete the illusion. But thanks to the Old Boss's contacts in the higher echelons of German authorities, it was unlikely the house would be raided. Additionally, Frans was in the SS, and German was the language of the house. Frau Kochmann, the ever-reliable family cook who'd come with them from Riga, helped the family keep up appearances.

So, when the doorbell rang on a cold evening in February 1944, followed by shouts of "Open up!" everyone panicked. Boeder was in the basement, but Meyer Viol, who had trouble enduring life in hiding and often came upstairs for a breath of fresh air, was with the Old

Boss in the smoking room listening to Radio Orange, and the Railroad Man had just come downstairs. The family never knew why they were raided; perhaps one of the deliverymen noticed something and tipped off the SD, raising suspicions as to why so many German naval officers visited Briva Latvija. There were also rumors about Admiral Canaris at the time, so the Nazis decided to come have a look for themselves.

There was no time for the houseguests to return to their hiding places, though Frau Kochmann stalled as much as she could. She played grumpy (which she was by nature—a dramatic moment certainly wasn't going to change that). *"Ja, ja!"* she hollered at the four men in black hats standing on the doorstep, fiddling loudly with her keys as if she couldn't find the right one. Her act gave everyone the extra minute they needed. While Meyer Viol ran upstairs, dashed out onto the balcony, and attempted to hide in a wall of ivy, the Railroad Man went through the kitchen and ran out through the backyard into a typical Voorburg street lined with row houses. He kept going until he reached Uncle Wim, who hid him in the tower of the Sint-Martinus Catholic church on Oosteinde.

But Meyer Viol wasn't as lucky. "What are you doing here?" the SD agent asked the young man standing against the wall trying in vain to disappear into the ivy. Out of desperation, he'd even scattered a fistful of leaves on his head. "Can't you see?" he replied in German, his eyes full of contempt, "I'm hiding from you!" He was promptly handcuffed, and what followed was anything but funny.

The only one who kept a cool head through the whole ordeal was the Old Boss. He switched stations on the radio (which he had a license to own), took the two glasses into the kitchen, and righted the overturned chairs. When the agents entered the room, he was calmly working at his desk. How the Old Boss pulled it off in such little time was a mystery. The highest-ranking SD agent was ushered into the smoking room, and the door shut behind him. Half an hour later he emerged and ordered his men to release Meyer Viol. The four uninvited guests politely bid the household a good evening and left. Even Peter Meyer Viol struggled to describe it in his memoir. "He saved my life," was all he wrote.

It's possible that Meyer Viol, bilingual in German and Dutch, had been selected by Kriminalkommissar Munt to participate in an informal meeting he was trying to arrange with the Resistance youth to create understanding for the German perspective and to try to improve the image of the occupying forces. It seemed like a logical initiative of a decent person who was tired of being treated as less than human because of his nationality, rank, and uniform. As idealistic as it may seem, a significant amount of work was going on behind the scenes in Munt's division to establish enough trust for this meeting. The arrest of one of the invited participants would have ruined everything. And Munt's meeting did take place shortly after the Nazis' visit to Briva Latvija, and Meyer Viol and Jimmy were among the ten participants, but it didn't lead to the mutual understanding Munt had hoped for. When word of his efforts began to circulate in Nazi circles, Munt's relationship with Reichskommisar Seyss-Inquart and Joseph Schreieder, who led the Nazi counterespionage department in the Netherlands, suffered. Munt was seen as soft—but remarkably, he wasn't fired.

The Old Boss, on good terms with the reasonable Munt, but not with the fanatical Schreieder (the man behind England Game), was now in danger. This became clear two months later, in April 1944, when he was arrested and interrogated by the Gestapo. He could no longer count on any special treatment from Munt; if someone blew the whistle on the Old Boss—and someone certainly would—the consequences would be serious. The interrogators mostly asked him about Bert Westenberg. Schreieder's assiduous spies had discovered that Westenberg and the Old Boss were good friends in Riga in the interwar period. They'd gotten to know each other in the timber trade, and both had returned to the Netherlands as the Soviets were preparing to invade Latvia in 1939. As the leader of the Amsterdam Zuid Resistance, Westenberg was a high-value target for the Gestapo, and the agents thought they might be able to extract information from his former companion. An hour later, they arrested Jimmy, who was questioned about his connection to Peter Meyer Viol, who'd since gone into hiding elsewhere. The Gestapo had inadvertently picked up on Westenberg's trail by arresting the Old Boss. The Resistance fighter was, in fact, hiding at the Binckhorst industrial complex in The Hague, where Jimmy brought him food every day. He could do this without attracting any attention because he was working as an administrator at the nearby Stork's ring fan factory, which the Old Boss had bought.

If either of the Münninghoffs had talked, Westenberg would undoubtedly have been arrested and shot. But neither of them did. Father and son were interrogated separately. They didn't even know the other was there until, thanks to the negligence of one of the guards, they crossed paths in a hallway. The Old Boss swept his hand across his mouth, as if wiping, but Jimmy understood immediately: *Don't say a word.* That gesture gave him strength, he later explained. Finally, he had a chance to prove to his father—the man who had always seen him as a disabled mama's boy—that he was capable of doing something right.

Jimmy's interrogators started by asking him if he knew anyone by the name of Bert, and he answered without missing a beat: "Yes, Bert ten Brink. We were in school at Katwijk. He was two grades behind me." This disarmingly effortless reply, along with Jimmy's noticeable disability (his right shoulder was higher than his left and his right arm conspicuously thin) and effortless German—not to mention the Baltic German crusaders pin on his lapel (which the Old Boss wasn't happy about)—was enough to convince the interrogators to let him go. He was released within the hour.

The Old Boss didn't get off so lightly. The interrogators remained hands-off, but he was kept overnight in prison for further interrogation. That gave his friends in the German Navy a chance to act, and they came marching into the Binnenhof, and gave the Gestapo commander a piece of their minds: "Either shoot him for being a spy or let him go. The fact is, we need him!" They explained that the Old Boss had set up a production line that was extremely important to the Third Reich, naturally leaving out that they also needed his intel for a secret attack on Hitler set to take place barely two months later.

What they said about my grandfather's production line was correct, and that was ultimately the reason the Old Boss—who'd denied having any relationship with Bert Westenberg whatsoever—was released that same day. My grandfather had a license to produce a Swedish gas generator at his Binckhorst factory, and Berlin had officially declared this machine indispensable to the war effort. In other words, the Old Boss had made himself essential to German authorities; once the importance of his production line was confirmed, there was no reason to interrogate him further. The Gestapo agents apologized profusely and returned him to Briva Latvija by private car. The Nazis never bothered him again.

The Old Boss's connections to Sweden gave him the opportunity to travel to Stockholm on a regular basis, yet another Joan Münninghoff–style business venture, carried out in secret.

It turned out the Old Boss hadn't started his business in Latvia on his own but with his younger brother, Tom. His brother also settled in Riga, where he quickly gained a reputation for being a wild womanizer, and Joan worried about him. Even after his face was partially burned with hydrochloric acid in a factory accident, his activities didn't diminish.

My father, who visited him regularly as an adolescent in the 1930s, was still baffled by him: "He looked like a crumpled rag doll, with a large, dark brown burn spot on his forehead, a blunt, chewed-up nose, and scars all over. But he managed to compensate for his appearance with his personality. He was a good talker and a born charmer; women were head over heels for him. So you see—it's not looks that matter, it's what's behind them. You could laugh with the guy, and he was downright wasteful with money—which I of course took advantage of. The women did too, by the way. How he got his hands on all that money was a mystery to me. But, of course, I didn't think about it that much at that age."

Tom's Casanova reputation in Latvian high society didn't sit well with my socially sensitive grandfather, and he wanted to distance himself from his brother, so the Old Boss made Tom director of his textile factory in Bauska, a small town on the Lithuanian border. In 1939, the two brothers didn't flee Latvia together. Tom managed to avoid the Soviets by escaping to neutral Sweden in a speedboat across the Baltic Sea. He eventually ended up in Stockholm, where he had some good business contacts. There he married the girl he'd been dating, Käthe Endel, whose father had been the Swedish consul general in Riga. Thanks to her, he managed to obtain Swedish nationality without any trouble.

These circumstances offered interesting possibilities in wartime, and so the brothers managed to put aside their differences in order to face the challenges at hand: surviving the war and subsequently recovering their lost possessions. An excellent opportunity presented itself in 1942, when my grandfather secured the rights to produce the Kaelle gas generator in the Netherlands. The machine, a peat-fired engine, was a product of Swedish fan factory Svenska Fläktfabriken, and would become extremely valuable as fuel became increasingly scarce. Not only was the machine important for the Dutch, but it became indispensable to the Germans, who needed to transport supplies and troops and had little hope of conquering the Caucasian oil fields.

How did Joan Münninghoff obtain that license and convince the Nazis to let him take a test drive in a car with a specially designed Kaelle engine, which would get him to Riga in three days? Obviously, Uncle Tom and his father-in-law had lent him a helping hand from Stockholm. But how he managed to make the high-level connections within the Nazi administration that were necessary to establish a profitable relationship with Sweden and travel to Stockholm is, in retrospect, less clear. My grandfather made use of a contact he'd made in the early days of the occupation: German banker Otto Rebholz, who'd come to the Netherlands in 1924 as a young lawyer and eventually become a naturalized Dutch citizen. Rebholz's firm specialized in international stockbroking and was able to build up a lot of contacts in Germany at the beginning of the war, thanks to Rebholz. It came as no surprise that after Berlin appointed a special commissary for De Nederlandsche Bank in 1941, Rebholz became the first point of contact. Rebholz proved himself to be a diligent friend to his compatriots; he personally carried out a number of transactions for Seyss-Inquart on the Dutch stock market, where assets formerly held by Jews were free for the taking.

My grandfather had known Rebholz in Berlin in the 1920s, so, in 1942, he decided to invite him for dinner. The men discussed the peat-fired engine in the smoking room over a glass of cognac. That evening Rebholz became the cofounder of the Dutch-Baltic peat company Nebalturf. The company would harvest peat in Latvia, which would be used to fuel the new Swedish engines, but it goes without saying that Joan Münninghoff's underlying motivation was to regain some control of his Latvian holdings.

Thanks to his new partner's ties to Berlin, my grandfather obtained papers to travel to Germany, Latvia, and even Sweden on business at a time when it was virtually impossible to travel freely. In summer 1943, after the Old Boss visited Minister Rosenberg at the Reich's Ministry for the Occupied Eastern Territories in Berlin, the Kaelle peat-fired engine was elevated to a matter of imperial interest. From then on, there was nothing in the way of my grandfather carrying out the project. Shortly afterward, my grandfather left on a test drive to Riga, accompanied by a lawyer friend. Once he got there, he developed "engine trouble" and managed to stay for a week longer than planned, enough time for him to check on his holdings in Latvia and take a few appropriate measures.

It was clear that repatriation to Latvia was not advisable. Although the Germans had things somewhat under control, the horrors of war were everywhere. The Jewish population, once approximately 30 percent of the more than half a million people in Riga, was gone. Nearly all Latvian Jews had been killed, deported, or forced into death camps outside the city. There was also a growing sense of malaise from the eastern front. The small country seemed to be collapsing under pressure from the Soviet Union, and Riga was so paralyzed by the looming prospect of Bolshevik reoccupation that there was hardly any business or industry to speak of.

The Old Boss understood that, as far as his factories and other holdings went, there was nothing to do but wait and hope. However, he decided to keep abreast of happenings in Riga by making deals with "the Lords of the Kudra," a cartel of Latvian peat farmers with a lofty-sounding name who were eager for a steady customer in these uncertain times. For the Old Boss, the main motivation behind this was to keep Xeno and some Dutch friends out of the Germans' forced labor system, the *Arbeitseinsatz*, by hiring them to oversee the peat-harvesting process in Latvia.

All his factories were now under German authority, so the Old Boss focused his attention on the items from his villa. With the help of the Riga police, of which Uncle Arno was again the commander, my grandfather managed to have all the items loaded onto a barge. One week later, the shipment was delivered to Voorburg, much to the family's surprise. Most members of the Münninghoff household had abhorred the Tudor-style chairs and sofas (a judgment that I came to share), and no one thought the Old Boss would waste his energy trying to salvage them.

But that's just how he was. Joan Münninghoff didn't give up what belonged to him, and if someone took something from him, he wouldn't rest until he had it back. The fact that he managed, in the middle of the war, at a time when logistics were incredibly difficult, to have this rather insignificant cargo transported all the way from Latvia to the Netherlands with relative ease is further evidence of his tireless persistence, not to mention the quality of his connections.

The parts for the peat-fired engine—a ninety-pound box that could be mounted on the hood of a vehicle—went into production immediately after the test drive, and were assembled at the Stork's ring fan factory in The Hague. Demand exploded, not only among the Germans, but also among the Dutch. My uncle Tom was eventually able to buy the Grand Hotel in Malmö with the profits. The factories couldn't keep up with demand; delivery time quickly grew to four months, which some people found too long.

One such person was the owner of Huifkar Cigars in Oisterwijk. During the war, this incorrigible bon vivant lived in the luxurious Hotel des Indes in The Hague, renting an extra room next to his suite just to store his massive cigar collection. He proposed paying my grandfather in cigars, a highly valuable commodity during those years, and the Old Boss, an avid cigar smoker himself, agreed. My grandfather took his new stock to one of his German Navy friends who traveled regularly to Berlin to meet with Rear Admiral Von Puttkamer, another cigar fanatic, and one of Hitler's personal adjutants. The arrival of high-quality Dutch cigars from Huifkar, a famous brand in connoisseurs' circles, was received with great enthusiasm by Von Puttkamer. In fact, he was so delighted that he became good friends with the much lower-ranking lieutenant who delivered them. Von Puttkamer, who'd been wounded in the bombing on July 20, 1944, and met with Hitler daily, sometimes casually shared information about the Führer's daily affairs and other secrets from Berlin's highest circles, much of which was repeated in the Old Boss's parlor in Voorburg. This was one of the ways the Old Boss remained thoroughly informed on the upcoming attack on Hitler. During his visits to Stockholm, he was able to pass this information on to MI6 agents.

ELEVEN

Frans Münninghoff could have considered himself lucky. It wasn't exactly what he'd hoped for, he told me later, but when the SS sent you somewhere, you went. It turned out the Nazis needed more than battlefield pawns, and at the last minute, Frans was sent to the Russian front as an interpreter for regimental staff. From Lublin, the Viking Division set off toward the apocalyptic battlefield on the other side of the Russian border. Meanwhile, my father was able to take shelter in the officers' quarters, surrounded by topographic maps, canteens, and field telephones. His best friend from Riga, Wolf Metzkeris, was a tank commander, killed just days after deploying. Many of Frans's friends met the same fate; troubled, Frans asked to be transferred to the front lines. Better interpreters had arrived from Berlin by then, so he was sent to the front, leaving the officers shaking their heads at his disregard for his own life.

One Sunday morning, years later, my father poured himself his first drink at eight in the morning, as he often did, and I prepared for one of his endless stories about the Russian front. His big brown eyes welled up with tears, but as a teenager I found it hard to show compassion.

It was always the same ritual. "How are things at school?" he'd ask, and then, without really waiting for an answer, he'd launch into a story. "Listen, did I ever tell you about Pauli, winter of '43? You weren't even born yet. We were lying in the trenches, he didn't give a damn about any of it, I knew him from Riga, he had this long blonde hair. He stood up and started combing it, to provoke the Russians, or maybe he had gone crazy, yeah, he'd probably gone crazy. I yelled at him to take cover—*Pauli, are you crazy? Get down!* But he just laughed and kept on combing his hair, with those long strokes. The bullet went straight through his forehead. It didn't take a sniper to shoot him, he was a sitting duck. You know what I mean?"

I shrugged.

He looked at me helplessly, eyes full of indignation, as if I were some kind of military psychiatrist, then took a sip and went on. "We were in Georgia, winter of '42 to '43. Tip of the sword. There were eighteen of us, mostly Balts. All we had to do was survive the winter and wait for the spring offensive. We all spoke Russian, there were even a few local Mingrelians and Cossacks among us. Anyway, we assimilated into the local community and rode around unarmed on mules. The villagers were friendly enough. Stalin and his cronies weren't all that popular in the Caucasus—I'll tell you about that later. Sure, he was the hero of the Ossetians because he came from their tribe and all, but everybody else'd had enough of him by then. And once we were snowed in a kind of solidarity developed. We were in it together, y'know? United against two common enemies—nature and the Bolsheviks."

"Communication with headquarters was at a complete standstill; we were mostly forgotten, useless in the bigger picture. But what a great village, Bully! They didn't care what was going on in the world, whether there was peace or war. When the winter was over and Stalingrad had fallen and everything had thawed and things were working again, we were ordered to rejoin the general forces. Looking back, we'd've been better off not going—then we would've at least had a chance. But we didn't even think about it back then. I was wounded twice after that, but y'know, if I'd've stayed behind, the Soviets would've killed me after the war."

By the time he finished telling me his stories, he'd drunk about a quart of gin.

Of all my father's war stories, there was one he told rarely, quickly, and without embellishment, as if he himself were in awe. I think this must've been the moment he was closest to death. I still remember the first time he told it to me.

My parents were out somewhere, and I was poking around the house and found a giant sword behind the wardrobe in their bedroom. The dark wood scabbard was lined with leather, and its handle was trimmed with copper and looked like a bird's head. Despite the dullness of the copper and the worn leather, there was something murderously fascinating about the weapon. When my parents came home, I couldn't keep the discovery to myself.

My father smiled at my excitement, took the sword into the living room, poured himself a glass, and began to tell me the story.

"This is a sabre, Bully, not a sword. It belonged to an officer in the Red Army. It's my only war trophy. It was summer 1942, and I was in Ukraine with my regiment. I'd just married your mother in Hamburg. A couple of Wera's relatives let us stay at their farm in Lübeck to have a break from the chaos and violence of the war. But on the battlefield, things took a turn for the worse, so I was called back. Did you know Ukraine was known as the granary of Europe?

"Our troops were assembled in the forest. We were planning an attack, and I was sent out to recon the area with a few other guys. We had to cross this giant cornfield; ten yards in and you were lost. Surrounded by six-foot-high stalks, you lose all orientation. Well, they should've sent the Luftwaffe to check it out first, but they didn't. Anyway, not long into it, we'd lost all contact with each other. We couldn't turn back; that would have been seen as disobeying orders. Calling out was impossible because there were Russians hiding in the field. So, I trudged on, pushing through the corn stalks—it was like being in some kind of jungle."

My father slowly extracted the sabre from its sheath with great care. "All of a sudden, I stepped into a clearing about the size of our front yard. At the exact same moment someone stepped out of the corn across

"After a few months," my father continued, "their attitude changed, and the people in our occupied territories became bitter enemies. It was Hitler's idiotic Lebensraum and his plan to make Russians and Ukrainians slaves of his *Herrenvolk*. You can read about that in the history books, but there was another reason that they turned against us: they feared retaliation from the partisans, who were hiding in the woods by the thousands, often under the command of Red Army officers. At night they'd come into the villages and execute anyone who was collaborating with us.

"We didn't do much about it because we'd already moved on by then—we only left behind a garrison in larger cities. But of course it made people less willing to work with us. The last time I worked as an interpreter was in 1943, in Cherkasy on the Dnieper River. I had to help interrogate a couple of prisoners of war. It was a grim scene, and the SS interrogators quickly concluded that they weren't going to get the answers they'd been hoping for. They were officers, a couple of assholes from Saxony, but as a sergeant I couldn't protest, so I just interpreted. But soon enough, I realized that things were going to go much differently than before.

"In the early days, prisoners were housed in camp and eventually taken to Germany or one of the occupied territories to work. Tens of thousands of Russians, guarded by just a few men from the Wehrmacht, were transported without any major incident. They could've taken those guards out, but they didn't—they were happy to be alive and happy that the Germans weren't the man-eating warriors their propaganda machine had made them out to be. And we were winning, so we were in high spirits and always treated their officers politely, offering them food and coffee during interrogations.

"But this time it was different; we were just coming out of the Battle of Stalingrad and were in retreat. Morale was low, and we were nervous and on edge. The Russian POWs bore the brunt of it. During a smoke break, a Baltic acquaintance said that after interrogation, the prisoners were loaded into trucks in groups of twenty and shot in a ditch on the edge of Cherkasy. I still wonder how I had the nerve to do what I did next.

"I went to the barn where the prisoners were being held and pulled out the next one in line for interrogation. He was a young kid with a friendly, open face and dark eyes. He'd been sitting on the ground with a picture of his wife and son in his hand, and I couldn't take it. I pulled him up by the belt, dragged him outside, whispered in his ear that he needed to get the hell out of there because they were going to kill him, and gave him a hard push toward the edge of the woods. He didn't have to be told twice, and a few seconds later he was swallowed up by the forest.

"Well, another sergeant had just walked outside and saw the whole thing. My story that the prisoner had gotten away from me didn't hold, and I was handcuffed and set to appear before the court martial. He'd sentence me to death—that, I knew. But by a miracle, I was saved. A commander from a nearby unit was visiting at the time, and it happened that he'd been a friend of my mother's family and had been at my christening. So, when he heard the name Münninghoff, he asked to speak to my commander in private. I don't know how he did it, but somehow, without making a big fuss, he managed to have me transferred to a suicide unit with the storm troops, instead of me going before the firing squad. I never heard from him again."

My father never said the name of the man who'd saved him, and he never spoke about his time in the storm troops. The unit was given high-risk missions, like fighting to the death to defend the equipment necessary for retreat. Before long, my father was wounded in the leg and taken to a hospital in Bamberg. After a few months, he was declared fully recovered and given two weeks to return to the front. I've always considered his going straight to Posen and getting my mother pregnant the actions of a dead man walking who knew his time was running out.

TWELVE

News that Frans and Wera had married in Hamburg on May 11, 1942, reached the residents of Briva Latvija a few weeks later. The reactions were lukewarm. The Old Boss said that Frans was an adult and free to do as he pleased. "But I forbid him to show up here in uniform," he added darkly in the same breath.

When my father heard this, he decided to avoid Briva Latvija for as long as the war lasted. Omi, who was extremely proud of her son, tried to persuade him to change his mind and visit, but he refused. Throughout the war, Frans Münninghoff only appeared at the house in Voorburg once, in the spring of 1941 before his marriage on his first leave. He arrived in uniform ready for a fight, fully aware that, by doing so, he had crossed a line with his father forever: he, the eldest son, was a warrior, and there was nothing the Old Boss could do about it. With his shiny boots, SS bars, and brash confidence, he made an indelible impression on the people in the neighborhood—not that he cared. The Netherlands and its people meant nothing to him.

Fortunately, the Old Boss was out of town, and after two weeks, Frans left. Omi saw him off, along with the other members of the household who adored him: Jimmy, Titty, Frau Kochmann, and a few aunts and uncles who lived nearby.

Once my father was married, he instantly moved up in the Nazi apparatus. As the new head of a household, he was entitled to higher wages, but the changes for Wera were more dramatic. Her minor administrative position at the theatre in Posen was deemed unsuitable for the wife of an SS sergeant, so she was given a new job working for Deutsche Volksliste, an institution of the Nazi Party that was classifying inhabitants of Nazi-occupied territories into levels of purity.

"I was pretty annoyed," my mother said. "Things were nice at the theatre, and all of a sudden I had to go work for the Deutsche Volksliste. We checked everyone's ancestry to figure out how much German blood a person had. It had a direct impact on people's daily lives; the color of your passport was determined by the amount of German heritage. Blue for 'pure German,' also known as *Volksdeutsche*, green for half-German, and orange for less than half. The orange stood out immediately, easier to stigmatize.

"There were five girls working in the office. We were all from Riga and Reval. Our job was to type the information into the passports, so it wasn't that different from typing programs at the theatre where I worked before. And none of us had a choice—we were all married to men in the SS. It was depressing: we were right in the middle of the Nazi machine, and our boss, Mr. Strickner from Austria, was a bully. If he had even the slightest suspicion that the information submitted wasn't accurate, that they were hiding a Jewish ancestor, for example—which happened a lot—he'd have that person brought in for an interview.

"And they were rough. Strickner would shout and deliver one blow after another. We heard everything, and we were scared to death. But of course, we couldn't say anything. And if Strickner told them their case would be subject to further research, we'd just look the other way. Because everyone knew what *further research* meant: house search, arrest, concentration camp, or worse."

My mother was there when Heinrich Himmler, the *Reichsführer* of the SS and perhaps the most powerful man in the country, visited the offices. Himmler was the mastermind behind the whole project, and he came to see how his brainchild was developing.

"I knew exactly what was going to happen," my mother said. "Strickner was sweet on me, and he thought he'd please me by letting me present the flowers to Himmler. He must have thought a girl like me would consider it an honor. Strickner had written a welcome speech dripping with Nazi pathos, and I had to learn it by heart and deliver it. Well, I wasn't having it, let me tell you. I had taken a few acting classes at the theatre, so I made a good show of acting shy and forgetting my lines. I looked desperately at the crowd and even managed to blush.

"Strickner apologized and tried to send me away, but Himmler wouldn't have it. 'When such a beautiful woman brings you flowers, she doesn't have to say anything, the gesture speaks for itself,' he said, surprisingly charming for a man like him. Fortunately, he didn't *sieg heil*, he just shook my hand. He had small fingers, and his hand was clammy and cold."

I asked if Strickner gave her trouble after Himmler left, and she shook her head. "No, he was too impressed, and Himmler himself said it was no big deal. Strickner kept courting me for a while after that, but I was newly married, what did he expect? Some of the other girls were more accommodating—maybe out of fear or self-interest—but not me. And I can make myself totally unapproachable if I want to." She flashed me a smug smile, still proud of turning down that creep a half century earlier.

My parents' first year of marriage was spent apart, and neither of them had a particular talent for writing. My mother didn't write anything about her life in Posen, and my father said nothing about his experiences in the Caucasus, or afterward. And I don't think he ever said anything to her about his disgrace at Cherkasy. The first sign that he was even still alive was a telegram from Bavaria in 1943: *Wounded, at hospital in Bamberg. Franz.* Wera went to him immediately.

"The hospital was in a state of total anarchy," she said. "Your father greeted me saying, '*Heil Hitlerchen*' sarcastically in front of everyone. There was a tenderness in his voice, too, as if he were saying, *Hello, darling*. He didn't get into trouble. On the contrary, everyone, including the nurses and doctors, burst into laughter. 'Look, he's hanging there,' said a soldier with only two fingers left on each of his hands. He pointed to a portrait of Hitler hanging upside down on the wall and stuck his fingers out at him. I understood, of course. There were three hundred men in the room, all of whom had lost an arm or a leg, in some cases even more. Their lives had been completely destroyed. When I walked in, all eyes were on me, some men whistled. I didn't mind, I understood. I felt for them—to be honest, I wanted to go around and give them all a kiss and pray to Blessed Mary to perform a miracle for each one of them.

"But the time of miracles had passed—well, maybe not completely because my Frans got to keep his leg. And he made a relatively quick recovery. Two months later, he was sent home to Posen on leave, where I could care for him."

My father's return to Posen was primarily a reconfirmation of their marriage, which had been put on hold because of the war. During this time, I was hastily conceived, and they discussed leaving military life. As far as Wera was concerned, it was time to start thinking about a regular married life. No one believed in a Nazi victory anymore—the imperial eagle was commonly called the vulture of doom, and Wera couldn't help but notice, in Bamberg and beyond, an air of defeat among the troops. Hadn't Frans picked up on this as well? And he could get out, or at least be transferred to a better post: three years on the front, wounded, an Iron Cross, and on top of that, he wasn't even German! He was a foreign mercenary with a contract that could be terminated, wasn't he?

At first, my father wouldn't hear of it. But in the fall of 1943, he received word that another dear childhood friend, Manfred Dolgoi, had been killed. Germany had lost the major tank offensive at Kursk, and it was clear that revenge against the Bolsheviks was impossible. So Frans did a bit of soul-searching.

"I realized I'd sacrificed myself for a senseless fight, and that Wera was right: even though I felt like a German, I wasn't. I had two passports: Dutch and Latvian. It was confusing, but it would allow me to end my contract with the SS without being executed as a deserter. Of course I still needed to come up with an excuse and a new plan.

"And then General Andrey Vlasov announced he was forming an armed force called the *Russkaya Osvoboditelnaya Armiya*, the Russian Liberation Army. I'd met some of the people in it during the campaign; they were anti-Bolshevik Russian patriots, a group I'd always felt represents the good side of Russia. Sure, you could call them traitors because they defected to our side, but as far as I'm concerned, the Soviet Union wasn't Russia. Again, I wasn't there to fight the Russians, I was there to fight the Bolsheviks. I explained this to the SS leadership, and they said a decision would be made in August 1944."

But that didn't happen. In early spring 1944, two months before my mother had me, my father was wounded again during a rearguard action in Estonia. His shoulder blade in splinters, he was evacuated to Posen and operated on by an overworked surgeon. My father said: "He stuck the knife in with one eye closed, smoke wafting up from the cigarette permanently dangling from the corner of his mouth. I could tell he knew what he was doing, and when it was over, he said, 'Bravo! With a wound like that, you'll probably survive the war!' I knew he was right."

Two weeks later, still healing from his wound, his arm in a sling, my father joined the *Landsturm*, a special formation of lightly wounded or recovering soldiers under the command of the Baron Degenhardt, whom he'd ridden with in Latvia. Their job was to maintain order in Posen. The city served as the largest railway junction in the Eastern territories, and it was in shambles. At the end of February 1944, about six weeks before my birth, the Soviets' first massive bombing destroyed much of the city center, sending the population into panicked chaos. On top of that, there were rumors of an impending invasion of Soviet troops.

From above, Posen must've looked like a pan of squirming worms. A large portion of the population had packed their belongings and was attempting to flee, on foot, on horseback, by car, or by wagon. There were the poorly trained, hastily formed military units scraped together from every corner of the German Reich arriving at the train station on their way to the front, where they were being sent to stop the tidal wave of troops from Asia. The sirens were going off more frequently, driving the people into shelters. Posen was paralyzed with fear. The despair was inescapable; everyone was acutely aware of the fact that they were in the final phases of an unwinnable war, that they were being dragged into an apocalypse, and the chances of survival were slim.

And then, during those dark days, I was born on April 13, 1944.

Wera was living in a small house on Langemarckstrasse, not far from the center of Posen. She'd moved in with her mother and paternal grandmother, Anna, who'd raised her in London. Grandma Anna had left England in 1939 to spend her final years in her native country, in the quiet countryside of Schleswig-Holstein near the Danish border. But when she heard that Nadia wasn't able to care for the pregnant Wera on her own, the robust woman showed up unannounced with a suitcase full of bacon and sausages and declared she was there to handle the arrangements surrounding the birth of her first great-grandchild. She was probably the only person in Germany who wanted to travel *to* Posen rather than *from* it.

The city hospital where my mother was to give birth wasn't far from the central station, but seeing as the station had already been bombed and there was no reason for the enemy to return, it was actually a good location. "Or so we thought," my mother said. "But, since there were still trains coming and going, the Allies decided, on the very Thursday you were born, to drop a few more bombs on it for good measure. I started having contractions at five o'clock in the morning. Public transportation was hell and there were no taxis anymore, so Frans and Grandma Anna helped me walk to the hospital. My mother stayed home to prevent looters.

"Things could've really gone wrong," she went on. "The second we went out, a bullet hit the doorframe next to my head. Two men were chasing each other on bicycles, shooting. It wasn't all that unusual at the end of the war; people were starting to take measures into their own hands. I was in shock and furious: how dare those two idiots endanger me, in my condition! *'Ihr Schießer!'* I shouted after them. Of course, what I meant was *Ihr Scheißer!*—you bastards!—but in my state, I accidently called them what they were—shooters! Your father got a good laugh out of it.

"When we got to the hospital, no sooner was I settled into the delivery room than the air raid siren went off. An hour later, I had settled back into bed, and the second wave of attacks began. Clinging to your father's neck, I ran down to the basement again. Everyone was angry and desperate. No one thought about anyone but themselves. I stood because no one even offered me a seat. People were cursing and crying and shouting that it was the end. And all of a sudden, in his booming military voice, your father bellowed *'Ruhe!'* and the room instantly fell silent. He was in uniform, wearing the Iron Cross, and a member of the Landsturm, after all."

She continued: "Then, in the sudden silence, he announced that a child was about to be born. That's all he said, but his words had an incredible effect. It was as if everyone suddenly realized that there was still a glimmer of hope, and rather than worrying over the end, they could focus on the beginning, that every birth is a new start. I got a spot on the bench, and people became kind and caring. A sense of solidarity filled the room—it was a wonderful sensation.

"In the end, you were born in the hospital delivery room at around one in the afternoon. A little while later, the third air raid siren sounded, and this time they took me into the shelter on a stretcher, with you on my belly. People gave me wet cloths to shield you from dust and debris. Turned out to be a good idea—two bombs went off so close that part of the ceiling collapsed and caught fire. Later, after we'd climbed out of the rubble, they found that three people had suffocated, and the entire basement had burned."

We were sent home two days later due to overcrowding, but back on Langemarckstrasse, there was still little peace for the mother and child. Toward the end of April, the sirens went off again, and this time we suffered a direct hit: my parents returned from the shelter to find that their house had been almost completely destroyed. "It was macabre. Only one house on the whole street was hit, and it was ours," my mother said. "It was as if they'd specifically targeted us. While we tried to gather a few things, mainly clothes and food, I left you in a basket with a neighbor a block away. And guess what? An hour later there was another siren! Grandma Anna and Nadia ran to the shelter, and I sprinted toward you. But when I got there, the door was locked. The neighbor had gone to fetch water and left you inside!

"I thought I would go crazy. Panicking, I screamed with all my might 'Can anybody help me?' in a voice so terrifying that it still gives me chills. A Polish man walked by, gave me a friendly look, said something in Polish, and kicked the door with such force that the lock broke. He bowed subtly and disappeared. I'll never forget it."

My father wasn't there during any of this. He'd gone to visit the Von Kluge family—distant relatives on an estate outside of Posen—to ask if my mother and I could stay there with the rest of her family entourage for a little while. Even though they hardly knew each other—they were acquainted more through the family chronicles than personal contact—the Von Kluge family welcomed us with open arms.

It was a time of milk and honey for us. Resources were still abundant on the estate; there was all the dairy a mother could wish for and no shortage of food. The Prussians' strict, autarkic approach to rural management had paid off: everything was organized down to the last detail, the administration was impeccable, and the distribution of goods flawlessly executed; no one had anything to complain about. It was no wonder that after weighing a meager six pounds at birth, I quickly grew to a whopping nine pounds, and my mother started calling me Bully— her chubby little bull. She wasn't aware of the pejorative connotation in English, and of course I can't blame her, but for someone with the beautiful first name Alexander, I've been plagued by this unfortunate nickname my entire life.

My mother's first and best friend in the Von Kluge family was Astrid, who was the same age as she was. Astrid was a distinguished-looking woman who spoke in a German that, when I met her in the Netherlands years later, was music to my ears. For me, any idea that German was a harsh language was completely undermined by Astrid von Kluge and, of course, by my mother, who constantly whispered German words of love into my ear.

THIRTEEN

The members of the Von Kluge family were preparing for their own evacuation as well. There were already reports from Courland that any landowners who had not left their property on time or who refused to leave altogether were hung before their staff's eyes by the Soviet invaders. The Von Kluges planned to go to Baden-Württemberg, where they had a country house near Ulm. The family kindly invited Wera, Anna, and Nadia to join them, but they decided to flee to Schleswig-Holstein instead. The sleepy Danish-German countryside was far enough west that it seemed unlikely that the Russians would ever make it there. And there were hardly any militarily strategic targets in the region, and they had close family living there.

My father was back in arms and wasn't consulted. They'd assumed he was terminating his contract with the SS and transferring to Andrey Vlasov's Russian Liberation Army, as he'd said. In reality, Frans had managed to string along his SS employers for weeks by signing up for the Russian Liberation Army and then claiming to have communication problems (not particularly unbelievable given that telephone and telegraph wires were constantly failing); that fall, however, he disappeared altogether, and after a while he was reported missing. No one, not even Wera, knew that he'd deserted and gone into hiding.

In Voorburg, the family had been entirely unaware of our situation, but they eventually received enough information to understand how dire it was, especially with the advance of the Soviets. My grandfather had become obsessed with my status as heir to the family name, and was determined to keep his branch of the family tree intact. So, in the early summer of 1944, the Old Boss decided to bring my mother and me to the Netherlands. He planned to pick us up by car himself; he had a number of individuals' addresses where he could sleep and get gas along the way. It was a dangerous undertaking, given the constant threat of air raids, but traveling by train was just as dangerous, if not more so. A problem arose, however: that July, my grandfather received an urgent request from the Dutch government in London to facilitate the transfer of a high-ranking official from the Ministry of Trade and Industry to the British capital.

It was a top-secret mission and one that had been in preparation for a long time. Now the end of the war was in sight following Normandy, so they needed to act swiftly. The Dutch government in London had realized they'd need detailed information about the current state of the economy in order to begin reconstruction immediately after libera-tion. To this end, they approached Eduard Koning, director general of the Dutch Ministry of Trade and Industry. This was in itself a delicate undertaking, for the Department of Special Economic Affairs, the cen-ter of Dutch economic policy during the war, was entirely in the hands of the Dutch National Socialist Movement, the NSB. Koning was one of the few trustworthy Dutchmen at the top, though he'd kept his feel-ings about his fanatic Nazi superiors to himself. A young civil servant secretly playing a leading role in the Dutch Student Resistance managed to get Koning in touch with my grandfather. The Old Boss happened to live just across from Koning at Briva Latvija, which facilitated their relationship.

It turned out that Eduard Koning and Joan Münninghoff worked very well together. They were both dedicated to the cause, which resulted in a fruitful collaboration and easy communication. Often one word was enough. Back in December 1942, the duo had already made a German-approved trip to Stockholm on the pretense of studying Swedish gas generators. Despite its neutrality, the Swedish capital was swarming with spies, agents, and snitches, but Uncle Tom knew the city like the back of his hand and could shake followers and guide people to safe houses.

This wasn't as important during their first trip; both men were on their best behavior, so as not to arouse suspicion among the Germans. However, for their second trip in January 1944, things had changed. Once again, they traveled to Stockholm under the pretext of studying Swedish gas generators and relevant fuels, but the real purpose of their trip was to learn more about what kind of information the Dutch government in exile needed. Anton Speekenbrink from the Ministry of Trade, Industry, and Shipping was brought over from London, and Tom arranged a safe house where the men could talk in private for an entire day.

The third trip was scheduled for the end of March 1944 to deliver the information, either encoded in the generator documents or safely stored in Koning's memory. But Koning contracted scarlet fever, so the trip had to be postponed. Once he had recovered, London insisted that the project continue: The D-Day invasion had been successful, and the tides of the war had officially turned. It was only a matter of time until Germany capitulated, which meant that every day counted for preparing for Queen Wilhelmina's return to Holland and the reinstatement of the Dutch government.

So on July 23, 1944, Koning and Münninghoff left for their third and final mission. They flew to Stockholm via Berlin—getting the impression that the German government officials were so preoccupied with the recent attack on Hitler that they didn't have time for travel documents. The two Dutchmen's papers were arranged in no time, and they weren't questioned or stopped once along the way. The first few days went according to plan. They visited a few Kaelle establishments and other related institutions with feigned interest, and then they went into action. Tom took Koning to a secret location, where a security agent from London met him and brought him to a tiny airport outside of Stockholm, where a small plane was waiting to take him to London. By the time my grandfather informed the Stockholm police of his travel companion's disappearance the next morning, Koning was having tea at Arlington House, where he gave a detailed overview of the state of affairs in various sectors of the Dutch economy. I still have the list of sectors from an internal report that was sent to my family years later: coal, liquid fuels, lubricants, iron and steel, nonferrous metals, wood, building materials, leather, rubber, paper, textiles, chemicals, insecticides, paint, and pharmaceuticals.

According to the report, Koning was very detailed in his explanations. In his description of the state of the rubber industry, he mentioned "the need to manufacture rings for preserving jars." Apparently, he foresaw a massive wave of home canning in the event of postliberation food shortages. And in his description of the decreasing numbers of bicycles on the streets, he added that there had been a "competition for a bicycle tire substitute," but that the winning solution was ultimately not feasible because the Germans refused to allot "the necessary amount of steel." At the end of the section, he explained that "a durable solution made entirely of wood was being produced by Bruynzeel in Zaandam. However, demand is so high, this is just a drop in the bucket."

When he'd left home for Stockholm in 1944, Koning had written his family a letter of farewell that read "*adieu*, and until the end of the war." Before leaving for London that night, he asked my grandfather to take care of his wife and children. And the Old Boss did, just as he provided food and other aid to others through the war. I've heard testimonies of my grandfather regularly showing up at hospitals (probably just Catholic ones, though I'm not sure) to hand out boxes of bacon, chicken, eggs, wheat, and, of course, cigarettes. He even gave these boxes to people he passed on the street.

Obviously, this sparked jealousy. Rumors started flying around, and this ultimately created an air of doubt around the Old Boss. Joan Münninghoff was fraternizing with the enemy, after all, not to mention that his son had fought for the Nazis! All of this was true, of course, but it was only part of the truth. Still, a few chickens and slabs of bacon weren't enough to change that image.

So his plans to bring Wera and me to Voorburg were put on hold. Eventually, however, the Old Boss found a solution: before he left for Stockholm, he had his son Xeno, who'd just gotten his driver's license, prepare to bring us safely to the Netherlands. I've thought about this a lot. My uncle Xeno, not even nineteen years old, jumped into the family Chrysler in August 1944 and began the 620-mile trip east, a journey that would bring him much closer to the battlefields and the horrors of the war, all to pick up a woman he barely knew and her child, all for the sake of the cursed family line. It was no task for an eighteen-year-old boy, but Xeno accepted it without question. In early September 1944, he finally reached the Von Kluge family estate. "Shot at twice," he reported breathlessly when he stepped out of the car. He received a hero's welcome from the noble family.

He'd arrived just in time. Most of the staff had already left, and the family was ready to escape. Finally, the time had come. On their last evening at the estate, the family pulled out all the stops: a suckling pig from their own stalls appeared on the table, and the very best wines from Bordeaux were brought up from the cellar. The family gathered around the fire with glasses of cognac and shared memories of better times, back before the war, when their worries were few. With the sounds of artillery fire audible in the distance, they sang, cried, prayed, and promised to find each other again after the war, wherever they were.

It was a promise they couldn't keep. On their way to Ulm, the Van Kluges ended up in a long line of refugees that was bombed; Astrid was the only member of the family to survive. Grandma Anna returned to Schleswig-Holstein, where she lived seven more years, never seeing Wera or me again. Nadia was scared by the way the Old Boss had treated my mother in Riga, and if it had been up to her, Wera and I would've gone with her to Palenberg, not far from the Dutch-German border, where she had a few Baltic-Russian friends. But Wera longed for Frans, whom no one had seen or heard from since he'd disappeared. Wera knew that if he survived, he'd eventually return to his parents' house in Voorburg.

Three days later, Xeno triumphantly drove up the driveway to Briva Latvija, having traveled nonstop for more than forty-eight hours. He was proud to prove himself to his father; he'd delivered us alive and well, mission accomplished. To my mother's surprise, Xeno said almost nothing to her the entire journey. "When I tried to thank him for all he had done for us, he just looked the other way. I never really understood that."

So we made it to Briva Latvija in Voorburg. Mad Tuesday had just passed, and the Hunger Winter was yet to come.

FOURTEEN

As soon as we arrived, the women—led by Omi—made a beeline for the bassinet. Their eyes welled up with tears at the sight of me, and they praised my unexpectedly good constitution. When Omi lifted me up out of the basket, I let out a loud burp, and everyone cheered. My grandfather poured champagne and said that he couldn't think of a better present for their twenty-fifth wedding anniversary, which they would be celebrating next month. My mother and I were given the largest guest room on the first floor. Assuming Frans survived the war, the family could live there together. At that point, however, Frans's whereabouts were still unknown.

It was the start of a difficult period for my mother. My grandfather was distant and condescending toward her—he still hoped for a future for my father in the Netherlands with a Dutch wife, preferably with status and connections. Wera soon realized that Briva Latvija would never be her permanent home, but she was passive by nature and decided to wait and see how things turned out. She hoped for a happy ending but couldn't convince herself that one would come. She tried to make herself as invisible as possible in the daily household goings-on; her only status was derived from the fact that she happened to be my mother. The women in the house were nice to her, at least, and I—the son and heir—was her guarantee that she would be allowed to stay. What else could she do? She didn't have any family in the Netherlands, and her mother was in Germany. All she could do was wait for Frans to come home; she was profoundly alone.

In daily life at Briva Latvija, she was almost completely ignored by my grandfather and at best tolerated by Xeno. Jimmy, on the other hand, adored and doted on her, which was naturally confusing. But the biggest questions were all about Frans. Where was he? Would he make it home alive? How would he react when he found her there? Could these two children of the war, Frans and Wera, build a new future together in the Netherlands? Would they manage to stay together? Or was he already dead, and in all the chaos, word just hadn't reached Voorburg yet? It all took a toll on Wera's nervous system. She suffered long migraines and fell into deep states of depression; our family doctor, Van Tilburg, didn't know how to help. Once she stopped breastfeeding around Christmas, she spent most of the day in her room with the curtains closed, leaving my care to Omi and the household staff. The Old Boss made sure I was baptized and accounted for in the parish register of the Sint-Martinus Catholic church in Voorburg.

Time dragged slowly. The Hunger Winter had a murderous grip on the western part of the country, but thanks to its richly stocked cellars, Briva Latvija was virtually unaffected. However, there was still no word from Frans. The Old Boss had his suspicions, but he bore them in silence. "If Frans is dead, we would have heard something by now" was his way of encouraging the family to keep faith. By then, he'd turned his focus toward renewing international contacts after the war ended. Neither the British government nor MI6 made any further requests for his services; after two successful operations and with the end of the war in sight, there was no reason to expose their contact in The Hague to greater risk.

It was my grandmother who brought sunshine to the house. Thanks to her increasing deafness, she missed most of the subtle barbs exchanged in household conversations and could thunder through the brooding silences with me laughing joyfully on her hip. She'd sing Russian songs and play games with me, and her silliness served to lighten the mood around the house—if only for a little while.

In the early morning of March 3, 1945, Omi was with me doing gymnastics in the yard. Whenever the weather was warm enough, she'd spread a big white sheet out on the grass and move my arms and legs up and down, spouting encouragement and praise in Russian like a first-rate Russian *matushka*, completely devoted—heart and soul—to her grandchild. For the record, I doubt the pilots could have seen us from up there, but the story was that the big white sheet spread out in the middle of a field probably looked like an excellent target to the RAF pilots flying overhead at approximately nine o'clock that morning. They had orders to bomb the V-2 rocket launchers in Haagse Bos, but their target had been wrongly marked, and was actually farther north. The sound must have been deafening when a major load left the Bezuidenhout neighborhood in ruins, but Omi didn't hear it. She was laughing in the sun when a terrified Frau Kochmann ran out and rushed her inside. Once she realized what was going on, she sprang into action, transforming back into the nurse she'd once been in Astrakhan instantaneously. She made a giant pot of soup and prepared blankets and first aid for anyone who might need them. At least fifteen people received food and medical care at Briva Latvija that day.

The Netherlands was liberated from the Nazis on May 5. At Briva Latvija the Dutch flag flew high, and all was calm. In the end, no one in the celebrating masses dared to point a finger at Joan Münninghoff; he'd built up too great a reputation for helping those in need. And even when Frans finally showed up on June 1, there were no angry masses waiting for him. Briva Latvija was like a fortress that had somehow transcended the standard measurements of good and evil. Something had happened all right, but it didn't lend itself to simple assessment. It had all taken place on another level, in a cloud of mystery and secrets, like in any war.

Frans, in his own way, had done quite well. In August 1944, when he deserted, he sought refuge with his uncle Walter Lehmann, who had acquired the Ostrowo estate in Vorpommern with his wife, Litty, during Heim ins Reich. The couple took Frans in, no questions asked, despite the danger; deserters were being hunted down and hanged by the thousands in those final days of Hitler's Reich, and those who sheltered them risked the same punishment. But as a surgeon and director of the regional hospital, Uncle Walter was a man of standing. He had personally carried out a number of major surgeries on leading Nazi officials and enjoyed the full confidence of the local Nazi leadership. His stately villa would never be searched, and Frans could stay there as long as he wanted. Uncle Walter was too much of a family man to turn him away.

Frans remained there in hiding until March 1945 and spent a lot of time with his cousin Kurt Strandmann. They had spent their childhood together in Riga; in fact, it had been Kurt and his fanatical parents who'd awakened the radical anti-Bolshevik sentiments in Frans that ultimately led him to join the SS. Naturally, Kurt had enlisted as well, but unlike Frans, he hadn't made it to the dreaded Soviet lines. His unit had lasted until Moscow, and like anyone who dared to use his brain, he began to wonder why the Führer's plan for a decisive attack on the enemy's capital was constantly failing. One day, however, a mortar salvo put an end to his reflections. When he woke from anesthesia, his right leg had been amputated, and he was sent home for further treatment.

At Ostrowo, the friendship between Frans and Kurt, which had been so abruptly interrupted when the war broke out, continued to flourish. As boys, they'd marched into hell; as rough, disillusioned men, they'd managed to make it out alive. What now? They had no idea what their futures held. The fact that Frans was a de facto deserter by not reporting to Vlasov as promised was of no concern to his family members. He'd been wounded twice, even awarded the Iron Cross (which Kurt had not). In their eyes, he was a war hero.

Their conversations around the fireplace increasingly turned toward the obvious disadvantages of having a Führer from a petit bourgeois background who, in his narrow-mindedness and need to be right, had ruined the entire military operation by refusing to listen to his highly capable Baltic generals. In their eyes, Hitler had let himself be overwhelmed by pathos and ruthless violence, which ultimately cost millions of people their lives, and Germany the war. Germany could have won, the men at Ostrowo believed, but instead they'd lost everything, and the thought of following the deranged Austrian corporal into suicide, as many in Berlin had, was absurd.

When the Russians began a final offensive on the Vistula River in January 1945 and pushed to the banks of the Oder in almost no time, the former frontline soldiers knew that they needed to escape as soon as possible. Panic rippled across the beautiful Pomeranian landscape, and masses of refugees headed west in terror, carrying what they could in suitcases and backpacks, on carts and horse-drawn wagons. Frans and Kurt decided joining them wasn't their best option. They knew the Nazi regime was on the brink of collapse, and Germany was about to enter into a long dark period. They also knew that given their Baltic backgrounds, they were better off staying out of the hands of the Soviets. Their choices of destination were obvious ones. Frans would try to get to his parents' house in Voorburg, a plan that seemed possible given that he still had a Dutch passport and could pass for a forced laborer returning home. And Kurt had some relatives in Brussels who would surely take him in. As a crippled veteran, he figured he wouldn't have too much trouble, and he could always use his Latvian passport to bluff his way across the border. Emboldened by their desperate courage, the two men said goodbye to Uncle Walter and left him with their weapons and a few belongings that they weren't ready to part with, but that they knew they'd better not have on their person in case they were detained by Allied forces. For Walter, who took refuge at his holiday home in the woodland resort town of Varel, near Oldenburg, keeping things like the Iron Cross and the Soviet sabre was a matter of honor.

In the early '50s, when we went to visit him at Christmas, the Iron Cross lay under the Christmas tree, along with a pile of photographs of my father and his war comrades in uniform. Beaming, Uncle Walter told how he'd wrapped everything in oilpaper and buried it at the edge of the forest behind his house.

How Kurt managed to cross the border into Belgium without any problems is a mystery. But once he reached the Belgian capital, he managed, with the help of a Latvian representative, to arrange the necessary papers to obtain an apartment in the French-speaking district of Ixelles. He did what so many did in those chaotic months: he took advantage of the confusion, the lack of proper administration, and the fact that so many documents had been lost in bombings or confiscated or destroyed by the fleeing Germans. Anyone who could put on a good poker face and deliver a convincing story had a chance of deceiving the Allied military authorities, who, although they were technically in charge, were anything but well informed. Under those circumstances, a wooden leg and a Latvian passport in the hands of a born storyteller were as good as gold.

But my father was a daredevil and incredibly naive; he had no story to tell—he just got lucky. He tagged along with the caravan of refugees until he finally reached Lübeck, where he could catch his breath in the same place he'd spent his honeymoon. Then he continued via Hamburg and eventually crossed the border into the Netherlands in Oldenzaal. He was exhausted, but he had a Dutch passport, spoke Dutch, and had parents living in Voorburg—that was enough to convince the Allies working at the displaced-persons camp in Winterswijk. On June 1, he showed up at the front door of Briva Latvija, where he would be coldly rejected by his father, and his marriage to Wera would dissolve without a fight.

Wera flung her arms around his neck with joy and showered him with kisses, while he stood there like a guard at Buckingham Palace. That something was broken between the two of them was clear. He was dog-tired, he said, and still recovering from his injury. He wanted to go to bed, alone.

He slept for twenty-four hours straight, and when he woke and saw Wera, who hadn't left his side the whole time, sitting in a chair beside the bed, he rolled over to face the wall. The reflex was unmistakable. At first there was just deep, silent disappointment, followed by their first real exchange of words.

He couldn't handle it, he said. The memories of the war were over-running everything. He felt as if he were carrying the weight of his fallen comrades—some of whom he had known in Riga—on his shoulders. Why did he deserve to live?

"Don't say things like that," she cried. "You're alive—you have a child and a wife."

He roared back at her like a wounded animal. He should be dead, and he almost *was* dead. He could still see himself lying in the gray, melting snow in Cherkasy, bleeding out like a slaughtered cow in the Ukrainian countryside, just as the soft, wet earth was awakening from its winter sleep. For months he'd managed to survive by sheer luck, but his luck had run out. He'd been struck in an artillery salvo, and he was finally going to die. The thought gave him a strange sense of peace; finally, the score between him and his friends would be settled. Until all of a sudden, out of nowhere, a medic appeared. Silently, as if it were a matter of course, he bandaged Frans's leg, lifted him onto a stretcher, and hauled him to the field hospital. The worst thing about it was that the medic, whose name he didn't know, was killed half an hour later, when the Katyusha rockets plowed through the battlefield one more time, just for good measure. The young man had been out looking for more wounded. Frans lay in the putrid field hospital for hours, sobbing. He cried for the medic, for Wolfi Metzkeris, for Manfred Dolgoi, and for all the others who'd been less lucky than he'd been. Couldn't Wera understand that, god damn it? She was certainly more understanding than his father, who'd greeted him with a look of contempt and simply stated that measures would need to be taken.

As in immediately. Now that his oldest son had come home alive, arrangements needed to be made.

Wera had only nodded, crying softly in desperation, overwhelmed by the memories of their happy times together in Riga, when they'd been carefree teenagers with the world at their fingertips, when life was full of promise and possibility. Now, she found herself yoked with a damaged young man with steel armor around his soul.

"But we were destined for each other," she said with tears in her eyes.

And with that, Frans softened. He wrapped his arms around her, and they sat together at the edge of the bed, rocking back and forth, tenderly stroking each other between kisses and tears, whispering that maybe everything would be all right in the end.

FIFTEEN

But it wasn't all right.

It was a mixture of bitterness about the course of the war, which had stolen the lives of nearly all of his friends, and the lack of recognition—not to mention gratitude—for his sacrifice that drove my father away from Briva Latvija within just a few weeks. Frans was horrified to realize that his father wasn't the least bit proud of him; the Old Boss forbade him to talk about his experiences in Russia and advised him to integrate into Dutch society as quickly as possible, as he'd always been supposed to do. My grandfather would have preferred that his son find himself a Dutch wife, but Frans and Wera were married and had a son, a fact that a virtuous Catholic like my grandfather had no choice but to accept.

But for the sake of the family name and Frans's future, cleansing the house of anything that smelled remotely of Germany, not to mention the Nazis, became a matter of primary importance. And given his service with the SS, keeping Frans out of the Special Court of Justice was going to be incredibly difficult. Fortunately, my grandfather had some good Catholic friends in high places, so Frans might be spared, provided that he obediently assumed his Dutch identity. Surely that wasn't too much to ask? After all, hadn't he spent his formative high school years in the Netherlands? And as far as Latvia was concerned, the family could never return, not with the way things had panned out.

The country had become a province of the USSR and would remain so for a long time. They would be lucky if they managed to recover even a fraction of the family's assets from the Soviets via legal means. Either way, the children, and Omi as well, would have to abandon the thought of ever returning to their paradise of prewar Riga. Everyone was forced to accept the family's fate. As far as my grandfather was concerned, this meant that the primary language of the house would from then on be Dutch. German would only be allowed if there was absolutely no other way to make oneself understood. The process of total assimilation would be executed with a strong hand, and my grandfather, the Old Boss, would make sure it succeeded.

My father was furious. All of his hate for the Netherlands and disgust for his own Dutch identity boiled over into a teeth-grinding, fist-clenching *No* to everything his father demanded. Speak Dutch? The language of those petty, conservative dandies he'd always despised, even after eight years of jumping from one Dutch school to the next at his father's command? The language of those spineless cowards who'd let their country be conquered without a fight, most of whom hadn't even dared to resist? On the contrary! Some of them had even collaborated with Germany and joined the NSB! Nothing was more despicable! They were traitors to their own country!

Lost in his fury, he was desperately searching for something to hold on to. He realized he needed to leave the Netherlands as fast as possible, not only because they'd be looking for him, but also because he needed support from people who understood what he'd been through. But what about Wera and Bully? They could come later; he needed to take care of himself first. Supporting his family meant that he would remain forever attached to Briva Latvija and its inhabitants—let the Old Boss do it, he thought, he certainly could afford to.

At the end of June, less than a month after he'd come home from the war, Frans left Briva Latvija suddenly after yet another argument with Wera. He went on foot and hitchhiked—purely by instinct—to

Oss. When he got there, he tried to track down Robert, one of his classmates from the Saint Nicholas Institute in the early 1930s. At the hollow echo of the doorbell, a woman hesitantly cracked open the door. He could tell she lived alone and there was something wrong in the house. When he introduced himself, she embraced him with a sob and quickly pulled him inside. "I'm Martha," she said. "Do you remember me?" He nodded and looked around. He used to play here sometimes, not so much because Robert was a friend, but more because he lived in Oss and was allowed to go home on the weekends occasionally. Her husband, a wine merchant as Frans remembered, had died before the war in an accident, Martha explained. And as for her son, Robert . . . Well, he'd disappeared without a trace. He just woke up one morning, jumped on his bike, and left. "See you tonight!" he called, waving cheerfully, but he never came back. Or at least that was what she'd told the neighbors, and Frans at first.

But the flimsy cover story didn't hold water, not in the neighborhood and certainly not with Frans. After Frans gave a full account of what had happened to him, she confessed that Robert, like many Catholic boys from the area, had enlisted in the SS and was sent to the eastern front. All she'd ever heard from Robert was that he'd been sent to Russia, so now she listened wide-eyed to Frans's stories, desperate to hear everything. It was as if a messenger from the eastern front had shown up on her doorstep. After three years of imagining Robert's macabre fate alone in her misery, she hung on to Frans's every word.

Frans told her what really happened. And although he had never seen Robert on the battlefield, what he described had most likely been the same for her son. She went to the cellar—still full of supplies stocked by her late husband—and returned with a bottle of jenever. "Schnapps!" Frans exclaimed with joy. She poured him three, four glasses and even a small one for herself.

Frans stayed with Martha in Oss for no less than ten weeks. He didn't go outside, slept during the day, and told his story over and over each night as he drank himself into a stupor. He needed it—both the alcohol and Martha's listening ear. All the attention he'd been yearning for in Voorburg he found in Oss with Martha. And with every drink, he seemed to be able to make a little more sense of his own story in the war. "You understand, Martha?" was always the last thing he said before his head dropped to his chest, as if struck by a belated Russian sniper, and he fell into a deep sleep.

Martha did understand, but she also knew that the situation wasn't sustainable. There were lists of people who were wanted for collaborating with the NSB and the SS circulating around the country, and even in Brabant, brigades were searching houses. Frans couldn't stay there, that she knew. So, when he asked her to help him cross the border into Belgium, she enlisted the help of an old friend of her husband's who had access to smuggling routes across the Brabant countryside. By the end of September, Frans was gone.

SIXTEEN

For Wera, this was catastrophic. After just three years of marriage, she was faced with the total loss of her husband a second time. He'd once again disappeared without a trace, and no one heard a word from him. Her initial response was to calm herself with a logical explanation. Stubbornly, she insisted that he'd gone because he was understandably traumatized by the war. Frans had returned home damaged goods, she could tell the moment she saw him standing in the doorway. Suddenly, she knew what she needed to do: she had to obey the Old Boss and learn Dutch. She had to become Dutch. Surely, once the dust had settled, Frans would come home and make the best of the situation.

And Wera tried, she really did. She learned our language with its difficult syntax, and spoke it until the day she died, a half century later. On her deathbed, she talked to her grandchildren on the phone in Dutch. Just as she spoke it to all the good-for-nothing Dutchmen she crossed paths with during Frans's absence. My mother was a beautiful, romantic woman and incredibly naive. She yearned for love. The Dutch university students who visited Briva Latvija in the fall of 1945 at the invitation of Jimmy and Xeno—they were studying in Amsterdam and Delft respectively—were crazy about her. Naturally, she noticed, but her loyalty to the man who, like all the other boys from Riga, had taken up arms, kept her from reciprocating at first. Of course, having a baby crawling around was hardly conducive to any kind of romantic activity.

Although, when I was two years old (this is my earliest memory), I was sprawled out on a mattress on top of a dresser. My mother had just changed my diaper, and I was lying there waiting for something to happen. But nothing did, because Wera had finally succumbed to Jimmy's advances. My uncle Jimmy had, despite being left disabled from polio, grown up to be quite the Casanova, and he took advantage of my father's absence to capture my mother's heart. Fidgety by nature, I flipped over on my belly and noticed that there was a window open right in front of me, so I crawled over to it. I didn't yet fully understand the three-dimensional nature of the world, or the dangers of falling out of windows. Without the slightest hesitation, I leaned out and toppled ten feet down to the ground.

This memory is reconstructed based on what Wera and Jimmy told me later. What I actually remember is this: my mother burst out of the pantry in her dressing gown, looking bewildered, in retrospect probably a combination of fear, remorse, shame, anxiety, and above all, love—wild, panicked motherly love. She looked like a strange bird with her colorful robe fluttering behind her. I also remember a man in a blue jumpsuit installing a wrought iron railing in front of the window I'd fallen from. I knew there was a connection between my fall and that man's work, but I didn't know, of course, that I had just escaped death. It's a concept that two-year-olds simply can't grasp. Something had happened to me, and my mother swept me up in her warm embrace. It wasn't until much later that I heard what had really saved me that Sunday morning. The workers building a new driveway had left several bags of cement and a pile of sand right under my window. It was that dusty cushion that saved my life.

The whole event left my grandparents, my grandfather in particular, deeply shaken. The fact that Jimmy played a role in it was soon forgotten; they blamed everything on my mother and her behavior. After all, she had made herself available, not only to Jimmy, but to an entire line of suitors. And it really had gotten to that point. Wera had been abandoned by her husband. Dazed and indecisive, she was living with a family that didn't want her. In search of a sympathetic ear and someone who could take her away from the Münninghoff family that had so coldly rejected her, she couldn't resist the charming young gentlemen who crossed her path. And they did their very best to cheer her up, for a little while. She began going out, leaving me at Briva Latvija, where Omi, and sometimes Frau Kochmann, put me to bed.

I don't know exactly what my mother was feeling, but I can certainly understand it. A beautiful woman in her late twenties owes it to herself to embrace the opportunities that life has to offer her. But the men she went out with had their own Dutch agenda and weren't capable of or interested in developing a long-term relationship with her. The feeling was mutual; none of them, she told me later, seemed to understand her internal struggles or her specific problems. She remained overwhelmed by her deep longing for Frans.

By the end of 1945, Frans seemed to be finally getting a grip on himself. He had gone by train to Eindhoven, where he'd been met by an acquaintance of Martha's and transported across the border to Belgium via the small village of Netersel. He traveled via a smuggling route through the woods and across the fields with a clear goal in mind: Brussels. He would move in with Kurt and contact Guus van Blaem, a boy he'd been friends with at Huize Katwijk in The Hague at the end of the 1930s. He had heard that Guus was involved in some interesting business ventures in Brussels and Antwerp, including the arms trade. Weapons—now, that was one field in which Frans could call himself an expert.

When he arrived in Brussels, he found that Kurt was already involved in a number of clandestine activities in which Frans could certainly put his specific experiences to good use. That very first evening, Kurt invited to his home a Latvian man by the name of Alfred Valdemanis, who was setting up Nazi escape routes to South America. When he heard the name, Frans hesitated: an ethnic Latvian? Could he be trusted? But Kurt assured him that Alfred was perfectly trustworthy and that he had plenty of good contacts who could help him.

During their conversation, which lasted three bottles of vodka and went on until four o'clock in the morning, Alfred explained that there were thousands of former SS members hiding all over Europe, and most of them were just waiting for an opportunity to escape to Brazil, Argentina, or some other South American country. Apparently, there was a lot of money to be made in it. "Did you know that anyone who worked for the SS is suspected of war crimes, even people like you who only ever engaged in honest frontline combat? Don't think for a second you're going to get a fair trial," Valdemanis said. He offered Frans a job as a guide along the escape route: "You pick up customers, escort them to the port, and put them on the ship. We take it from there. Who knows, maybe after a while you can start a new life over there yourself."

Frans expressed interest at first, but then began to realize just how dangerous such a mission would be. And come to think of it, he didn't want to leave Europe. Yes, he'd probably be arrested in the Netherlands for fighting for a foreign militia, but over time and with the help of his father's connections, he'd find a way out of it. In fact, what he wanted was to go to Germany and help the country rebuild, but first he had to figure out a way to do it. After the second bottle of vodka was empty, he suddenly blurted out that he didn't think it was right that Alfred and Kurt intended to get rich from human trafficking, taking advantage of their old comrades. "No, I don't think I'm cut out for it," he finally mumbled. "Let me do something with weapons. I'd be much better at that."

Kurt and Alfred looked at him suspiciously, and an icy chill fell over the room, even after Alfred was gone, when Frans was left alone with Kurt. Suddenly, he understood: there was life before the war, which in his and Kurt's case had been essentially paradise; then there was life during the war, when friendships were sacred, and the greatest, most miserable tasks were carried out without question; and then there was life after the war, their life now. In this life, a man had to be sly and calculating. It was a life that Kurt Strandmann was clearly cut out for, certainly more so than Frans.

After sleeping off his hangover, my disillusioned father said goodbye to Kurt the next afternoon and set out in search of Guus, the only person in Brussels he knew. When he finally rang the doorbell at the address he'd been given, he was greeted by a cheerful, attractive brunette whom he'd only ever heard of: Mimousse van Blaem. She was Guus's first cousin—and also his legal wife. With a hopeful smile, Frans introduced himself to her. She'd heard of him as well, and she welcomed him with a kiss on the cheek and ushered him inside.

It was love at first sight.

SEVENTEEN

Mimousse was the daughter of an arrogant ear, nose, and throat doctor, Toine van Blaem, and a Belgian baroness, Elisabeth de Heusch de la Zangrye. Their marriage, which had been sealed in the final days of the First World War, was generally viewed among the degenerating Belgian nobility as a mésalliance. After fathering four children in record time and still finding no acceptance among the Belgian elite, Toine—an incorrigible womanizer—finally decided to throw in the towel. He abandoned his family for a Dutch patient, a woman of great wealth but without the pretension of Belgian nobility. The baroness and her four children moved in with her parents on the Ridderborn Estate, tucked away deep in the hills of Belgian Limburg.

Castle life at Ridderborn around 1930 was no fairy tale—that was something that Mimousse (her real name was Marie Ghislaine, but such a somber name required a frivolous nickname like Mimousse) and her sisters, Yvonne, Jacquot, and Edith, fully agreed on. Ridderborn was more of a cloister than a castle, and Granny, as we later called the baroness, held herself and her children to strict Catholic standards (with the tacit approval of her frail, old, God-fearing parents), which offered little opportunity to experience any form of worldly pleasure. It was as if her life's work was to transform her failed marriage to the lascivious, authoritarian Van Blaem into a valid entry ticket into heaven.

As a result, Mimousse and her sisters grew up to be naive, headstrong girls well versed in the staunch etiquette of Belgian nobility. (The fork should be laid with the curved side up and not like a pitchfork, as the Dutch do it; the second-to-the-lowest button on one's vest is to be left open *à la Albert*, etc. She relayed it all to me, the Dutch teenager, in tremendous detail.) Mimousse and her sisters were removed from the harsh realities of the 1930s, and the Belgian boarding school they attended certainly didn't change that. The school was run by Benedictine nuns who valued discipline over all else, and whose didactic pedagogy was drenched in piety and religious contemplation. Most of the girls eagerly looked forward to the long holidays, when they could spend a few weeks in the ordinary world among normal people, but for Mimousse and her sisters, holidays were wasted on incredibly boring visits to uncles and aunts, who wanted to make sure that, mésalliance or not, the young ladies at Ridderborn— though without title—were still being raised in a respectable manner.

Fortunately, the Ridderborn girls found salvation in the arrival of Bob Pietersma, a cheerful Dutch agricultural scientist who'd been hired to overhaul the estate's grounds and make the land profitable again. He soon caught the eye of the divorced baroness, who, despite all the tragedies life had thrown at her, was still quite becoming, and the two began a passionate affair. Before long, she declared herself willing to leave her life of self-imposed celibacy and follow Pietersma to the ends of the earth—which was good, because he'd applied to work as a plantation manager in the Dutch East Indies and received an assignment in Java.

In fact, Ridderborn was to be his last job in Europe; he was all ready to go to the Indies—forever, it seemed. Would Elisabeth . . . ? Granny didn't hesitate for a moment. She agreed to go with him, and of course, the children were welcome to come along as well. He loved children and had developed a strong bond with Yvonne, Jacquot, and Edith, who were all in their teenage years and desperate for a father figure. The girls happily packed their suitcases with their mother. But for Mimousse, the oldest, emigration wasn't an option. Unlike her sisters, who wanted nothing to do with their father, she was determined to find Toine van Blaem. She needed to understand why he'd abandoned his family. "I felt like I would never find peace if I didn't try to figure it out, and Granny never said a word about him," she told me later.

She graduated from boarding school at eighteen, and set out for the Netherlands at twenty, leaving her bewildered mother in tears. She bought the train ticket with her own savings; she didn't need anyone. No one was going to stand in her way. She was on a mission to find out who her father was, to see for herself what his side of the family—despised in Belgium—was really like, and to understand why he'd deliberately disappeared from her life.

At first, the pompous doctor didn't recognize her when she came to his office in Breda, and true to form, he tried to seduce the beautiful young woman with his famous charm. "It's me, Mimousse!" she cried out, interrupting him. The scales fell from his eyes, and he turned away in embarrassment. Overwhelmed with emotion, he asked her to leave. "I'm so ashamed," he admitted. Toine's confession allowed Mimousse to become an angel of forgiveness, and she took full advantage of the opportunity. A little while later, father and daughter were sobbing in each other's arms, and Mimousse was allowed to stay.

From that day forward, Toine van Blaem put his best foot forward with Mimousse. His second wife, Annette, with whom he had had no children, had never pushed him to reunite with his daughters, though they bore his name. Sunny by nature and averse to all pretension, the wealthy shipowner's daughter had always been bemused by what she referred to as "the dusty Catholic upper class." They lived their whole lives locked up in stuffy castles in the countryside, where there was no sea wind to blow through their hair, where they could never let go and laugh, and where there was no adventure to speak of. "Let them suffocate in their provincial pettiness, Toine," she said, in the rare instances when the topic of Ridderborn came up. "To hell with those barons and princes!"

She and Toine—after it became clear she couldn't have children—would occasionally muse about the four daughters who seemed to have disappeared from their lives for good. So the fact that his eldest daughter had sought them out on her own accord was nothing short of a gift from heaven. The largest guest room in the house was immediately set up for Mimousse, and the next day, like it or not, she would go to the city with Annette to go shopping. Although Breda was by no means a desirable paradise in 1938, there was no turning back for the refugee from Ridderborn. Her mother had married the ambitious Pietersma and followed him to the East Indies with her other three daughters, and Ridderborn was left to its ancient inhabitants to deteriorate into a haunted castle. Mimousse had made up her mind: she would stay with her father in the Netherlands.

Mimousse's decision came with certain obligations for Toine and Annette, and the couple acted accordingly. To make his daughter's life in Breda a bit livelier, Toine introduced Mimousse to Guidi and Guus, his brother Theo's sons. Theo van Blaem was a notary in nearby Kaatsheuvel who, in 1939, already had a terrible reputation, and it only got worse during the war. He'd worked in Urmond, where he'd been involved in large-scale embezzlements of capital from local Jews who'd fled Germany, which led to encounters with Otto Rebholz and his money-laundering scheme in Amsterdam. Eventually, it all came out, and by the end of the war, Theo van Blaem was facing indictment, which, even without a prison sentence, would put an end to his career as a notary.

But true to form, my grandfather came up with a scheme to make it all go away, since Rebholz's involvement in the Van Blaem affair could potentially harm him as well. He heard about Van Blaem's situation because Guus and Guidi had been in school with Jimmy and Xeno during the war. He spent the last year of the war using quiet diplomacy and hush money payments to quell any potential commotion around Theo van Blaem, and with the help of the Jesuits at Huize Katwijk, where the Old Boss was a major donor, he was incredibly successful in doing so. After liberation, no one in Urmond or the surrounding area knew anything about Van Blaem's embezzled Jewish assets.

If anyone thought that Van Blaem might express gratitude for Joan Münninghoff, they'd be mistaken. The infamous notary was fully aware that he had a wealthy moneylender by the throat and didn't balk at the opportunity to use my grandfather's connection with Rebholz as blackmail. After the war, my grandfather ended up paying for most of Guidi's education to become a notary himself—until 1947, that is, when Theo van Blaem fell down the stairs, broke his neck, and died. Apparently the Old Boss didn't look all that surprised when he heard the news.

Given the circumstances, it was fortunate that Guus didn't have any particular plans for his education. He preferred a libertine lifestyle full of challenges to a gentlemanly existence in The Hague financed by Joan Münninghoff. Guus had fallen head over heels for his cousin Mimousse, and the two got married and moved to Brussels, a cosmopolitan city that offered countless possibilities to anyone who could see past all the postwar chaos. Guus van Blaem's life had been a hodgepodge of fantastic scams, improbable affairs with wealthy women, and quasidelusional ideas for which he—contrary to everyone's expectations—managed to find financial backers. He moved to the Belgian capital, where he intended to fully devote himself to all kinds of shady pursuits.

The arms trade was just one of them. He was also involved in human trafficking and narcotics, which were in high demand among a small segment of the Dutch elite. My grandfather didn't care about any of that. For someone who had been so quick to ask for money during the war, Guus had thankfully disappeared without a trace—or so the Old Boss thought. But all that changed the day Frans showed up at his house. My father's arrival brought a new dimension to the relationship between Guus van Blaem and the Münninghoff family, and all of a sudden, new opportunities to earn easy money presented themselves.

For Frans, staying with Guus and Mimousse in Brussels was his first opportunity to take his future into his own hands. He no longer felt bound to the Netherlands or his family. His father had more than turned his back on him. Worse, he'd exploited Frans's position in the war to keep up appearances with the Germans: *My son, as you know, is fighting in Russia, where he was wounded and received the Iron Cross for bravery . . .* He couldn't have asked for a better entrance ticket into the upper echelons of German society. At the same time, while rubbing shoulders with the Dutch, he was sure to allude to the fact that he disapproved of his son's actions, but there was nothing he could do. Embittered to the core by this betrayal and consumed by powerless resentment, Frans did everything he could to suppress all thoughts of his father.

One thing was certain: he no longer had a home in Voorburg. His mother didn't dare to oppose the Old Boss, nor did Xeno, Jimmy, or Titty. The latter two resented the Old Boss as much as Frans did, but Xeno was another story. He adored his father and managed to work his way into the position of right-hand man. He accompanied his father on all his business trips around Europe, which was slowly rising from the ashes of the war. Xeno was first and foremost the Old Boss's driver— Grandpa couldn't see well at night and would often insist on driving straight through to keep their tight itinerary. The Old Boss didn't allow himself any frivolities during this hectic period—he knew there were plenty of opportunities to be had, and if he didn't seize them, someone else would. Therefore, speed and efficiency were of the essence.

Father and son visited a long list of prewar contacts in Sweden, Finland, Denmark, England, France, Spain, Portugal, Czechoslovakia, and, of course, Germany to see if they might pick up where they had left off. They also made new contacts along the carefully planned route. Time and again, Xeno was impressed by his father's meticulous preparations and extensive knowledge of business and languages. Xeno proved himself to be an attentive student.

"Xeno is a quick learner and recognizes the opportunities these times have to offer us," his father said. "I think he will be my successor."

So what was left for Frans at Briva Latvija? He had a wife and child, but the flame between them had been ruthlessly extinguished by the war. He couldn't be with her anymore; there was no choice but to build a new future for himself, to divorce Wera and find another woman. She could keep the child as far as he was concerned. The only way forward was to leave his past behind.

Frans Münninghoff exuded an aura of wartime melancholy and heroism. He took refuge in Belgium, where no one knew him, and he could show off his wounded leg and peddle a concocted story that started on the beaches of Normandy and ended in the Ardennes. With his handsome, masculine features, his war-trained physique, and his velvety brown eyes, he made a profound impression on both men and women alike. Mimousse was fed up with her swindler husband's embarrassing activities, and after a second miscarriage, her relationship with the notary's son was falling apart.

Although she knew the truth about Frans (Guus had told her about him long before), that Frans had fought for the Germans in Russia wasn't a major obstacle for her. She asked if he'd ever committed any war crimes, and he replied with a passionate "No, I fought!" and she believed him completely. That was all she needed to know; from then on, she devoted her life to the tragic hero. Six months later, she left Guus and moved into Frans's tiny apartment in Brussels. They weren't thinking about marriage yet—first, they needed to make some money.

In the end, Frans managed to avoid the police for a long time. It wasn't until August 1946, after he'd been working in the arms trade for months, that he was picked up during an inspection at the Port of Antwerp; and it's not clear to what extent Guus played a role in this. In the end, the public prosecutor in Brussels didn't know what to make of him, because although he had a reputation among weapons dealers for being a technical expert, there was no proof he'd been actually involved in any deals. And once his identity was established and linked to the family in Voorburg, the authorities decided that the easiest solution was to deport him for having been in Belgium illegally. On September 4, he was handed over to the Dutch police in Roosendaal and transported to the prison in Scheveningen. By then, there was a warrant out for his arrest for fighting in a foreign military.

EIGHTEEN

It seemed inevitable that Frans would have to appear before the Dutch court and be sentenced to at least a few years for having joined a foreign military. This, in addition to having been in the SS, was bound to damage the Münninghoff family's reputation. The Old Boss absolutely couldn't afford this while he was trying to reconstruct his business empire, so he made sure it didn't happen. The Old Boss had started planning for this the moment Frans had left the house in 1945, and as usual, his foresight proved impressively accurate.

When Frans was finally arrested, Joan Münninghoff went straight to his old friends from the Catholic establishment, starting with Henri Kolfschoten, the brother of Father Constant from Riga, who would go on to become the Dutch minister of justice. Once again, the smoking room at Briva Latvija was host to an elite Jesuit think tank. Shrouded in thick clouds of cigar smoke, the powerful men put their heads together and hatched a plan to keep Frans's punishment minimal.

They agreed that from a strictly legal point of view, there was nothing they could do—Frans had been an SS sergeant, and the judges could easily take a hard-line approach, triggering a surge of negativity from the general public. Nevertheless, the Cold War was brewing, and the former Soviet allies were starting to look more and more like a new enemy. This turn, my grandfather suggested, could open doors for someone like Frans, who spoke Russian and had extensive knowledge of the country, to avoid prosecution by offering his services to the Dutch Intelligence Service.

Kolfschoten concurred, but his response was cautious. It wouldn't be that simple, and he had no idea how to get his friend's son in touch with the right people. Moreover, the Dutch Intelligence Service didn't exist yet; at the time, the Dutch security force was more or less an uncoordinated group of windbags blown in from London. "Leave it to me," the Old Boss said with a grin, and the two friends concluded the conversation with a glass of cognac. By the time Kolfschoten left Briva Latvija that evening, Grandpa already had a plan: his eldest son would have to quietly leave the country—that was all there was to it. And the Old Boss would see to it that he did.

Among my grandfather's many carefully constructed business contacts was Pierre Sweerts, a Belgian adventurer who'd joined the SS and managed to work his way up to the level of *Hauptsturmführer*. When the tide began to turn, Sweerts pretended to be an Allied spy resurfacing after a long period undercover. In the world of Dutch secret services, which was primarily populated by romantic adventurers, fantasists, and charlatans, Sweerts managed to obtain a rather prominent position. He was the kind of person who enjoyed the fact that when his name came up, people would exchange knowing glances and say he was someone to be careful around—though no one knew for sure exactly why. Sweerts had at least twelve pseudonyms, which he used interchangeably, and even played against each other. Arie van der Molen was his most successful; it was under this name he'd been interrogated, and shortly thereafter hired, by MI6 as a specialist on the Netherlands. He became the head of Special Counterintelligence, which was housed in Blauwkapel, an old fortress, in Utrecht.

My grandfather needed a cunning, energetic workhorse, and Sweerts was the ideal candidate. As the Old Boss was closing deals all over Europe, it was critical that he have insider information on all background issues. It was a period when new elites were being formed, and old structures were resisting their imminent demolition. Some of his prewar networks had become unusable, and it was important to know which doors not to knock on. In short, he needed someone who could get the lay of the land first, and Sweerts could carry out intelligence work like no other.

The Old Boss first met Sweerts during a London-commissioned evaluation of the Old Boss's wartime activities with MI6. My grandfather was immediately intrigued by the eloquent, intelligent man, who recounted in flowery language tales of the many predicaments he'd weaseled his way out of. After a few discreet inquiries confirmed that Sweerts's stories were true, my grandfather asked Sweerts to be his "special employee," as he called it, and offered him a considerable amount of money. No one would know about their professional relationship. For the sake of appearances, Sweerts would keep his job in Utrecht, which conveniently called for periods of untraceable absence, offering a curtain behind which they could silently carry out all kinds of dealings.

When the Utrecht police finally arrested Sweerts at home in 1947, he had sixty-eight false passports, "financed by a Dutch millionaire, a certain M., from The Hague," as reported by *Het Vrije Volk*. Perhaps due to the strangeness of the times, the socialist daily newspaper didn't publish my grandfather's name. Maybe they didn't know it. There was still a lot of faith in the authorities at the time, and true investigative journalism didn't exist yet. The intended recipients of all those passports weren't made public either. It became clear that the international Roman Catholic network, urged by the Vatican to step up the fight against communism, had been involved. The church had a vested interest in protecting certain people—people with specific skills important to the Holy Roman cause that would be lost if they were arrested and tried for war crimes. But this wasn't something that could be disclosed publicly and so was kept secret in the postwar Netherlands.

During the three months that my father was in prison in Scheveningen, Sweerts, under his pseudonym Arie van der Molen, visited him on numerous occasions at the Old Boss's request. "He spoke French and German very well, but his Dutch was terrible," my father told me. "I liked the guy. I thought he must be from Luxembourg or something. He told me that he was an intelligence agent and that he had examined my file and come to the conclusion that I was the right man to carry out a few missions for the Allies." This was pretty much all my father ever told me about this period of his life.

Van der Molen's message was clear: as someone who'd previously worked for the SS, Frans Münninghoff would face serious consequences if he were taken before the Dutch court. There was, however, a way to avoid that. After all, he spoke Russian, didn't he? He would be sent into the Soviet-occupied zone in Berlin "to investigate the various conditions and systems put in practice by the Russians," as stated in a May 1947 police interrogation report. At that, my father politely asked Van der Molen if he was blind. "I would never pass for a spy!" he cried out with laughter. "There's nothing Slavic about this face. They'll be suspicious, and before you know it, they'll arrest me, learn that I'm a deserter, and execute me. This plan of yours is worthless, Van der Molen. I'm not interested."

After a week, Sweerts gave up and came with a new proposition. OK, they wouldn't send him to Berlin. But what about South America?

"To do what?" my father asked.

Sweerts assumed my father didn't know about the escape routes that were set up with the Vatican's support to help SS members flee to Paraguay and Argentina. So when Sweerts said Frans's primary job in South America would be investigating underground Communist activities, Frans was immediately suspicious. Thanks to Kurt and Valdemanis, my father knew that there were tremendous amounts of money to be made in assisting SS war criminals and that there was hardly any Communist activity in South America. "If you're asking me to spy on my old comrades, Van der Molen, I won't do it. It's against my principles," he said, and with a sad smile he added: *"Meine Ehre heißt Treue"*—"My honor is called loyalty."

Having exhausted all options, Sweerts decided to play hardball. He didn't visit my father for weeks, and in the meantime, he made sure that Frans's living conditions in the prison gradually became unbearable. Sweerts, who had friends in the prison administration, had my father transferred and placed in proximity to Hanns Rauter, the infamous leader of the Dutch SS. Rauter had been seriously wounded in an attack by the Dutch Resistance in March 1945 and was in the hospital until the end of the war. He was being held in the same wing of the Scheveningen prison where countless Resistance fighters had waited for death. The cells were small, dark, and cold; Rauter had grown accustomed to them, but for Frans, they were hell.

Even worse, however, were his encounters with Rauter during their daily one-hour period in the tiny walled prison yard covered in barbed wire. Rauter, who was being held in solitary confinement until trial, was suspicious of his unexpected companion and immediately began to interrogate him with typical Nazi superiority. "They sent you to the Russian front? And now you're here? In the Dutch slammer? How did that happen?" My father wanted to portray himself as a dutiful solider sent to the eastern front, and he couldn't let this man, a direct employee of Heinrich Himmler, find out that he had deserted at the end of 1944. But Rauter, it turned out, was very well informed of Frans's situation— he was probably tipped off by one of Sweerts's prison connections— and the confrontations between the two of them took a turn for the worse. Rauter proved to be even harsher than Frans's own father. He didn't believe any of Frans's stories and said in no uncertain terms that the Third Reich had collapsed because of despicable lowlifes like Frans Münninghoff, who, as far as Rauter was concerned, deserved the bullet.

My father completely collapsed, and when Sweerts came back in mid-November to cash in on his cleverly orchestrated scheme, Frans was as pliable as wax. Yes, he would go to South America, and yes, he was prepared to do whatever Van der Molen asked of him, anything to get out of that miserable place. A few days later, on November 26, Frans Münninghoff was driven out of Scheveningen in a Special Counterintelligence car, headed for an unknown destination.

Sweerts must have thought he had broken my father enough that his assignment from the Old Boss was nearly complete, that Frans felt so isolated and hopeless that he was the only beacon of hope in his hazy, sad reality. Sweerts took him back to his apartment in Utrecht and plied him with good food, plenty of jenever and whisky, and rest. After five weeks with Rauter in prison, it was exactly what my father needed. One week later, Sweerts decided that it was time to discuss his next steps.

"Your destination will be Argentina, but you'll travel via Paraguay, because border control is less strict there. Just give the guards a few dollars and they'll be happy. You'd have a harder time in Buenos Aires—those Argentines have gotten full of themselves since the end of the war. With all these high-ranking Nazis fleeing to their country, they feel like they've got to show the world that there's no messing with them. It's a matter of national pride, you know." Sweerts let out a disdainful snort.

"You, an unimportant Nazi, would be immediately arrested in Argentina, which is why we have chosen Paraguay. We have an apartment for you in Asunción, and you'll have a few months to get acclimated. You'll have to study Spanish intensively, because you'll need to be able to find your way around there. I don't have to tell you how important it is to speak the local language as a refugee. You'll only move on when we tell you to move on.

"Eventually, our people will get you across the Paraguay River. It'll be a piece of cake, that border leaks like a sieve. There is little difference in standard of living between the countries, and they aren't at war with each other, so border security isn't a priority. Then you'll take the bus to Buenos Aires. We have people there, too, but they don't have a German background, so no way of getting in with the *alte Kameraden*. That's where you and your Baltic connections come in. To make things easier, we've decided you won't have to report on anyone—you took issue with that if I remember correctly. All you'll have to do is introduce our people into the SS circles forming there. We think it'll take a year or two, maybe less, depending on how you play it.

"Did you know that your uncle Helmuth von Russow fled to South America as well? He attempted the crossing on a sailboat with a friend, but they got caught in a heavy storm off the coast of Brazil and were rescued by a luxury passenger ship. They couldn't believe their eyes when they saw two bearded, half-naked seafarers floating in the water. A young woman from São Paolo immediately fell in love with your uncle, and now he's with her on her father's rubber plantation in the Brazilian countryside. They're about to get married, and Von Russow'll be rich overnight. Determination and a sense of adventure can really pay off."

Sweerts fell quiet for a moment and looked at my father. Frans was stunned: Uncle Helmuth, the gentle herbalist from Reval, his favorite uncle, had managed to escape the war. If anyone would receive him with open arms and understanding, it was Uncle Helmuth.

Sweerts must have been able to read his mind. "Once you get our people into the right circles, we'll consider your mission accomplished. Rest assured, we won't burden you with other jobs. But let's not beat around the bush here: your father told me about your uncle Helmuth. He's set aside a considerable amount of money for you to start a new life in Brazil. Helmuth will help you with that. The only condition is that you never come back to the Netherlands or Europe again. Your father doesn't want you here. I'm sorry to be the one to tell you this, but a policeman came to ask him questions about you a few weeks ago, and he told him that you were dead to him."

These words had a profound effect on Frans, but not the one Sweerts expected. It was one thing that he'd turned his back on his father, but such a strong and definitive rejection in return was a blow to the gut. What was more miserable than a father rejecting his own son, declaring him dead? And Sweerts wasn't really trying to help him stay out of jail—he was just another of the Old Boss's servants, willing to go to any lengths to carry out the job he'd been hired to do. Frans was suddenly overwhelmed with a profound sense of malaise: What was left of the camaraderie he'd cherished during his four years in the war? In hindsight, those were—despite all the death around him—the best years of his life. Because where was Frans Münninghoff now? Everyone, his own father included, was just trying to use him.

Everyone except Mimousse, that is; she'd even visited him regularly in prison before he was placed in solitary confinement.

"I understand," Frans said to Sweerts, "and I agree. But first give me some time to say goodbye to my girlfriend. I'm sure my father told you she lives in Brussels. I want to marry her, but I don't know if she'll come with me on this South American adventure." Sweerts promised that after a while she would be allowed to join Frans in Argentina. "Good," Frans replied. "But I can't leave without seeing her first. Can you make sure that I can go to Brussels?"

On December 1, 1946, he found himself standing on Mimousse's doorstep in Ixelles. She flung her arms around his neck with a cry of joy and he swept her upstairs to the bedroom. Sweerts had given him until the first week of 1947, and he intended to use the little time he had left to make his relationship with Mimousse van Blaem a success.

NINETEEN

One of the few residents of Briva Latvija who had no contempt for Guus van Blaem was Titty, the only sister of the brothers Münninghoff. Like Frans, who was one year older, Titty had attended Dutch schools in the 1930s, but she'd had hardly any contact with Frans at all during that time. After graduating from Sacré Coeur College in 1940, she came to Voorburg. Titty had artistic ambitions. Around the age of fifteen, she discovered she had a talent for drawing and sculpting, and once she moved to Voorburg, she enrolled at the art academy in The Hague. Tall, somber, and skinny, with a large hooked nose, Titty wasn't exactly a beauty. She wasn't especially feminine and had the jet-black eyes of a religious icon, which gave her a serious, almost threatening look—or at least that was how I perceived her as a child.

Among her friends, she'd acquired the obscure nickname Munningbull. The name fulfilled itself. If she had one drink too many, which happened often, she would become hysterically aggressive. This was always terrifying to see, or I should say to hear, because the entire house shook with her heavy, smoky voice. She rarely got along with the Old Boss, but she was Omi's favorite. She was named Erica after Omi, who'd even had a special Roman colonnade built near the house, "so Titty's wedding guests won't get wet if it rains," she explained to my grandfather. He laughed and shook his head as he signed the builder's contract.

Half a century later, when I visited the old house, transformed into a Soviet military institution, there were a few workers taking a smoke break under that colonnade. Suddenly, I felt sorry for my aunt, who could never have lived up to this magnificent structure. For a while, it seemed that Titty would never marry; she had no suitors, and though she did her best to act disinterestedly emancipated, it caused her great sadness.

But that changed when Guus van Blaem came into her life. After he'd lost Mimousse to Frans, he was left adrift for some time. He'd had to give up his dealings in Antwerp's underworld because of growing threats from the arms-trade mafia, which considered him a nuisance. And there was the fact that the Belgian police were showing interest in him because—as he later told it—they saw him as an ideal undercover agent. He didn't even consider it—a job like that would land him at the bottom of the Scheldt River with a concrete block chained to his feet. So, in the end, he took refuge in the Netherlands.

First, he went to stay with his brother Guidi, who'd since graduated as a junior notary and started an office in Kaatsheuvel. Guus lived on his brother's income for a while, but all his absurd projects kept his brother from work, so after a few weeks Guidi asked him to leave. He knew where to go—to Voorburg of course, where the master of the house would surely receive him. When Guus arrived at Briva Latvija, however, he found a house full of women. The Old Boss and Xeno were constantly abroad, Jimmy had moved to Amsterdam to study, and Frans was in Brussels with Mimousse.

Guus showed up at their door with a bouquet of flowers in hand and was announced by a disdainful Frau Kochmann. From the moment she met him, my grandmother distrusted that handsome charmer and all his big ideas. But she had a big Russian heart and couldn't leave him stranded, especially not after hearing his tale of betrayal in Brussels and the role her Frans had played in it. She decided he could stay with them for the time being, on the condition that he find his own accommodation as quickly as possible. She didn't trouble herself with him any further and went back to her social life. Omi had no idea of the damage this decision would cause: to Guus, Titty and Wera were defenseless prey. Guus seized the opportunity to completely devote himself to the young ladies of Briva Latvija. Every day he'd "just drop in," as he'd cheerfully put it. And though Frau Kochmann made her objections known, both young women soon fell under the spell of the attractive, well-dressed man. Guus was, above all, a gifted conversationalist, and the only person paying any attention to the two women at the time.

It didn't take long for them both to fall in love. Titty was so taken by him that after just four months she begged her parents to let her marry him. The Old Boss was wholly against the idea, but when it came out that Titty was pregnant with Guus's child, the devout Catholic couldn't bear the thought of his daughter having a child out of wedlock. After a few explosive confrontations, he had no choice but to consent. However, he took precautions: his notary friend who drew up the pre-nuptial agreement in the spring of 1947 confessed over drinks that he'd never seen a more humiliating document in his career. But Guus didn't mind: he had his foot in the door with the Münninghoffs, and one day his time would come.

How Guus, happily married to Titty, still managed to win Wera's affection is a secret behind which hides a tormented woman's heart. Although she didn't want to admit it, my mother was still wait-ing for Frans to return. When she learned he was being held in the Scheveningen prison, she wanted to go to him right away, but the Old Boss told her that his son was not allowed visitors. She had no way of verifying this, so she was forced to resign herself to the fact that she would not be able to see her husband. But that didn't assuage her long-ing for Frans. During an eerie New Year's Eve party at Briva Latvija that was completely spoiled by family feuds, Wera made a secret resolution: 1947 would be the year that she and Frans would get back together.

However, when Guus told her what Frans was doing in Brussels in January, her hopes were dashed. Frans was so enthralled with Mimousse that he'd abandoned his duty with the Dutch Intelligence Service. Wera hadn't known anything about it; with growing horror she listened as Guus gently caressed her hand and offered her his comforting embrace. Paraguay, espionage, Argentina, Mimousse joining him there later, Brazil as a final destination—nowhere in the entire scenario was there any mention of Wera. The fact that Mimousse had rejected the whole plan and persuaded Frans to go into hiding in Belgium didn't help her. She realized Frans's heart was closed to her forever.

She gazed at Guus desperately. "How will I go on with my child? I can't stay in this house with these people who hate me. They would be all too happy to see me disappear to the other side of the world." Guus offered some reassurance. She was still married to Frans, wasn't she? She could stay at Briva Latvija for the time being—after all, her son was the heir to the family name, and he was only three. Better times would come; he would personally see to it. The fact that he married Titty two months later was, in his opinion, not the slightest obstacle.

Meanwhile, dark clouds were gathering above my father's head. At the end of the first week of January 1947, Sweerts contacted him as agreed, and Frans did everything in his power to stay in his love nest with Mimousse a bit longer. "I've never been so in love, you've got to understand! Just leave me alone for a while!"

Sweerts chuckled and handed Frans Münninghoff a pile of documents. "Here's your passport, so you can start getting used to your new identity," he said. "Your name is Martin Alphonsius Jacobus Fons, born on July 4, 1923, in The Hague. You were demobilized from the Allied Expeditionary Forces—here's your soldier's paybook—and you have a visa for Paraguay. It's 100 percent authentic, by the way. You have your father's connections with the consul in Lisbon to thank for that. It is the only real travel document of the lot. The rest are all fake, but good fakes—rest assured."

Sweerts smiled sarcastically, but he was clearly impressed by the expertly falsified documents. "And just to be on the safe side—you never know when you might need it—I got you a Latvian passport as well. It was issued by the Latvian consulate in Bern. In that case, your name is Alfred Valdemanis—I believe you knew him in Brussels, but he unfortunately passed away. I won't tell the circumstances; the important thing is that you have an emergency exit. In many countries, the authorities feel sorry for Latvian refugees, so this passport will get you across the border, as long as you come up with a good story."

Sweerts glanced at Mimousse, who had entered the room despite being told not to. "Well, all right then, I'll give you one more week with your girlfriend, but after that you've got to go, otherwise our whole itinerary will be thrown off. There are people in South America waiting for you, understand?"

Frans nodded and promised that he'd be ready to go next week. But Mimousse had already convinced him otherwise. That same day, the young couple left for Ridderborn Castle, where the lonely old baron and baroness greeted them with surprise and were all too happy to make a wing available to their granddaughter and her fiancé. There, the two made plans for the future, none of which included a South American adventure.

Naturally, Sweerts was furious when he discovered he'd been deceived. He blamed himself for his overconfidence. He should've kept a better eye on Frans, but the boy had seemed so willing to go along with their plans that Sweerts hadn't bothered to take any precautions. Not that he had any doubt that he would catch up with Frans sooner or later—his Belgian network was so wide Frans wouldn't be able to hide for long. The real difficulty was having to tell the Old Boss that he'd failed to get his son to South America. He managed to locate Frans and Mimousse after just four days, and this time he put them under surveillance. Then he headed back to Briva Latvija to discuss the situation with his client.

To his surprise, the Old Boss was remarkably calm about it. "Well, at least we can say we did our best, right, Mr. Sweerts?" the Old Boss replied. "But if my son refuses to cooperate and instead chooses to stay with his new girlfriend, there's not much we can do about it, is there? He'll have to bear the consequences himself."

"I'm afraid that the consequences could be quite severe," Sweerts answered. "I'll be forced to have Belgian police arrest Frans, because, apart from the fact that I can't let this go, your son's position is hopeless. He's got no way out, no one who can help him, and he could quickly fall into the wrong people's hands. You know how precarious things are these days. So I'll have him arrested—keeping an eye on things from a distance of course. We used to be able to carry out arrests a few years ago with a small, well-trained team, but that's not possible anymore."

He swallowed the *unfortunately* and fell silent for a moment, as if fondly recalling the well-orchestrated methods used during the war. "And that means," Sweerts continued, "that he'll probably be extradited to the Netherlands, and it'll be impossible to avoid publicity. In Belgium, he'll be arrested for carrying falsified documents; I personally gave him three fake documents, and he most certainly has them on his person. But the Dutch public prosecutor will have a much stronger case against him. They'll try him for fighting for a foreign military and, if possible, for war crimes. You know how things are here right now: too many cases have been dismissed, and they need a war criminal they can unambiguously punish."

My grandfather's sharp gaze drained the color from Sweerts's face. "My apologies," he stammered. "What I meant to say, of course, is that they will try him as a former member of the SS, and it's going to take a lot of work to convince them that your son doesn't fit the Dutch image of an SS sergeant."

"Mr. Sweerts," the Old Boss replied stiffly, "let's assume that my son has not committed any war crimes, as he consistently claims. The public prosecutor will have to produce evidence to the contrary, which I believe they won't be able to find. Even if there were evidence of such a crime, relations with the Soviets are far too tense for them to get their hands on it. For the rest, I have secured the legal support of two of the best lawyers in the Netherlands, Mr. De Pont and Mr. Bart van Dal. They're already preparing my son's defense, and I can assure you that Frans's citizenship will play a decisive role.

"The key question in the case will be whether he joined the SS as a Dutchman or a Latvian—if the former, he hangs; if the latter, he walks. Either way, documents will be required, which offers us some room for maneuvering, and in this respect, I am optimistic for the future. Of course, I would've preferred my son leave the country quietly and build a future for himself with his uncle Helmuth in Brazil, but clearly, he doesn't want that. Be that as it may, I can't overlook the fact that you failed to carry out the job you were hired to do.

"With greater conscientiousness and resolve on your part, the Paraguay plan could have worked, but it seems that you made an insurmountable error in a key phase of this operation. This forces me to call our collaboration into question, and I therefore suggest that we end our relationship for the time being."

The Old Boss rose to his feet, walked over to the safe in the smoking room, and took out a thick envelope. "Your fee, as agreed," he said coolly. "Feel free to count it."

Sweerts's response was neutral. "That won't be necessary, thank you. I'll make sure that your son returns to the Netherlands, even if as a prisoner of the queen. But if I understand what you've said, there's a good chance of a favorable outcome for his case, and I'm glad. Frans is a good boy. He deserves a better future than the one he is facing now: a life permanently on the run."

The two men left the smoking room and stood in the vestibule. My grandfather switched on the light outside. "I assume that my son will be treated properly both during and after his arrest," he said hoarsely, without acknowledging Sweerts's comment on his son's character.

"Of course," Sweerts assured him. "That we have to do this instead of the Paraguay option is upsetting enough. Well, Mr. Münninghoff, I wish you a pleasant evening. Maybe we'll meet again another time?" There was no answer. "In any case, I would be happy to be of service should the need arise." At that, he nodded and disappeared into the night. No hands were shaken.

TWENTY

Sweerts did indeed have the arrest and extradition of Frans Münninghoff under control. It took a few weeks for him to arrange everything with his contacts in the Netherlands and Belgium, but once in place everything went smoothly. On the night of February 12, 1947, Frans and Mimousse were taken from their beds at Ridderborn Castle, while the police raided Mimousse's apartment in Brussels. In one of the rooms, they discovered a vast amount of pharmaceuticals that Guus had been selling on the black market. Deeply immersed in their affair, the couple had left that room untouched.

This complicated things at first, because the Belgians suddenly had a pretty serious case against the lovers as well. But within a month, Sweerts managed to arrange things so that the only suspect was Guus van Blaem, currently living in the Netherlands. Mimousse was released, and the Belgian gendarmes delivered Frans to the Breda police on March 13. Two days later, he was again locked up in the Scheveningen prison, and within forty-eight hours he was at the interrogation table of the Politieke Recherche Afdeling on the Lange Voorhout in The Hague. It remained to be seen whether the Old Boss had the right connections behind the scenes to secure a safe future for his son—or at least to avoid the kind of disaster that would damage his business reputation.

At first, it didn't seem to work. The Public Prosecution Service had appointed Johannes Zaaijer as procurator general. Zaaijer, who was well known for taking a hard line (he was the public prosecutor against Rauter, a trial that ended with the death penalty), would leave no stone unturned. If it turned out that Frans Münninghoff was indeed a war criminal, Zaaijer would see to it that he was severely punished.

The interrogation reports reveal that my father was able to confuse his interrogators. "He is a very obscure figure," they note helplessly in their report. They asked that his detention be extended by three months, and their request was granted. In the meantime, Frans explained in detail how much suffering his Dutch nationality had brought him in high school, how he'd been influenced by his mother's German family during his holidays, and how, out of resentment for his father, he'd run away from home after the Germans invaded the Netherlands and enlisted in the SS in The Hague. "So I could go to Posen, where my girl was living—we were engaged at the time," he said.

His interrogators understood this, but they couldn't understand the unlikely discrepancy between the Old Boss's patriotism and the anti-Dutch sentiments of his eldest son. They'd never encountered such opposing attitudes between father and son, and refused to believe that such a disparity was possible. Frans's story was seen as an attempt to frame his service in a foreign military outside the realm of punishable offense. On top of that, at the time of enlistment, Frans had a Dutch passport, issued in 1940 when the family settled in Voorburg.

Frans argued in vain that this passport "was not valid" to him at the time. "It was forced on me by my father. The man had absolutely no idea what I cared about. My heart was with Wera and my friends in the Baltics. When we fled Latvia in 1939, I tried to run away to family in Hannover, but my father had me picked up by the German police and brought to Voorburg. There was nothing I could do, but I didn't consider myself a Dutchman. I was only nineteen; I had to do what my father told me," he said, according to the interrogation report.

"But once the war is over and your side had lost, you suddenly wanted to become Dutch again?" one of the agents asked, handing him a second, brand-new Dutch passport issued on September 4, 1944, in the name of Frans Münninghoff.

All of a sudden, my father lost his sense of certainty. He hadn't known about this passport, but he suspected the Old Boss had it issued during the war in case he needed to return to the Netherlands, where it was relatively safe. Meanwhile, he knew, thanks to his lawyers, that no matter what, he needed to avoid admitting that at any point between 1940 and 1945 he'd known he was a Dutch citizen. The fact that he had a Dutch passport, or two for that matter, would work against him; according to Article 101 of the Dutch Penal Code, that fact alone would be enough to put him behind bars for years for serving in a foreign military as a Dutchman.

But Frans Münninghoff had no trouble denying his Dutch citizenship. After all, he'd always despised the Netherlands and the Dutch. He launched into a detailed explanation, claiming that the reason he'd had Dutch papers was that being Latvian could endanger him with the Soviets. The USSR has always had it out for the Baltics! He mentioned the recent case of three Lithuanians who were sent home from a refugee camp in Belgium by the Allies, only to be picked up by the Bolsheviks and executed without a trial. With a Latvian passport he would have met the same end. What's more, during his years on the Russian front, he'd made contacts with an anti-Communist resistance organization with headquarters in Kiev and Moscow (he made this story up on the spot). The head of the organization was a starets in the Orthodox Church who went by Dionisios—just a pseudonym, of course. But pretty soon the whole world would know his name.

His interrogators listened in fascination. These kinds of stories of international intrigue were much more interesting than the piddly Dutch countryside tales they were used to hearing. They seemed to understand the dilemma the young man had found himself in.

"So, you want to be Dutch now, but didn't consider yourself Dutch during the war?" was their final conclusion.

Frans confirmed this. "I considered the Germans less my enemies than you, only because I saw them as allies of my homeland, Latvia," he explained emphatically, just as his lawyers had instructed. "But now, everything has changed. The Latvia of my youth no longer exists, and I understand that I have no choice but to become Dutch."

The Public Prosecution Service was also looking for evidence of war crimes. For Frans, this was almost unspeakable. When his interrogators brought it up, he exploded with anger and contempt. "You have no idea what it was like on the Russian front! We were there to fight Bolsheviks, not rape women, murder children, or burn villages. And all this about the concentration camps and gas chambers and genocide of Jews—I never heard anything about it when we were fighting in Ukraine. I know now, of course, but I don't know what I'm supposed to do about it.

"Look," he continued. "We lost the war. So that means you get to decide what's true. You can accuse us of anything and everything, and there's nothing we can say, because no one will believe our side of the story. All I can say is that there were some damn fine people with us in the Waffen-SS. And think about it: I was on the front lines. *Immer vorwärts!* Onward! We didn't know about anything happening behind us. Kill the enemy and stay alive, that was all that mattered."

It was the same story he bombarded me with as a teenager in the late '50s and early '60s in The Hague. I knew better than to challenge him, but I had learned all about the extermination camps from my high school teachers and the despicable role the SS had played. But on Sunday mornings at our kitchen table, my indignant father vehemently denied all of it.

"You have to understand," he'd explain, "there was a difference between the ordinary SS and the Waffen-SS. And in the Waffen-SS, it was the Balts, and the others were Imperial Germans. But there were plenty of good guys among them as well, except the Saxons. We were proud to be part of the elite, the very best Germany and the surrounding countries had to offer. I swear, Bully, with my hand over my heart, we were there to fight, and by fight, I mean fight to the death, but we never sank to the point of committing war crimes against innocent civilians, Jews or otherwise. It was beneath our dignity and against our honor as soldiers.

"That's why I let that Russian soldier at the interrogation center go, even though it put me in danger. Because I knew he'd be shot. So whatever they're saying about us now, all these terrible stories they're concocting, all I can say is that when we meet each other, we can look each other in the eye with no shame, because our conscience is clean."

It was interesting how he'd avoid *I* in these conversations, relying on the collective *we*. Was he still in touch with some of the men he'd fought with? And what kind of people were they?

In the 1960s, when I was living a nomadic existence, bouncing from one rental to the next, I decided to track down my father's old friend Hans Erich Seuberlich, a renowned German children's book author and career military officer who lived in Munich, in the south of Bavaria. He was a clean-cut gentleman: impeccably groomed, well dressed, living in a beautiful house with a BMW in the driveway. He was a man of prestige in postwar Germany, someone who'd done his part to breathe new life into the bombed-out wasteland Germany had become. It was thanks to people like him that the exhausted German population was eventually able to reclaim their prominent position on the European continent. Seuberlich's contribution had been in the form of twenty-some children's books, each one offering a much-needed sense of optimism and lofty values like loyalty and honesty—all against the backdrop of modern-day fashions, rock 'n' roll, and German youth zipping around on Vespas. These images helped the generation of the 1950s believe that, despite everything, they could still be a part of the new, better Europe.

During the war, Seuberlich had distinguished himself as a member of the Sonderverband Brandenburg, a commando unit under *Abwehr* commander Wilhelm Canaris. Under Admiral Canaris, he carried out dangerous operations in Ukraine, where he'd met my father on the front lines when he'd been a sergeant in the Viking Division combat unit. The two men knew each other well—they'd both been born in Riga in 1920, had attended the same primary school, and had the same friends. The connection went back generations: a century earlier, a Seuberlich had been appointed godmother to Omi's father. My father and the famous children's book author could've been lifelong friends had my grandfather not decided to force Dutch culture on his eldest son by sending him to that boarding school in Oss.

Like my father, Seuberlich passed through one of Posen's centers for displaced Balts early on in the war. The two young men found each other there and rekindled their friendship over drinks at Café Schwan. When Seuberlich advanced to the rank of officer, he and my father lost touch, but their chance encounter in Ukraine was a joyous reunion. They talked for hours, exchanging war stories. Given Seuberlich's reputation, I was hoping he'd be able to provide a reliable opinion of my father, so I contacted him to ask if I could come visit, and he agreed.

"A real daredevil, your father," he said. "I understand he's in a difficult position in the Netherlands. You probably didn't know this, but he visited me a few years ago in Bonn, where I was serving as a colonel in the Bundeswehr at the time. He asked me if I could get him a job in the German military. I couldn't help him. Unfortunately, he was too old— that's what I told him, at least. But the real problem, *lieber* Alexander, was in his head, and it probably still is. He, like so many others, can't let go of the war." Seuberlich walked over to the giant window showing an impressive view of the Alps. As if planned, an eagle swooped across the clear evening sky, a symbol of the new Germany that Seuberlich was a part of and my father was not.

"And in a country like the Netherlands," Seuberlich continued, "where German collaboration and oppression went hand in hand—perhaps more so than in any other country in Europe—it's even harder to find the right path." Seuberlich cast a thoughtful glance out the window, where the sun was quickly setting behind the snowy peaks. "You don't have to worry," he continued. "If Frans had committed any war crimes, I would know. I would've picked up on it that time we met in Ukraine. You can see it in a man's eyes if he has something shameful to hide. You can tell by the way he talks. I didn't see that in your father, rest assured.

"He didn't have the character for such acts. His sense of humor was too good for that, though that sounds strange. He killed people, of course. Dozens, maybe more. His unit had quite a reputation, and he'd already received the Iron Cross in 1943. But that doesn't make him a war criminal. He had a boyish love for combat, and he was good at it.

"He told me once how, just a few weeks before we met, he'd taken out a Russian lieutenant with a spade during a mission in a cornfield. I'm sure you've heard the story. But I think that moment says a lot about him. When the situation called for it, he was resolved, efficient, and merciless—qualities that are useful in a war. But in times like these, we need people with empathy, knowledge, and foresight. Now he's landed in the business world, much to his own chagrin, where you have to be able to talk to people, keep up appearances when things go wrong, and even deceive business partners when necessary.

"Frans doesn't have it in him. He'll always long for that short period in his life when honesty, camaraderie, and loyalty were unconditional—that was the world he functioned so well in. The war was his finest hour. That time he came to visit, he begged me to get him a position in the Bundeswehr. He was prepared to become a German citizen, live in Germany without his family if necessary—whatever it took. I tried to explain that the new German army is completely different, that he would be confronted with tremendous bureaucracy and a new generation of German boys who definitely didn't have the discipline he was used to. I think he holds the fact that I didn't help him against me. In any case, that meeting in Bonn was the only time I've seen him since. I think it boils down to his naivety and impulsiveness. It's a shame, really, because he is a convivial man. You could have a lot of fun with him."

TWENTY-ONE

Convivial or not, Frans Münninghoff was still in prison in Scheveningen in 1947, and the Dutch interrogators were determined to paint him as a war criminal. But after months of interrogation, they had gotten nowhere. The Soviets refused to provide the information that would verify Frans's story, which had to do with the fact that the Netherlands had been the last western country to recognize the USSR, in 1942, and was extremely critical of the ruling powers in Moscow. Furthermore, relations with the Soviets had become increasingly tense with the onset of the Cold War, and a wall of mistrust had been built between East and West.

Wera was called in for questioning in June, and the detectives tried to extract incriminating information from her. They knew that her marriage to Frans had fallen apart, and they hit her with one question after another. But despite her frazzled nerves, my mother didn't give them what they wanted. She told them how they'd met in Riga, and how she'd seen him at the end of 1940 at Café Schwan in Posen. "He was wearing a German uniform with a diagonal belt across his chest and carrying a weapon. There was a band around his upper arm that read Dolmetscher, or interpreter. I fell in love with him all over again, though we hadn't seen each other for over a year. Then the war began. He didn't write, but he visited me twice in Posen, where I got a job with the government. We got married on May 11, 1942, in Hamburg. Why there? I had family in the countryside there, some distant relatives of my mother's, and they could still afford a few luxuries, so we went to celebrate our marriage and let them spoil us for a little while. No, we never considered getting married in the Netherlands. Frans had a bad relationship with his father and didn't plan on ever returning to Voorburg."

At this point in the report, Wera begins to recite the lawyers' version of the story almost verbatim. She mentioned, without offering details, Frans's injury in the spring of 1943 at Cherkasy and his admission to the hospital in Bamberg. She saw him again later that summer, when he returned to Posen on sick leave. It was then that I was conceived, but there's no mention of this in the interrogation report, nor of the fact that my father returned to Posen after his second injury in early 1944 and was there when I was born.

"After that, to the best of my knowledge, Frans was dismissed from military service," my mother continued. "How he eventually returned to his parents' home in the Netherlands, I have no idea. I had been living there since September 1944, when Xeno came to rescue me and my child from the impending Russian attack on Posen. Then, on June 1, 1945, Frans suddenly showed up at the front door in Voorburg.

"It was a difficult period for us," she continued. "He couldn't cope with the misery of the war, and on top of it all, his father was incredibly hard on him. So, after a few weeks, Frans left again without telling me where he was going. I haven't seen him since. You asked if he was in the SS. I'm afraid I don't know, because he never told me about his experiences in the war." But hadn't she been able to tell by his uniform whether or not he was in the SS? they asked. Wera responded like a true ingenue: "I'm afraid not, I don't know anything about those kinds of things." Once again, those drama classes she had taken at the theatre in Posen paid off.

She did well in the interrogation room, nearly everyone in the family agreed. When it was over, Jimmy, Titty, and Omi genuinely believed that they'd leave the sweet girl from Riga alone after that, and she'd be allowed to stay at Briva Latvija with little Bully, the heir to the Münninghoff family name. But the Old Boss and Xeno disagreed, and they made their opinion known during their short stops at Briva Latvija between business trips. Despite her excellent performance in the interrogation room and the fact that she hadn't betrayed Frans, Wera still had to go. How, between all his business woes, my grandfather found the time and energy to plan for my mother's destruction is a mystery to me, but he did. As usual, when the Old Boss set his mind to something, there was no talking him out of it. This time, however, it took much longer for his plans to succeed.

The same Van Dal who would later secure Frans's release was also working behind the scenes to make Wera disappear legally. It just so happened that Van Dal and Mimousse had been childhood sweethearts, and the Old Boss was correct in thinking that this would only increase his motivation to help her. The young attorney didn't waste any time. On August 8, 1947, he saw to it that Frans and Wera were declared divorced. However, since his son was in prison, the Old Boss's plans to have my guardianship transferred from Wera to himself were, for the time being, hopeless. The court ruled in October 1947 that Wera would be granted custody of me, and Frans, while still behind bars, would still be coguardian. But he wouldn't be in prison for much longer.

By the fall of 1947, the political climate in the Netherlands was changing. The cries for revenge that had been so loud in the months after the war were gradually being replaced by the feeling that what the country needed most for reconstruction was an irreproachable legal system. And in order for such a system to exist, criminal cases needed to be examined in detail, not dismissed on emotional grounds. Henri Kolfschoten may have only served as minister of justice for a short time, but by the time he resigned in 1946, he'd managed to expedite more than 70,000 cases against alleged political delinquents. In nearly three-quarters of these cases, particularly those involving lighter offenses, the door for release was conditionally opened.

Kolfschoten's successor, Johan van Maarseveen, yet another Catholic and a member of my grandfather's social network, accelerated this trend. A few serious cases, such as Hanns Rauter's, were kept open just in case the courts needed a bone to throw at an angry public, but by 1947, the number of political prisoners had been reduced to 25,000, keeping pace with the target set by the House of Representatives in 1946.

Frans Münninghoff, however, was not among those who were released. The new challenge for my grandfather was to make sure that his son's case was classified as a minor offense. He managed to secure Van Maarseveen's support in this matter, but the minister was still sensitive to the priorities of the times, and rightfully so. "As a minister, I don't have any direct influence on your son's case, Joan," he explained to my grandfather in his smoking room, after examining Frans's situation in detail. "We've just opted to implement more transparent judicial procedures. I'm mainly dealing with Zaaijer here. He's just as fervent as he was in May 1945. True, he hasn't made much progress against Frans, and the detention order can't be extended forever, but he'll just take more decisive action. I'll see if I can enlist a few contacts to help Zaaijer understand your son's side of the story; but if he gets the chance to use those passports to force a conviction, he'll take it."

The Old Boss nodded. Both he and Van Maarseveen, as well as the Kolfschotens, knew that the law wouldn't be sufficient in this matter, that they'd have to resort to other means. This was something the Old Boss had long prepared for.

What happened next suggests that intensive discussions with Zaaijer had indeed been going on behind the scenes. In September, it seemed as if the procurator general's mind had been made up: he asked the Department of Justice to check whether Frans Münninghoff had a criminal record. When he received word in early October that the person in question "is unknown in the criminal record" (which is remarkable given my father's misadventures in Belgium), Zaaijer arrived at the same conclusion that had been announced the day before at Frans's sentencing: three years in prison "for voluntary military service for a foreign power as a Dutch citizen while fully aware that said power was at war with the Netherlands."

Less than two weeks later the Special Court of Justice of The Hague (one of the eight courts specifically established for serious cases) reached a different conclusion: "Conviction pursuant to Article 101 of the Penal Code is excluded on the account of the person in question's Latvian nationality. The young man had never been to the Netherlands"—as stated in a letter to Zaaijer, to my utter surprise—"and it is entirely logical that Frans Münninghoff regarded Russia as a greater enemy than Germany."

How that court came to such a conclusion, so diametrically opposed to the judgment of the highly respected Johannes Zaaijer, I'll never know. And how could they believe that my father, who'd spent nearly eight years in Dutch schools, had never been in the Netherlands? It's clear from the judgment that they'd been in a hurry to close the case, and a decision had already been made behind closed doors. And that was true. The ambitious Bart van Dal had taken over as defense attorney on his own while his colleague was handling more lucrative matters in the Münninghoff family empire. Indeed "Bartie," as our family affectionately called him, had worked out quite a deal with the Justice Department.

But for the plan to work, they had to make sure that Zaaijer didn't lose face. To achieve this, my grandfather enlisted the help of Van Maarseveen, the Kolfschoten brothers, and even Emanuel Sassen, a Catholic and the future minister of Overseas Territories, and Laurens Deckers, member of the Council of State and the Catholic People's Party minister of Defense and Agriculture before the war. These men frequented the smoking room at Briva Latvija to discuss their tactics and work out the finer details of their plan. Although Zaaijer was by no means a papist, the Roman Catholic delegation ultimately managed to convince the officer of justice to do their bidding.

There's an incredible correspondence that confirms this fact. "On January 12, 1948, the Minister of Justice informed me in writing that His Excellency was of the opinion that your client had not lost his Dutch nationality," Zaaijer wrote to Van Dal on January 15. Therefore, as the letter continued, the criminal prosecution had every right to proceed. In other words, Minister Van Maarseveen had formally agreed with Zaaijer. However, this was all part of a charade, because then, completely out of the blue, Zaaijer added: "But I am inclined to overlook this, considering that internally this man was more Latvian than Dutch. There are indeed mitigating circumstances for the Balts."

The notion that my father was "internally more Latvian" is entirely inaccurate: my father considered himself first and foremost a Balt of German-Russian descent with a few Dutch genes unfortunately thrown into the mix. Definitely not Latvian. In his eyes, the Latvians were provincial people whose language he spoke fairly well—the only Latvians he'd really known were the household help.

Of course Bartie van Dal didn't mention any of this in his defense. Instead, he passionately told the story of a young man who had seen the beautiful Latvia of his youth pulverized by the Bolsheviks and decided to join the Germans in the fight against their common enemy. Psychological examinations weren't standard practice in criminal cases, and besides, what did people in the Netherlands know about Latvia, a country that had been swallowed up by the USSR and disappeared behind the Iron Curtain? Back then, a good criminal defense came down to eloquence, persuasiveness, and a network of friends in high places. Bartie van Dal took care of the former, and my grandfather's Catholic brotherhood handled the latter.

There was also a personal meeting with Zaaijer on January 28, in which Van Dal gave his assurance in writing that Frans Münninghoff would "leave the Netherlands as soon as possible to settle abroad permanently, that everything would be done to ensure a swift departure, and that the person in question would behave discreetly until that time. The person in question's father has also given me his word that he will do everything in his power to encourage his son's quick departure." In a letter to the Old Boss, Van Dal summarizes his conversation with Zaaijer and concludes by expressing the hope that the father's word "would be reason enough to release Frans Münninghoff." Under the assumption that Frans would soon be leaving for South America, the Ministry of Justice concluded: "One might ask whether it is in the national interest to prevent such a departure because of prosecution for acts that Münninghoff carried out as a Latvian. The charges are hereby dismissed."

Rarely has a dismissal ever been formulated so curtly. Is this a sign of irritation on the part of Zaaijer and his colleagues after realizing that the Old Boss had pulled a fast one on them? We'll never know. On January 30, 1948, after ten months in prison, my father was finally released.

TWENTY-TWO

But the fact that Frans Münninghoff was a free man didn't mean that he'd regained his citizenship rights. He may have escaped conviction and the accompanying publicity, but Zaaijer's note in the margin of the Ministry of Justice's statement is telling: "He remains, however, a somewhat shady figure. I consider this more a matter for the Aliens Department." Two officials from the Aliens Department promptly visited my father at Briva Latvija, where he was staying after being released from prison, and confiscated his passport and identity card. It was a short, firm conversation carried out behind closed doors; my grandfather was in the room as well. The iciness was palpable, both between the two officials and my family, and between the Old Boss and my father. No one looked each other in the eye.

My grandfather confirmed again that plans were underway to send Frans to South America—that is, if his son would cooperate. My father stared straight ahead with a spiteful look on his face, and only mumbled a confirmation when he was explicitly asked for one. The gentlemen from the Aliens Department got a good read on the situation, and as they were leaving, they turned to my father and said: "You would be advised to stay out of trouble."

The two officials were hardly out of sight when the house was shaken to its foundation in the most violent explosion of anger Frans ever had in front of his father. "I felt so humiliated, Bully," he told me.

"You have no idea. The way those two Dutch bastards just walked in and told me to stay out of trouble, and my father was on their side, because that's how it felt. I accused the Old Boss of everything I could think of—from sleeping with the enemy to being a terrible father to betraying me, the boy he'd wanted so badly to make a Dutchman, and who he'd manipulated throughout the war for his personal gain. After ten minutes or so, I ran out of steam. 'What kind of father are you, trying to send me out of the country? A father doesn't do that, does he?' I said finally. I felt betrayed and desperate, as you can imagine.

"And you know what he did next? He had sat there in front of me in silence the whole time, and when I was finally done, he took out a deck of cards! He didn't say a word. He started laying out a game of solitaire. He always did that when he needed to think. He'd set a pencil and notepad beside him and whenever a thought came to mind, he'd jot it down. And that's what he did! He didn't even look at me, he just let me stand there as he laid out those stupid cards. I had just poured my heart out to him, and he just shut me out. It was like I'd been shouting at a wall. I walked out of the room sobbing in anger, and he just sat there at his desk—no reaction whatsoever."

This oppressive status quo endured at Briva Latvija for nearly three years. Xeno and Jimmy lived there nominally, but they spent most of their time in Delft and Amsterdam respectively. Titty had moved in with Guus, Xeno was studying hydraulic engineering (but gave it up once he realized there was more money in his father's business empire), and Jimmy had enrolled in the political science department, which had a reputation for being one of the easier subjects, at the university.

Within a few months, Frans and Mimousse found shelter in an old, leaky houseboat called the *Juno*, which was anchored in the harbor of the Poortensdijk oil refinery on Junostraat in The Hague. But in the meantime, my father and the Old Boss established a kind of armed peace; they avoided each other as much as possible and kept conversation to a minimum. Frans was given an administrative position at the Old Boss's trading company, Poortensdijk, so there was nothing for the outside world to gossip about. But there was little more than tolerance between father and son, and to make matters worse, Mimousse—a depraved woman in my grandfather's Roman Catholic eyes—wasn't welcome at Briva Latvija. This wasn't just because she was divorced; apparently the Old Boss hired a detective to track down her baptismal record and found that she'd been a twenty-year-old woman when she'd deflowered the fourteen-year-old Guus. This disgrace barred her from the family for good, so when the *Juno* became available, Frans packed his suitcases with a sigh of relief and left.

From the boat, my father had a clear view of the factory that he would inherit just a few years later, but at that point the place was virtually useless to him. Management had been handed over to Wim, the Old Boss's brother, who turned out to have a surprising skill with the refinery's main products: oil and lubricants. In the laboratory Uncle Wim would test new formulas by dipping a finger into the batch and tasting it, which was either gratifying or horrifying for the lab assistants gathered to observe his unprecedented level of product involvement.

For Frans, whose life had been put on hold, so to speak, the job at Poortensdijk was frustrating. The administrative tasks he was expected to carry out were minimal, and he considered it an insult to his intelligence. So, in order to distinguish himself as more than just the owner's son, he donned a lab coat and began carrying out amateur experiments. At one point he was assisted by Count Stubendorff, a Russian immigrant who'd been a chemical engineer in St. Petersburg. My father liked wanderers like Stubendorff because he'd withdrawn from Dutch social life, not so much because he'd been told to, but because he was insecure about his run-ins with the authorities and harbored a deep aversion to all things Dutch.

Stubendorff—"Stubka"—was in his seventies and had a wooden leg from the Russian civil war. He and my young father, not yet thirty, turned out to be an excellent team. The factory workers, with whom Frans maintained a jovial bond (I think factory life appealed to his sense of soldierly camaraderie), couldn't understand a word Frans and Stubka were saying when they entered the laboratory speaking Russian (which was suspicious in those Cold War McCarthy years). They came across as both comical and mysterious. At one point, they were even investigated by the police, who were probably tipped off by a recently fired employee, but the officers didn't find anything incriminating. They concluded that the men's activities were nothing more than innocent science experiments.

It turned out that Stubendorff was working on a process to regenerate used oils, which seemed fairly innocuous. Years later, when I saw the manuscript of *From the Grave to the Cradle*, the manual he and my father wrote together, I was impressed by the detailed figures, clear diagrams, and painstaking descriptions of the oil regeneration process. But they never thought that Stubka had any other chemical tricks up his sleeve or that my father would use them for illegal purposes.

Of course, the South American emigration the Dutch government had agreed to for Frans never came to fruition. On the contrary, he applied for a normal passport in 1949 so he could carry out business for the Poortensdijk factory abroad—primarily in Belgium. His reason for cancelling his intercontinental travel plans was "financial problems related to the Nemaglas factory in Schiedam," where the Old Boss had set up a glass factory shortly after the war. There, he illegally housed seventy or so Bohemian glass makers, all of whom were professionals in their field, but according to the same report were "mostly ex-political delinquents."

It is downright remarkable that, though the authorities knew all this, my grandfather was able to carry on with business as usual. The same went for his brother Tom, who, after a few hiccups on his way back from Sweden (he was arrested at Schiphol in 1946 with forty-five pounds of gold bars in his luggage) was once again able to put his business acumen to work on Dutch soil. Uncle Tom arrived in Holland with a patent to produce Swedish tiles, bought a grinder, and started the Vibro stone factory, just a stone's throw away from Poortensdijk in the Binckhorst industrial complex. In need of raw material, he ground up the ruins of the Bezuidenhout bombing, which he was able to buy for next to nothing.

Glass and tiles: two essential materials for the Netherlands' postwar reconstruction. It was in the brothers' nature to respond immediately to demand—Tom even gave up his comfortable life in untouched Sweden for it. But the fact that the Dutch government allowed them to do so, when there were undoubtedly other entrepreneurs with a much cleaner track record, who hadn't tried to smuggle gold bars into the country or employ undocumented glass blowers, raises questions.

This time, my grandfather hadn't called on the higher powers that had proven effective in the case against my father. In Frans's case, the Catholic brotherhood had stepped up to protect the reputation of one of its most respected families. This was an economic favor, a token of appreciation for services rendered during the war. Trivial, in a way. Out of gratitude to my grandfather and Uncle Tom for their efforts in their wartime mission, Anton Speekenbrink—now a high-ranking official in the Netherlands—saw to it that the investigations into both the gold bars and the illegal glassworkers were closed, arguing that the country could surely benefit from two entrepreneurs like the Münninghoff brothers, who weren't afraid to take risks.

The Old Boss fell into financial trouble after a 1948 explosion in the Nemaglas factory—the bang was so loud it could be heard all the way in Rotterdam. The results of the official investigation were that a few pumps had broken down, but the Old Boss's confidential police sources had a different story: sabotage. The postwar production of window glass had been awarded exclusively to Glaverbel, a glass manufacturer in Liège, and Nemaglas had circumvented that agreement. Since it would take more than a year for the insurance company to pay out—and no glass could be produced in the meantime—the Old Boss's plans to send Frans to South America had to change. Or at least that was the story Bart van Dal gave the courts in 1949. The plan had been for Frans to stay with one of his father's partners, a glass manufacturer in Paraguay, but now this was impossible. Moreover, South America was no longer a viable option for trade. Surely, the Public Prosecution Service could understand; and no one could deny that Frans Münninghoff had been staying out of trouble—he was rarely seen in public and kept busy playing the good employee at the Poortensdijk factory. Since the court had definitively ruled that my father had not lost his Dutch citizenship, the authorities saw no reason to continue to deny him a Dutch passport. A surprising leniency.

Most surprising of all, however, is the fact that Wera and I managed to stay at Briva Latvija for almost three years. With a stubbornness that is almost incomprehensible, my mother continued to live in that giant house, though its owner openly speculated about her departure, assuming she'd leave me behind, of course. But she refused to go, and she had the support of Omi and Titty. And if anyone could win the frequent shouting matches on the subject, it was Titty. Whenever Wera's situation came up, Titty would rant about how her husband, Guus, was treated as well.

Despite Guus and Titty having two children, he was lower on the Old Boss's list than Wera; he wasn't even welcome at the table anymore. Not that there weren't good reasons for this: Guus had taken expensive Christmas presents that Titty had gotten from her parents, such as a fur coat and a diamond-and-amethyst ring, to the pawnshop. But Titty didn't want to hear it; she and Guus had plans to start their own gallery and studio. Couldn't her father see that she was happy with Guus, the man who had given her two wonderful children? That made the Old Boss laugh. His daughter was "in bondage," he shouted. (I can still hear him shouting the word *bondage*. I didn't find out what it meant until many years later, but I could tell by the venomous sting in his voice that it was something very bad.) He upheld his decree: Guus was no longer welcome at Briva Latvija.

My grandfather never went so far as to kick my mother out, seeing as her status was derived from the fact that I was heir to the family name. I was the firstborn son of his firstborn son, something my grandfather had transformed into a kind of mythical concept so as to justify the situation in his own mind. And when an argument would erupt at the dinner table for the umpteenth time, and everyone would start screaming, he'd often stand up and shout: "You just wait. When I die, I'm going to leave everything to Bully—with Xeno as executor. Surely, you don't expect me to throw it all to the dogs, do you?" The thought that Guus would indirectly gain part of the inheritance infuriated him. He would retreat to the smoking room alone, and you could tell by the angry thump of cards hitting the table that it was a matter of serious concern.

PART 2

WERA

TWENTY-THREE

As far as my grandfather was concerned, my mother's presence was no longer required. But before the family could send her away for good, a decision about me had to be made. The verdict on October 27, 1947, granting Wera custody of me with Frans as coguardian, was fiercely contested by the Münninghoff family after my father's release. Naturally, my grandfather played a leading role in all this.

Frans and Mimousse planned to get married and were busy building a new life together. Mimousse, who'd had two miscarriages with Guus, was determined to bring a child into the world to seal her fate with Frans and the family. My father acquiesced to her plans and showed no fatherly sentiment toward me whatsoever.

But the Old Boss saw the situation differently. Not only did he consider the idea of heir to the family name sacred, he'd also recently learned that he didn't have much time left to get his affairs in order. He was first diagnosed with throat cancer in 1936 and received regular treatment from the famous Palestinian doctor Hamid Chaoul, a man held in such high regard that the Nazis awarded him the title "honorary Aryan." Chaoul's radiation treatments had extended the lives of many a Nazi kingpin, and had also worked wonders on my grandfather; his voice sounded like a belt sander, but the disease itself was under control. But the war had thrown a wrench in his recovery as well. When travel to Berlin became impossible due to the war, one of Dr. Chaoul's protégés, Daniel den Hoed, took over my grandfather's treatment and continued to treat him after the war was over. At one point, one of Den Hoed's assistants made an incorrect diagnosis based on an incomplete examination. When my grandfather returned a year later for a checkup, the doctors discovered a tumor that had already grown past the point of possible recovery.

The Old Boss received the news stoically and shared it with no one, not even his wife. It was 1949 by then, and the doctors gave him two years at best. Thanks to new medications, some of which were still experimental, those two years would become almost five. But this made my grandfather even more intent on securing my future, and he would stop at nothing to have his way.

At first it didn't seem like the Münninghoff family would get very far in court. After Frans and Mimousse married on August 3, 1949, my grandfather immediately started the legal proceedings. Bartie van Dal argued that my custody should be given to my father because my mother was unable to care for me alone. "She lives with the child's grandparents, and they pay for everything," he claimed—which was true. Van Dal also brought up Wera wanting to leave the country because she had little chance of finding a job in the Netherlands as a foreigner. She was planning to go to Denmark, where her grandmother lived (in pitiful circumstances, Van Dal was sure to add), or to Germany to join her mother, who was barely scraping by as well. Van Dal thus concluded that the child—me—would be much better off with his father, a Dutch citizen, who was living a respectable life as a married man.

But at a hearing before the family court that October, the family's arguments were dismissed. Wera declared that she had no intention of going abroad. Perhaps the thought of it had crossed her mind in a moment of despair, she said, but she was looking for a job in the Netherlands as a domestic servant, preferably for a family with many children. Her son was going to preschool in Voorburg and was receiving plenty of love and care from both herself and the other residents at Briva Latvija. Naturally, the situation was far from normal, in light of her divorce, but that would change once she had found new accommodations. All in all, the family court didn't see any reason for a change in custody and rejected the request submitted by Joan and Frans Münninghoff, who, at least on paper, were working together on the case. In January 1950, the Old Boss submitted an appeal; this time he found a way to trap my mother in a nearly impossible position.

Briva Latvija had gotten too big for him, he announced. His children had all left the house, and Frau Kochmann had resigned, informing the family that she wished to spend her final years with her family in northern Germany. This meant that it was time for him to downsize; Wera would have to be out of the house by February 1, 1950. He and Omi moved into the Kurhaus Hotel in Scheveningen while they waited for the house to sell. In the end, they never did sell the house, but my grandfather believed this would put a knife to Wera's throat, and she would beg him to take over the care of her child. With her *testimonium paupertatis*, a transfer of custody might become a real possibility. But my mother didn't give in so easily. By the end of January, she'd found a job as a housekeeper in a guesthouse on Groot Hertoginnelaan in The Hague, where she'd earn sixty guilders a month in addition to free room and board for herself and me. Despite the fact that she spoke primarily German—which was hardly in fashion those days—she'd managed to secure employment and adhere to my grandfather's draconian deadline for her departure.

Where did Wera Lemcke, as she was once again called, get the nerve? Wera—the woman who'd always faded into the background, who haunted Briva Latvija like a ghost, always terrified of Xeno and the Old Boss—that same Wera was now demanding alimony! She knew that sixty guilders a month would hardly put clothes on my back and cover the costs of my education. But still, for a German woman who barely spoke Dutch to take a case to court in the Netherlands just five years after the war had ended was no small feat.

I didn't learn until many years later, through chance encounters with people who had known her at the time, that in her five years at Briva Latvija she had managed to build a following of men who were fond of or completely in love with her, whose patronage she could count on. Most of them came from Xeno and Jimmy's wealthy social circles and offered their moral, and, in some cases, financial support as the crisis escalated. And a few of them even went a step further and tried to use her in their shady business deals, for which a young, beautiful woman could be useful as part of an entourage.

Arrogant, fast-talking Karel Hofdijk fell hard for my mother when he met her in 1948 on the way to the beach. Whether it was her long dirty-blonde hair, her beautiful dancer's legs, her graceful gait, or her thoughtful, melancholic gaze, he was moved to sit down beside her in the sand and strike up a conversation. "Man, oh man, you were a real obstacle back then, you know that?" Hofdijk said when we met in the 1990s. My mother always insisted that I come along—to the beach, to parties, wherever she went. Most of the time I was put in a corner where I could keep myself busy, but at the beach, that was impossible. Eating ice cream, playing soccer, flying kites, jumping waves, building sandcastles—I wanted to do it all. I don't remember ever noticing that my mother was hanging out with the wrong guys or that I had interrupted them at just the right moment.

Karel Hofdijk was definitely one of those wrong guys. He was as much of a dreamer as Guus van Blaem, but more cunning. Exactly what kind of unsavory activities he was involved in, I'm not really sure, but one thing is certain: they eventually earned him a two-year sentence and tarnished my mother's reputation. Unbeknownst to her, he'd taken advantage of her on several occasions by bringing her to business dinners and introducing her as a Baltic princess and his future wife.

Since my mother was indeed a descendent of the royal Courland house of Lieven, she just smiled whenever the topic came up. And because she couldn't follow everything in Dutch, she unintentionally let people believe that Hofdijk was about to make a permanent entrance into an elite circle of Baltic exiles. In a time without databases or other modern tools, this was enough to create an aura of romantic promise around Hofdijk's activities, which greatly improved his credibility. It was Hofdijk who ultimately pushed Wera's alimony case through to court.

To my grandfather's unpleasant surprise, the judge again sided with Wera, at least nominally. Even though he made Frans tell the judge that Wera should have known marrying him was a bad idea, "seeing as I had no diploma and no career prospects" (it's painful to see how low my father would go at the Old Boss's command), the judge sentenced both men to pay fifty guilders each every month: half for Wera, and the other half, via the Guardianship Board, for me. These are absurdly small amounts, even for that time. What's more harrowing to me now, a half century later, is the fact that my father and grandfather did everything they could to reduce this amount to zero. Only after the judgment was upheld in a June 1950 appeal were the first payments made. But by then, something had already happened that would dramatically change my mother's and my life forever.

TWENTY-FOUR

Life on The Hague's elegant Groot Hertoginnelaan was extremely difficult for my mother and me. We moved into an attic room in a guesthouse run by a widow, Mrs. Roovers, at number 128. Next to the small room was a bathroom that we shared with an office clerk living in the other room. There were two windows in the slanted roof, which looked out to a few bare treetops and the hopelessly gray January sky.

My mother divided the room with a clothesline. The larger half was occupied by her bed, a low table, two chairs, and a closet. She hung sheets over the line to divide the space and gave me a somber look: "I know, my sweet boy—you had a beautiful room at Briva Latvija, with all your toys. And there was a sunroom where I used to read to you, and a garden where we played. So, it's going to be hard for you to live here in this new house. But you're a big boy, almost six years old, and you can keep your chin up, right? Mrs. Roovers is a nice lady—and you'll have to be polite and not say anything rude to her. Don't forget that there are four other people living in this house. I'm going to be working for them. You'll have to be very polite, now, because I can't have any trouble. Do you understand?"

I nodded, but on the inside I was filled with doubt and despair. After years of happiness at my grandparents' house, this new reality felt like a scary monster coming to get me. I missed my dog, Freddy, who had run off yet again, only this time no one had bothered to look for him. Every night I walked alone down the street after everyone else had gone home for dinner, shouting his name at the top of my lungs while crying, hoping that by some miracle, he'd managed to find his way back to me and would be waiting just around the corner, wagging his tail. Besides losing Freddy, I was soon overwhelmed by a growing sense of malaise. At first, I liked having a part of the attic room all to myself—with a little imagination, it was almost like living in a tent—but it became more and more oppressive as my mother's poverty stripped the joy from our lives.

On top of that, Mrs. Roovers's food was terrible. Spoiled by Frau Kochmann's hearty Baltic dishes, I couldn't stomach our landlady's cooking. She cooked in the central kitchen for everyone in the house, and since we didn't have a table of our own, we ate with Mrs. Roovers in the kitchen, which put me in a difficult position: I knew I wasn't helping my mother by criticizing her cooking, but sometimes I was unable to keep a straight face—especially when she made endives, which my mother invariably called chicory. Mrs. Roovers's baked endives were so bitter that I couldn't help but shudder in horror. Unfortunately, it was a cheap vegetable, so the loathsome recipe often appeared on the menu with potatoes and gravy.

Once, when I blatantly expressed disgust at the table, my mother gave me a hard smack on the side of the head. That was the first and only time in my life that she ever did such a thing. I immediately understood that it was an act of despair, one that was meant for Mrs. Roovers, who wasn't interested in making food palatable for a child, and even more so for my father and grandfather, who put us in this situation in the first place.

My mother managed to get me into the Duinoord School, a bastion of Protestant Christianity on Bentinckstraat. The school's director,

Mr. Van Westering, was a kindhearted man willing to admit a Catholic boy to his school, something rarely done in those sectarian postwar years. His only conditions were that I sing along with the daily psalms and prayers that he played on the organ and that I not flaunt my Catholic background. My mother's choice of school was likely an act of resistance against the Roman Catholic terror she'd experienced at Briva Latvija. After all, my grandfather was a fervent Catholic, and after I was baptized he'd insisted that, in addition to Holy Communion, I also receive Holy Confirmation, which meant that I'd had to learn my catechisms. I had participated willingly in this pious journey and accepted the Catholic traditions as a fact of life.

There was something mystical about it all that I was sensitive to at that young age—all that incomprehensible Latin and gold brocade, the lingering smell of incense in the church. I even set up my own altar in my room at Briva Latvija and played Holy Mass with Freddy, at the end of which I'd give the dog a big hug and praise him for sitting through the service so quietly.

Since Catholicism was all I'd known, I felt uncomfortable at the Duinoord School, where, much to my surprise, the other children didn't make the sign of the cross at the end of the morning prayer. Whenever I did, they'd ask, "What's that weird thing you're doing with your hands?" I knew if I kept it up, I'd make things harder for myself, so I had to get inventive. On my way back to class at the end of the morning hymns, I'd scratch my forehead, then check that the button over my sternum was fastened and round off the sacred operation by brushing the dust off my left shoulder, and then my right. I hoped that my grandfather's God wouldn't be too angry with me. My classmates never noticed this secret ritual; in fact, they weren't all that interested in me. Most of them knew each other from the Protestant preschools in the neighborhood and saw each other on Sundays and at Christian scout meetings. These were groups that I wasn't part of and that my mother was completely out of touch with—she was much too busy, poor, and un-Dutch for such things.

Surrounded by the older people shuffling around the guesthouse, most of whom treated the German cleaning lady's son with suspicion, I spent as much time as possible outside on the streets. My mother was fully occupied with household chores, and the situation only got worse when she took on extra work elsewhere. Two afternoons a week, she'd borrow Mrs. Roovers's bicycle and head back to the Bezuidenhout neighborhood, where, thanks to Omi, she worked as a companion for an elderly gentlewoman named Mathilde.

After she started, she told me: "I read Mathilde poems by Schiller and Goethe, she really enjoys that. Sometimes Heine or Uhland as well. And occasionally Keats or Shelley. Bully, you can't imagine how wonderful that is, after all the polishing and vacuuming around here. It reminds me of the old days, when I lived in London, and Granny used to read to me." Although I had no idea who those poets were, I understood that my mother took pleasure in doing something other than mopping floors and washing dishes, and I was happy when Mrs. Roovers adjusted my mother's work schedule. "Child, let's hope that luck is finally on your side. A gentlewoman! You couldn't ask for a job better than that!"

But for me, my mother's new job meant that I had to avoid the guesthouse until the evening. If my mother wasn't home (which was often the case—even on days when she didn't have to go to Mathilde's, she'd often have to run errands), Mrs. Roovers would send me straight upstairs, and I wouldn't be allowed back out. Anything was better than that. I found the small, dark attic room utterly depressing. So I became a boy of the streets, roaming the wilderness left behind in the giant ditches that the Nazis had plowed through the Statenkwartier at the end of the war as part of the Atlantic Wall project. Within a few weeks, I'd constructed fairly formidable headquarters for myself out of rubble;

from there I could keep a sharp eye on what was going on in the neighborhood. I realized soon that I needed to man the terrain, and started thinking about which classmates I would ask to join me.

But in the spring of 1950, my mother had an accident that changed everything. On her way biking to Mathilde's house, she was hit by a car. She broke an ankle, a couple of ribs, and dislocated her right shoulder. Mrs. Roovers picked me up from school and took me to see her at Zuidwal Hospital, where I found her in bed with a severe concussion, her face badly bruised. They kept her there for ten days. "It was my fault," was the first thing she said. "I was daydreaming on the bike."

All at once, our situation deteriorated dramatically. It would take months for her to recover, and in the meantime my mother couldn't work or care for me. Mrs. Roovers agreed to let us stay, but she reduced my mother's monthly salary to thirty guilders a month under the condition that my mother pay her back as soon as she was able to work again. For me, it was the start of a period of lonely freedom. No one was keeping an eye on me anymore at all, and since I didn't have any friends at school yet, I had no idea what to do with all those hours after school. At the end of the school day, all my classmates went home to their warm houses, where their mothers were waiting for them with tea and cookies. But no one ever thought to invite me, and I never dared to ask if I could come over.

Instead, I wandered alone through the antitank ditches, along the shops on Frederik Hendriklaan, until I finally went home around five. Like a little adult, I'd walk down the sidewalks and peer into shop windows; one day I was struck by the realization that there was nothing in those shops that I, or my mother, could buy. Still, I never resorted to shoplifting—not so much as a pear from the greengrocer. I was far too well raised for that. I hated Mrs. Roovers's guesthouse, and I was afraid that my mother would never recover and that I'd be condemned to an impoverished existence forever.

My mother was bedridden for nearly two months, and during that time, she had very few visitors. The fact that no one from Briva Latvija came by was expected, but Titty and Jimmy kept their distance as well. Every once in a while, one of my mother's former suitors would stop by, but that was rare; perhaps the circumstances and the boarders coming in and out scared them off. The only one who dropped by on a regular basis was Guus, who had two children with Titty by then and a third one on the way. In those dismal conditions, it didn't take much for him to win Wera's heart.

One day, a bouquet of roses in a vase appeared on her bedside table. I saw my mother's face light up with a smile; it had been a long time since I'd seen her look that way. "Come here, *Lieber Schatz*," she said and motioned for me to join her under the covers. I took off my shoes and jumped in bed beside her. Her ankle had healed by then and her ribs weren't too painful anymore, but I still had to be careful not to make her laugh too hard, even though I wanted to—anything to forget our daily misery for a moment.

I nuzzled my head between her warm breasts, sensing that she had something important to tell me. *"Najaaa,"* she began in her typical Baltic fashion—I'd grown up with *najaaa* at Briva Latvija and knew that it always heralded an important announcement. "You know, darling, pretty soon you won't be all alone anymore—God willing, of course," she added quickly, but I didn't understand what she met. I just listened, wide-eyed. "Soon you'll have a little brother or sister."

"Where's the baby going to sleep?" was my first question as soon as I understood. My mother looked at me in surprise. "You know what, silly goose, you're right. I'll have to think about that." I noticed that with this small, practical question, her flush of happiness disappeared. Out of love for my mother, I didn't ask any more questions, but in all honesty, I wasn't particularly happy about the thought of having a baby brother or sister. My whole life, it had always been me and my mother. We'd been rescued from Posen, we survived the difficult years at Briva

Latvija, and now, we were scraping by at the guesthouse, but through it all, one thing was certain: we were a team, inseparable. There was no room for a little intruder. From the moment I heard, I was wary of how the new arrival was going to change my life.

Tatiana Maria Wera Nadezhda Lemcke was born on February 4, 1951. Tatiana was a quiet little girl who was kept far away from me. I hardly noticed her growing in my mother's belly for nine months, and Wera didn't say much about it. When the time came for my mother to go to the hospital, I was sent to stay with a friend of hers in Rijswijk. I don't have any specific memories of that period, which can only mean that everyone was tiptoeing around me. The reaction from Briva Latvija, however, was mercilessly harsh. This was exactly the kind of thing my grandfather had been waiting for! If this child, born out of wedlock, wasn't proof that Alexander, the heir to his family name, needed to be rescued from the clutches of this morally depraved woman, what was?

At the Old Boss's insistence my father took the case to court again, this time with a new complaint. Frans wasn't particularly interested in the matter; he was completely absorbed in his life with Mimousse. Still childless, they were known to frequent the nightclubs in The Hague. They'd go out, dance, and drink, in anticipation of the baby and inheritance on the horizon. Mimousse spent every cent she had on those soirees, mostly in an effort to hang on to Frans. He was madly in love with her, and the young couple attracted a lot of attention among The Hague's beau monde without ever really making any connections; my father was much too skittish for that, which was something Mimousse understood.

They were clearly content with just each other, but pressure from the Old Boss left them no choice: on February 19, 1951, two weeks after Tatiana was born, Frans submitted his grievances to the court. According to his complaint, Wera was leading an unregulated life and didn't seem sufficiently concerned with her own day-to-day existence. This was evident in her current misfortune, which was no one's fault but her own. She was also spending time with the wrong sort—Hofdijk, for example (who was already the subject of a judicial investigation). And, most importantly in those prudish times, she was leading an immoral life. Imagine—an illegitimate child, while her own son was wandering the streets! My grandfather, it turned out, had hired detectives to follow me and my mother and came to court armed with a stack of reports, complete with a photo of me in an antitank ditch, looking rather unkempt.

On March 7, the case went before the judge, and Wera was called up for questioning. When she was accused of leading an immoral life, she replied in shock: "Absolutely not. I'm a divorced woman, and if I wish to seek a new partner, that's my right."

"But you had relations with Mr. Van Blaem, who's married to your ex-husband's sister and has two children with her. How do you explain that?" the judge asked.

My mother didn't understand the implications of the question. The Netherlands was a conservative country, but she'd never been bothered about its puritanical ways. She was consumed with one thing: true, honest love. After her disastrous relationship with Frans, this was what she had been looking for in Guus van Blaem, and she told the judge so. "I hoped to marry Guus, but he abandoned me," she said anxiously in the courtroom.

But the judge wasn't finished: "Couldn't you have done away with the child?" he asked unexpectedly. "You come from a country where abortion isn't unusual. Have you ever had an abortion?" It was a cruel question, perhaps one prompted by my grandfather. In 1951, abortion was still officially a crime in the Netherlands, and widely considered a mortal sin among people of faith.

My mother walked straight into the trap: "Yes, I had a few abortions over the past years. Abortion wasn't uncommon in Latvia, and because I was living with my in-laws, I was afraid of the problems an illegitimate child would bring. But now I live on my own, and I wanted to keep this child because I loved Guus and hoped to have a life with him."

This more or less sealed my fate, though it would take three months for the court to announce their decision. On June 20, my father received custody of me, with Mr. Joseph Sopers, related to Mimousse and a highly respected notary, as coguardian.

Wera had fled to her mother in Germany by then. She was horrified when she heard from her lawyer, who'd taken on the case pro bono and slept through most of the hearing, that her confession to having had multiple abortions had been a fatal mistake and that her child would surely be taken from her. In despair, she turned to Guus, who, despite everything, was one of the few people who could help her in this situation. She was the mother of his child, after all. In a gallant display of chivalry, Guus came to her rescue, and together they devised a precisely timed escape plan for April 12.

Guus showed up in Titty's DKW, and I got into the car without protest. Next to me in the back seat, securely bundled in her travel bassinet, was Tatiana, to whom I hardly paid any attention. I was disappointed and angry with my mother, who'd managed, the day before my birthday, to load us all up into a car with Guus and have him drive us off to God knows where. "We won't be coming back here," was all she said. Meanwhile, I was expecting a really good present from my grandparents—a pair of binoculars that I had asked for. I needed them to plan for upcoming battles from my headquarters in the antitank ditch. Then we were going to go eat *poffertjes* on the Malieveld.

No one would answer my questions about any of this. Guus's and Wera's minds were clearly elsewhere, and the mood in the car was tense. Finally, I gave up and fell into a dreamless sleep. When I woke up, we were driving through a dark, shadowy forest at dusk, the Brunssummerheide nature reserve in Limburg, as I later learned. I could just make out the contours of a giant monastery in the distance. All was quiet. A little while later we stopped in front of a roadblock.

My mother groaned and held Tatiana in her arms to calm her nerves. Guus tried to soothe her but was only partially successful. As far as she could tell, there was one immense risk: that the Old Boss would find out they had fled and notify Dutch border control to have us stopped. She knew how relentless he was and was terrified of what he might do. This was why the mission had to be carried out on that day, right before my birthday. No one would think she'd try to leave then, since plans had already been made for my birthday party.

A man in uniform stepped out of the border station. He asked in a funny Limburg accent to see our papers. A few minutes later, he came back and announced that everything was in order. "Where are you going?" he asked.

"To Palenberg," Wera replied. "My mother lives there." It was the first I'd heard of our destination. The word *Palenberg* meant nothing to me, and it did nothing to improve my mood. A few hours later, I turned seven in a city I had never heard of and with a woman I didn't know, who turned out to be my grandmother.

TWENTY-FIVE

Nadia hadn't remarried after the early death of her husband, Harry Lemcke. Passive by nature, she simply let life happen to her. Throughout the entire Heim ins Reich operation, she never left her daughter's side. For the first few months, they stayed in the provincial Prussian town Kolberg, where Nadia's heavy Russian accent aroused great suspicion and even led to a fight with the German woman at the bakery when she walked in and said "*Kheil Khitler.*" That was how she'd learned to say it, but she quickly realized that she shouldn't expect anyone to understand her Slavic accent on continental German soil. When Wera got a job in Posen, she followed her there, but by the time Xeno came to pick us up she declared the journey too dangerous for her. She ended up moving to Palenberg, where two childhood friends of hers lived. The town was conveniently located close to the border with the Netherlands, so that mother and daughter could be easily reunited after the war, hopefully within a few months.

But it had been seven years since they'd seen each other, so she was overjoyed when Wera showed up with me, her grandson, at her little house on Aachenerstrasse that night. Nadia had been informed of her daughter's plans and had set up the only extra room in the house for us. The conditions weren't much better than those on the Groot Hertoginnelaan, but at least we were with family. And the house was located on the edge of a promising-looking forest, as I discovered the next morning, when I woke up from another deep, comatose sleep. When I walked into the living room, I found my mother and grandmother at the table deep in conversation. Guus, who had spent the night on the couch, was already gone.

When the two women saw me, they jumped up and showered me with kisses. "Happy birthday!" Nadia cried over and over again with tears in her eyes. She beelined for the wardrobe and took a package wrapped in gray paper from a drawer. As I opened it, I could already see what my mother had gotten me from the corner of my eye: on the table was a pair of *Lederhosen* and a Hamburg-style mariner's cap, the ones everyone was wearing those days as the entire country desperately searched for a new German style. I bashfully unwrapped the present from my Russian grandmother and let out a squeal of delight: a model of an American tank! And it even drove—all you had to do was wind up the little key and let it go, and it would burst into an infernal racket and rumble around the room. Its caterpillar treads could even drive over small obstacles like a bump in the rug or a thin book. When it finally came to a halt against the leg of the sideboard, I picked it up and carefully placed it back in its cardboard box, printed with the magical toy's brand name: Schuco.

I gazed gratefully at my grandmother. "Are there any other kids around here?" I asked in German.

"You'll find out soon enough," my mother exclaimed. "Come on, put on your new cap and Lederhosen. Let us see what a German chap you are."

My first day in Palenberg was off to a festive start. There were homemade cakes, and I got as much lemonade as I wanted. That afternoon, Nadia's friends from Riga came to meet me. Olga gave me a pair of checkered handkerchiefs. "They belonged to my son, Egon," she said with tears in her eyes. "He died at Königsberg." I nodded and made a promise to myself never to use them.

The other woman, Nastia, gave me a wallet with one pfennig inside. "It's the start of a million, you know," she said at the sight of my disappointed face. This hadn't belonged to a fallen German soldier, so I put it straight into my pocket. Once the women had gotten a good look at me, they announced conspiratorially that they had important matters to discuss with Wera and Nadia that I wouldn't understand, and sent me outside to play with my new tank.

The lot next to Nadia's house was, in my eyes, ideal terrain for a massive battlefield for the tin soldiers and military action figures I'd brought with me from The Hague. Along the two-lane cement road that occasionally saw a car or delivery truck, the ground was soggy and—as I immediately checked—impassable for my super olive-green American tank with a white star on each side. I named him Charlie.

Just a few yards farther, the ground was dry, and there was a slight incline with a few bushes where I could position my secret backup troops. From there, they could launch a surprise attack in case my main guard—thirty Napoleonic soldiers in all different poses (a gift from Uncle Xeno)—ran into trouble. And if they needed to be liberated, there was a thicket nearby where I could place my collection of thirty Sioux (a gift from Uncle Jimmy). The faithful fighters, led by the famous Tecumseh, would know how to manage in the wooded terrain and defeat the evil enemy, I thought. I held on to Charlie as a secret weapon for the time being and went inside to fetch my tin brigade.

When I got back to the edge of the woods, there was a boy there waiting for me. He was a little bit bigger than I was and seemed older. He was wearing a mariner's cap like the one still perched on the top of my head.

"What are you doing?" he asked, as I emptied the contents of the bag on the ground and began preparing for battle. At first, I was overwhelmed by the prospect of having to speak German from now on and didn't answer.

"Just playing," I finally said.

Yes, the boy could see that I was playing, and wanted to join. Apparently, he had some soldiers of his own. He lived two houses away, on the other side of the street, and had seen me from his window. Since there were no other boys his age in the neighborhood to play with, he came out to meet me. "I'm Hans," he said with an outstretched hand. "Let's be friends. I'll be right back." After giving my hand a quick shake, he hurried home to get his toys.

He didn't leave me much time to think. We were preparing for battle, and this was the first time I'd had a real opponent. I'd never found any classmates to join me in The Hague, and I hadn't had a chance to tell anyone about my big plans in the antitank ditch yet. But there, in that strange town of Palenberg, all that was about to change.

I figured I would have to lay down some rules with my future opponent, who was also going to be my friend. But what kind of rules? In my lonely, solitary world, I'd been content to make all the decisions myself: sometimes the Sioux would win, sometimes the French, depending on my mood. But clearly that's not how this game would be played. Just to be sure, I took Charlie out of his box, wound him up with the key, put on his brakes, and hid him away behind a woodpile. Then I dispersed Tecumseh and his Sioux in the bushes and quickly dug a few parapets for my French grenadiers to hide behind.

That's when my new playmate returned, carrying two boxes under his arms. He solemnly laid them on the ground. "Check this out," he said. Inside, sixty beautiful tin soldiers were neatly displayed on a bed of blue velvet. They were extremely well maintained, painted, and polished down to the very last detail. On their helmets was the symbol of the SS, and one of them held a banner in a fiery, battle-ready position. "Waffen-SS, Viking Division," the boy said proudly, "complete and invincible."

Viking! That was the division my father had fought in! I couldn't suppress a cry of surprise but decided not to mention it for the time being. Then I showed off my men, but Hans wasn't impressed. "French! They can't fight at all," he said. "We conquered Paris in no time." I didn't know what to say and began to feel uncomfortable. The feeling only got worse when I showed him my secret Sioux. "Those are your backup troops?" he exclaimed in disbelief. "Ha! All right, let's play!"

We agreed we could each move ten men at a time, and after each turn, we would decide the new direction of fire. Once we agreed which soldiers had been shot, we would decide together which ones to carry off the battlefield. The goal was to capture the enemy's flag, in my case a dismal little soldier lugging a half-torched Napoleonic banner.

However, it became clear that Hans would be the one calling the shots on the battlefield. Despite my grenadiers being placed behind indisputably sound parapets, my new friend removed twelve of my men from the battlefield on his first turn. "*Panzerfaust* and flamethrowers," he explained, showing me the heavy armament that his SS men were carrying. "*Achtung*, Alexander. This group will plow right through and capture your flag in one go."

It took a lot of work to convince Hans that there were a few sharp-shooters among my grenadiers, who'd shot his soldiers carrying those powerful weapons, as well as a few of his foot soldiers. Hans eventually agreed to give up seven men. A little while later, however, two new black-helmeted troops appeared right in the middle of my front line carrying the same weapons, ready to sow death and destruction. Apparently, Hans had two of each! On top of that, he had a machine gun nest strategically lodged in a foxhole, which, he explained, had struck down at least twenty of my men with "devastating accuracy."

I agreed to give up sixteen men and sent the remaining two to carry out a desperate, but successful, attack on the machine gun. Then I ordered Tecumseh and twenty of his men to come to the rescue, kill-ing another eight of Hans's SS soldiers. My ten remaining Sioux were hiding around the edge of the enemy encampment, where the Viking Division's flag was located. There was no question that the enemy's forces were strong, but still I managed to take out ten of his men, arguing that the Sioux had a special talent for sneaking up from behind with a knife.

At that Hans burst into a fit of uncontrollable laughter. "Those guys? I'll need four men to guard my flag at most!" he jeered. "You bet-ter watch out, I'm about to advance." And with that, he ordered a major force of thirty men to charge at my puny Napoleonic soldier with his broken flag. We'd forgotten all about our agreement to only move ten soldiers at a time, and you could tell by our red-hot faces that we were completely absorbed in our fantasy world.

With mounting fury, I watched the battle unfold. Not only was Hans cheating by using more soldiers than he had left based on our mutually agreed number of victims, but I was also annoyed that he was being so rude about my toys—and on my birthday! So, when he finally arranged his SS troops around my flag with mathematical precision and demanded my surrender, I knew what I needed to do.

Less than three feet away, Charlie was standing by. He was already pointed in the right direction, and as soon as I took the brakes off, he advanced with deadly accuracy, his terrifying nose pointed right into Hans's Nazi forces. It was a sight to behold. As Hans's soldiers fell in all directions, Charlie continued his grim, triumphal march down the slope and, by coincidence, flattened the lower camp where the Viking flag was being held. My poor Napoleonic soldier was left unharmed, standing there with his flag still in hand, as if nothing had happened.

"I won!" I gasped, bewildered.

"No way!" Hans roared.

The friendly, self-assured superiority he'd had up to then was quickly replaced by horror, and then hate, and then sorrow. His blue eyes filled with big, wet tears. Suddenly, he let out a wild cry and threw himself at me. "I'm going to kill you! You think you can insult me like this? My father fought with them. He was wounded, you hear? Wounded!" He clawed at my eyes and slashed at my cheeks with his hard, sharp nails, holding me in a kind of choke hold. I realized that he was much stronger than me and began screaming for help. Within seconds, the four women ran out of Nadia's house and dragged us apart.

I was too shocked by Hans's sudden transformation and the things he'd said about his father to say anything meaningful. Much to my surprise, my mother put her arm around Hans, who was lost in a fit of rage.

All of a sudden, his shoulders sank, and he started to sob. She stroked his hair and whispered something in his ear. One of my grandmother's friends had the good sense to pick up Charlie, who'd gotten stuck in the mud by the curb and take him inside. After a few minutes, Hans seemed to calm down. His eyes red and puffy, he stammered something in a jerky voice with such a thick Aachen accent that I couldn't understand him. "All right, dear boy," my grandmother said, fawning over him. "Let's go inside and have some tea. It's Bully's birthday today."

I hadn't had the chance to tell Nadia that I hated the nickname Bully and wanted to be called by my real name. And I hadn't said anything to Hans about it being my birthday. But he hardly seemed to notice that my grandmother had revealed two of my secrets in one fell swoop. With the women's help, we collected our scattered soldiers in silence and went back to my grandmother's house. The tea was already waiting for us along with a supply of cake.

My mother, who'd been consoling Hans, noticed I was bleeding from a scratch on my cheek once we sat down. With a sense of care that seemed exaggerated, she began to clean and dab the wound. Hans looked at me guiltily. "Sorry," he said softly. "I didn't mean to, Alexander. Let's still be friends."

I was flooded by a wave of compassion and forgiveness, while a little voice in my brain told me it had been a dirty trick to launch my deadly tank on Hans when he had no way of defending himself. "Of course," I said, laying a hand on his shoulder as if dubbing him a knight.

"See?" the women exclaimed in excitement. Even my mother nodded in agreement, although I had grumpily brushed her hand away. "Now Bully has a dueling scar!" Nadia exclaimed. The ladies all laughed, but Hans and I didn't understand. We agreed that I would go to his house the next day, and he could show me his room. Since I'd never had a friend before, the thought of it kept me awake that night. And I couldn't stop thinking about the fact that our fathers had been comrades in the war.

TWENTY-SIX

The next morning Nadia stopped me as I was walking out the door to go to Hans's house after breakfast. "Don't be scared when you see Hans's father now. He's a nice man, but he looks terrible," she said, shaking her head. "Just awful. Maybe he would've been better off dead." And with that, she let me go and went into the kitchen to boil diapers for Tatiana, who was sleeping in the bassinet. I was gripped with fear. What was wrong with Hans's father? I couldn't ask my mother because she'd gone for a job interview at the American airbase in Aachen.

Now that my birthday had passed, I was no longer the center of attention; Wera had spent the morning nervously getting ready and barely acknowledged my questions. What are we doing in Palenberg? Are we going to stay here forever? Where am I going to go to school? "Darling, you go play with Hans and his friends. I've got to get this job with the Americans first, you understand? Otherwise, we won't be able to stay here. Haven't you noticed how poor your mother is? She certainly can't afford two extra mouths to feed, now can she?" she said as she put the finishing touches on her eyebrows with a black brush. "Now, wish me luck!" she exclaimed in her best American English. With a provocative little smile on her dark red lips, she gave me a pat on the head and set off for the bus stop. I thought she looked beautifully American, like Ava Gardner, and her convincing English accent certainly helped.

When I got to Hans's house, he opened the door before I could even ring the doorbell. "Come in," he said, ushering me inside. "I saw you coming. Let's go upstairs to my room."

All of a sudden, a woman around Nadia's age appeared. "Now, Hans, that's not the way we do things," she said, as if to clarify who the boss was in this house. "You need to introduce us to your new friend first." She reached out to shake my hand. "You must be Alexander, or should I call you Bully? Hans told me it was your birthday yesterday and that you two played together," she said, shepherding me into the next room.

I walked in and looked around. The house was four times the size of Nadia's. There was a heavy oak dining table in the front room with six old-fashioned chairs with twisted legs. In the corner by the window overlooking the street was a cozy sitting nook with three armchairs and a round coffee table. And to the back was a sunroom bathed in the tender light of spring. In the center of the room were two large leather couches and a glass coffee table, but the majority of the room was hidden from view by a Japanese folding screen. Along the walls were four massive bookcases, flanked by dark paintings of hunting scenes and still lifes. On the sideboard in the front room, I noticed two military portraits, one of which had a black ribbon in the corner. Hans's mother saw me looking at it and sighed. "Yes, dear, that was Hans's older brother, Peter. He died at Stalingrad, more than eight years ago. He would have been twenty-six now." She reached for her handkerchief to dry the tears that had suddenly welled up in her eyes.

The room filled with an uncomfortable silence. "How old are you, Hans?" I asked, with a strange emphasis on the familiar *you*, which immediately felt wrong.

"Hans is eleven. He was a late arrival," his mother replied quickly. "Have a seat over here, and I'll get you two some hot chocolate. You like hot chocolate, right?" And with that, she headed off to the kitchen. Hans noticed my confusion, so he explained in a calm, almost nurturing tone, "You're from Holland, aren't you? Well, it all worked out differently there than it did here. Of all my classmates, there isn't one who didn't lose a family member in the war. I didn't even know Peter. I remember his uniform more than his face. He was in the same SS division as my father."

He looked past me as if waiting for help to arrive from the backyard, and then whispered: "You have no idea how hard everything is for me. My father was a notary, one of the most important people in Palenberg. He was the fiduciary for hundreds of people in the city. Peter's funeral was huge. Every important person in Aachen came, and there was even a personal message from Himmler. Then two months later, my father was wounded."

Hans laughed dryly. "Wounded. The whole right side of his face was blown off, and his right leg and arm were so full of shrapnel they had to be amputated. He survived though, and now we live with a monster, Alexander. Thank God my mother still has a job at the high school."

I wanted to tell him about my own father and ask a million questions, but his mother came back with two steaming mugs of hot chocolate and set them down in front of us with a look of contrived happiness. "I'm so happy that Hans has finally found a friend," she said in a tone that was half-joking. "He really needed one."

The hot chocolate was extra sweet and had a chemical taste. We drank it in silence, and I decided not to mention my father for the time being. For starters, he wasn't there, so anything I would say about the Caucasus and the Iron Cross—that was pretty much all I knew about my father's war experiences at that point—would sound like I was bragging.

At least my father had made it home alive, and although he'd been wounded, he was still essentially in one piece, save for a few pieces of shrapnel and a couple of fist-sized scars on his upper leg and shoulder. That might make Hans and his mother jealous. I began to feel uncomfortable: Hans's mother had said that I needed to be introduced to "us," which meant that her husband, the monster Hans had told me about, was somewhere around here—maybe behind that screen. I shuddered at the thought and tried to imagine what a blown-off face might look like.

"Well, let's go," Hans said as soon as we'd finished the hot chocolate. "I'll show you my room, and then we can go outside."

"No funny business," his mother said as we ran upstairs. "Alexander is only seven."

"Old enough," Hans replied, to my delight.

Hans's room was perfectly positioned to keep watch over Nadia's house; both windows provided a direct view of our new home. I watched Nadia walk into the yard with a bucket full of Tatiana's diapers and hang them up one by one on the clothesline to dry. A little while later, she went back into the living room. Hans's room had a bed, a worktable with two chairs, and a small dormer window that jutted out about five feet toward the street. In the window was a tripod with a device at least six feet long mounted on top.

"It's a telescope," Hans said proudly. "It belongs to my father, but he can't use it anymore. It's a Zeiss." He pointed to the brand name modestly printed on the side. "Top quality before the war, from Jena— they really know how to cut a lens there." He adjusted a few of the knobs and rings and pointed it at a church tower off in the distance. "It's not really meant for looking at things on Earth," he continued. "Next time you'll have to come over on a clear night. Then you'll really be in for a treat! It's like all the stars in the sky are in this very room. Just look how close that church tower is in here."

Obediently I did as he said. The church tower had a clock that I could just barely make out with the naked eye, let alone read the time. But through the telescope, I could see that it was almost eleven. "Amazing," I murmured, mostly just to say something nice.

Hans beamed. "I've read a lot about the stars," he said, pointing to a few shelves laden with heavy books. "These are my father's too. He was a really good amateur astronomer." He sighed deeply. "But he's not interested anymore. I offered to read to him and even calibrate the telescope so he could take a look, but he doesn't want anything anymore. *I wish I could go to the stars,* he says sometimes. OK, Alexander, let's go outside."

On the way downstairs, Hans suddenly motioned for me to be quiet. There was a strange noise coming from the ground floor, occasionally interrupted by a soft squeak. "That's my father's wheelchair," Hans whispered suddenly, in a forbidden tone. "If you're really my friend, go downstairs and meet him. And if you're too chicken, I don't ever want to see you again."

All the blood drained from my face, but I also felt a sense of soldierly solidarity; my own father had escaped the war by the skin of his teeth, so who was I to refuse to meet a comrade who had seen the worst of it?

"OK," I replied with a shrug. "I can handle it."

"We'll see," Hans smiled bitterly and called downstairs. "Dad! My new friend, Alexander, is coming down to meet you!"

Through the railing, I saw a wheelchair make a few difficult turning movements and eventually come to a standstill a yard or two in front of the bottom of the stairs. I heard something that sounded like a groaning pant. There was no turning back, so down I went.

The true face of the war, revealed to me in that shadowy corridor at the bottom of the stairs in Hans's house, is maddening. My brain was initially overwhelmed by fear and disgust. How can you take pity on something you can't even identify? It breathed and moved, but it wasn't of this world.

Petrified, I just stood there taking in the destruction a Russian Katyusha salvo could wreak on a body. The right leg was gone at the hip, and the right arm stopped at the elbow. The right eye was completely gone, and the cheekbone underneath too, along with the right ear and cheek. All that was left was a kind of dark brown cavity of tissue with a miraculously undamaged set of teeth. The nose was still intact, and so were the lips, but it seemed they could no longer close. A steady stream of drool dripped from the mouth. He was held into the wheelchair by a few leather straps and could apparently maneuver using a complicated turning mechanism. A single blue eye stared back at me intently. There, pinned to his chest was the Iron Cross with all its deathly shine.

Hans came down the stairs behind me.

"Alexander moved in next door yesterday, with Frau Nadia," he said loudly. "He's from Holland."

A hint of kindness flickered behind the eye, and the man made a few gurgling noises. "He says, 'Welcome,'" Hans translated. "Come on, shake his hand and then we can go."

I obediently extended my right hand and instantly recoiled when the gesture wasn't reciprocated. I turned beet red, and in my confusion, I ended up sticking out both hands. Hans's father made such a ghastly sound that my first instinct was to run away, but Hans explained that this was how his father laughed. As he said this, I felt the man's left hand grip my right wrist like a vise. "Alexander." It sounded hollow, like it had been drawn up from a medieval abyss. The blue left eye held me in its inquisitive gaze. Only after what felt like an eternity did he loosen his grip, and Hans and I were able to go.

Outside was a crisp spring sun. Overcome with indefinable emotions, I followed Hans silently. I was struck by the realization that my father could've come out of the war looking like Hans's, but my dad had been lucky, and so was I. But could I ever really be friends with Hans and his classmates? Didn't he say all his classmates had lost someone in the war? Hans seemed to read my mind.

"You did well with my father," he said, and blurted out the question I'd been waiting for: "What about your dad? What happened to him in the war? Frau Nadia told me he was sent to the eastern front too."

"I don't really know," I lied. "I haven't seen him in a long time. My parents are divorced." I didn't know the German word for *divorced*, so for the sake of clarity I added, "Split up—y'know?"

He understood—it turned out that the German and Dutch words for *divorced* are almost the same. He mulled over my words for a moment.

"So, your father survived the war?" he finally said. "And what does he look like now, if you don't mind me asking?"

"He wasn't as badly wounded as your father," I replied, mustering all my courage, "but he was awarded the Iron Cross too, and he has a hole in his leg and shoulder. That's all I know."

Hans nodded sadly. The topic never came up again.

I was only in Palenberg for about three months, but in my memory, it felt like an entire year on a strange planet. Through Hans, I got to know a group of boys who had slingshot competitions; I don't remember any of their names, but I can still see their faces. There were no rival groups for us to fight with in Palenberg, but there was an empty bunker at the edge of the woods that we used as a base until the local police chased us out of it. Then we wandered around in search of new targets. Once one of us hit the window of an old dilapidated newspaper stand, and it turned out someone was inside. A fat woman charged out yelling and chased us down the street. I remember one morning I randomly shot my slingshot across Aachenerstrasse and hit the window of a Volkswagen van passing by. The driver chased me all the way to the village bar, where I escaped into a maze of stacked chairs and disappeared into a back alley like a rat.

The most significant event, I missed entirely. My grandfather showed up at Nadia's house unannounced to inform my mother that she'd lost the court case and that I would have to go back to the Netherlands to live with my father. His visit sent the house into a panic.

It was Sunday, and I'd gone out with Hans and some other boys to watch a local soccer match in Palenberg's shabby little stadium, which was basically a covered embankment next to a cow pasture that had been leveled and mowed for the purpose. We'd go there on Sundays to sell trinkets for a local peddler, who'd pay us a small commission on our sales. That day we were selling these plastic coin holders with special holes for German marks and one-, two-, ten-, and fifty-pfennig coins; you pushed the coins down on a little spring and could easily get them out with a flick of the thumb. This little device was touted as a great German postwar invention, and they were selling like hotcakes.

Soccer was incredibly popular, I think because it exuded the vitality that the Germans so desperately craved. Three years later, despite all the postwar oppression, Germany would win the world championships, bringing hope for a new European future. To all the haunted and despondent-looking men in the stands—many who'd been wounded in the war and ended up with makeshift prostheses—that soccer field in sad, gray Palenberg offered a sense of hope.

When I returned home at dusk, half a mark richer, I found my mother and Nadia sitting at the table looking noticeably distressed. They were sitting across from each other with their elbows on the table and their heads between their hands as if they were deeply engrossed in a game of chess. A lot had happened that afternoon that they didn't tell me about. The only thing my mother said was, "Your grandfather was here, and he was cruel to me."

Much later I learned that the Old Boss had presented her with a harsh reality: the court ruled that the boy must return to the Netherlands and live with his father. "I won't have my grandson running wild in this hick town," he said.

Wera stuttered helplessly, and Nadia, true to form, retreated into a corner with Tatiana. After less than half an hour, the angry man went back to Holland, chauffeured by Xeno in his silver-blue Chrysler. "Xeno was here too, but he didn't come inside," was the last bit of information I got from my mother before she burst into tears and wrapped me in a suffocating embrace until I finally managed to wriggle free from her frantic grip.

The following days were tense. All my mother's joy about getting the job as an interpreter at the American airbase was replaced by worry about how she might be able to keep her son, against the Dutch court ruling. It didn't help that she had to work from seven in the morning until eight in the evening and couldn't keep an eye on me. She didn't trust her mother, who already had her hands full with Tatiana and definitely wouldn't put up much of a fight if some official showed up to investigate a claim about a Dutch minor who'd been brought to Germany illegally. These fears took a toll on Wera's daily functioning; with all her nerves, she'd lie awake for hours at night and could barely eat. She began to look haggard and lost much of the infectious spontaneity that had earned her a place with the Americans. She had half a dozen suitors wrapped around her finger, and now they were forced to surrender to her maternal instinct. Wera wasn't going to stick around for drinks with the Americans in the mess hall after work; she took the first bus back to Palenberg every day, and when she got home and saw that I was still there and no official letters had come, she'd heave a sigh of relief and make the sign of the cross.

As time wore on, however, she relaxed a bit. Perhaps the Old Boss had been bluffing, and there was nothing to worry about, after all. There were so many postwar legal troubles, and the German and Dutch governments had never been much for cooperation. It could take years before a case like this was settled. If it was even still an issue by then.

In the meantime, Wera was planning to have me naturalized as a German citizen. She'd already consulted an acquaintance in Würzburg and made plans to go there with me to discuss the options in more detail. Once I was a German citizen, they couldn't force me out of Germany, she thought.

TWENTY-SEVEN

It must've been just after lunch, around two o'clock or so, that Dirk Sopers and Louise Marggraff parked their Volkswagen in the woods near Palenberg one Saturday in July. They took one last look at a recent photo of me and set off. Dirk was a thirtysomething industrialist from Brabant known for being a little rough around the edges. His brother was Joseph Sopers, the upstanding notary who'd been appointed by the Dutch court as my coguardian. Dirk's wife, Louise, descendent of one of the wealthiest families in the Netherlands, was a distant cousin of Mimousse. In her handbag was a wad of cotton and a vial of chloroform.

Hans would later confirm that he'd seen a red Beetle through his telescope (which we'd named "the all-seeing eye") that morning during his daily observations. The car came out of the forest, down Aachenerstrasse, and stopped after a few hundred yards. The car turned around in farmer Huber's driveway and disappeared back into the woods toward the Dutch border. Hans didn't think anything of it, and when we were playing in the street that afternoon, he didn't even mention it. He hadn't gotten a good look at the license plate; if he had, he would've noticed that it was Dutch, but even that wouldn't have set off any alarm bells because my mother hadn't told anyone about the Old Boss's threats. She considered the whole thing a private matter, so there was no reason for any of the neighbors to be on the lookout.

Wera was at the American base that day, where, among all her suitors, she'd chosen a young air force captain from Denver, Colorado. They had made plans to have lunch, and she'd spent the entire morning getting dressed for the occasion. For years, the last image I had of my mother was of a smiling beauty who had rediscovered her old flair.

After I finished lunch—the usual cup of soup, a grayish bit of processed bread with margarine, a sausage, and a glass of watery milk—I went out. Hans and a few of the other boys were waiting for me. The group was in low spirits; we had a long summer ahead of us, and didn't know what to do with ourselves. No one was going on vacation, so we were stuck there with each other. This led to yet another long debate about exactly what we were going to do with our time. Meanwhile, we threw pebbles at an empty paint can.

Under those circumstances, the sudden arrival of a strange man and woman on the street was exciting. They walked right up to me and asked, "Are you Bully?"

"Yes, I'm Bully," I replied, without batting an eye.

Looking back, I am still amazed by the innocence of my answer and my naivety in everything that followed. Given the Old Boss's visit and my mother's anxiety about me having to go back to the Netherlands, there should've been alarm bells going off in my head. But instead of running inside to Nadia, I was swept away by this strange couple. They told me they were from the Netherlands and that they wanted to take me out for ice cream.

"Countrymates!" I remember hollering at Hans and the others, who were watching from a distance. It was a strange word (*countrymen* was the word I was looking for), but they must've understood me, or at least pretended to, because they answered with a vague nod and returned to their deliberations. The plan of ice cream didn't work out: all the shops in Germany were closed on Saturday afternoons, and the fat woman who worked at the kiosk announced with malicious glee that she was sold out.

"Is there something else, something really nice that you'd like? That we could get for you next time?" the man asked. He'd taken off his blazer and hung it over his arm. It was hot; his bald head shone pink in the afternoon sun, and he was constantly dabbing the sweat from his neck with his handkerchief. We stood there indecisively; the small, dingy shops of the quiet suburb, with their cloudy windows still covered in the gray dust of the war, offered little inspiration. All of a sudden, I remembered a shop a few streets away whose window I'd gazed into for quite a long time just a few days ago. There was a model of the *Santa Maria*, and I was going to save my money to buy it. I asked my mother if she could give me an advance on my allowance because I was afraid someone else would get it before I did. It was a beautiful object, carefully sculpted down to the last detail. There were cannons menacingly peering out of portholes and golden-brown parchment sails emblazoned with dark red crosses billowing out as if the ship were sailing full force in the wind. Surrounded by all the other chintzy, pitiful toys in town (Nadia had had to go to Aachen to get Charlie), this *Santa Maria* was like something out of a dream.

I told all this to the man and woman, who smiled and listened intently. They seemed more than happy to follow me to the store window. The ship was still there! "We'll buy it for you," the man said, and he wrote down the name of the shop and the address. He wrote something else on another piece of paper and dropped it into the mailbox of the closed shop. "I wrote that we are going to come back to buy the ship and that they should hold it for us," he said. My heart burst with happiness; they were really going to do it!

"Oh, wait, I just remembered . . . ," the woman said as if she'd made a great discovery. "We still have a few bars of chocolate in the car. You like chocolate, don't you, Bully? The car isn't far from here. Come with me and we'll get them." She had applied more lipstick, which left smears of red on her long teeth. With her high, teased reddish-brown hair and long pointy nose, she looked a bit like a witch, which worried me a little, but then again, she had chocolate . . .

Dirk Sopers and Louise Marggraff must have done some reconnaissance in Palenberg that morning before they carried out the mission. This explains why we left Palenberg from the north side of town to reach the woods, and not from the south side as they'd come in, which would have taken them via Aachenerstrasse, past Nadia's house, where they would have been spotted. They'd told me where their car was parked, and I knew the place. It wasn't that far—a little over half a mile, the last four hundred yards through the woods. I followed the couple like an obedient little lamb.

The last thing I remember was the woman standing beside me, opening her handbag to get the keys to the red Volkswagen Beetle parked in front of us in a green, grassy field. The man, standing behind me, took her bag so she could open the car door—how else was she going to get the chocolate? The door opened, and the last thought that went through my mind was that I'd never seen such bright green grass or such a shiny red car.

TWENTY-EIGHT

I woke up in a bed in a whitewashed room with arched Romanesque windows, like a monastery cell. A ray of low, quivering sunlight beamed through the leaded glass windows, making a twinkling pattern of colorful spots on the dark wooden floor that held my attention for quite some time—time I needed to come to my senses. I had a feeling that something strange had happened to me, that I had been taken somewhere against my will.

My first conclusion was that I wasn't in any danger. I wasn't in a dungeon but lying in a clean bed in a sun-filled room. I thought about my mother: How long had I been gone? Did she know? I imagined how worried she would be and remembered how desperate she'd been the last time the Old Boss had visited. Suddenly it dawned on me what was happening. What time was it? I didn't have a watch, so I started to get out of bed to investigate.

There was a noise that indicated I wasn't alone in the room. On a stool in the corner was a large Surinamese woman in a white jacket. She smiled at me as she slowly stood up. "Stay there, I'll get your clothes," she said and opened the door to a long, tiled hallway. Since I was lying there in my underwear, I did as she said.

A few minutes later she came back with an outfit that I'd never seen before, but that I liked the look of: a pair of sharply creased white linen shorts with a leather belt and a soft light blue shirt, as if made of pure silk, thin beautifully made socks, and a pair of shiny, brown walking shoes with laces. Those shoes were a wonder to me, because the shoes I'd been used to were made from cheap, cardboard-like material left over from the war. It all fit perfectly. For the first time since I'd lived at Briva Latvija, I felt fashionable, which wasn't an entirely unpleasant feeling. The Surinamese woman smiled and took me over to the washing stand in the other corner of the room, where she combed my hair and ran a washcloth across my face. Only then did I realize that my arms, legs, hands, and feet, which were undoubtedly filthy after playing outside in Palenberg, had already been cleaned. Apparently, someone had bathed me before they put me in bed.

Palenberg—it was as if the town had already disappeared beyond the horizon. I studied my new clothes and examined the shoes that would undoubtedly lead me down another path in life, into a future that seemed more attractive to me than the poverty-stricken world I'd left behind on Aachenerstrasse. But what about my mother? And who were those people who had brought me here?

The Surinamese woman interrupted my musings. "Let's go then. Everybody is waiting for you," she said. I followed her slowly down the hallways lined with wainscoting and oak doors. Finally, we arrived at a large sunroom with doors that opened onto a tiled veranda. Beyond that was a large grass field, and off in the distance, I saw a group of men and women sitting at a long, festive table under a stand of beeches. There were coolers holding bottles of champagne, and I could hear crystal glasses clinking in the afternoon sun. The mood was expectant, cheerful. The women wore stylish summer dresses, and most of the men had taken off their jackets in the heat. Everyone was smoking, drinking, and chatting—it was like a scene from a Sicilian mafia movie.

At the head of the table, with his shirtsleeves held up by silver sleeve garters around his upper arms, was my grandfather, the Old Boss. He was the first person I recognized, and just as I did, he looked up and beamed. "There he is, at last," he cried triumphantly in his gruff voice. "Let's all raise a glass to the heir!" The Surinamese woman gently nudged me forward, out onto the terrace. Within seconds, I found myself standing before the table in my new outfit, my hair combed, my face washed. Everyone stood up, glass of champagne in hand, and gazed at me, completely caught up in the festivity of the moment.

The Old Boss and Omi, Xeno and Trees, Wim and Marie, Tom and his wife, Lyda—they all hugged and kissed me, as my grandfather made a predictable allusion to the parable of the prodigal son. Dr. Van Tilburg gave me a friendly pat on the shoulder and said I looked pretty good after everything I'd been through. I noticed right away that Jimmy, Titty, and Guus weren't there and knew instinctively that their absence was out of solidarity with my mother.

There were a few people I didn't know, such as the man who grabbed hold of my hand with a laugh. "Welcome to my castle!" he roared. "Welcome to Zionsburg!" His name was Ewald Marggraff, the brother of the woman who had kidnapped me. She was there, too, and approached me with a smile. "Louise, Aunt Louise to you now." A man with a droopy face and thick horn-rimmed glasses perched on his large nose introduced himself to me as well. "I'm Joseph Sopers, Uncle Joseph, your coguardian. I can imagine that this is all quite overwhelming for you. Try to keep your chin up, my boy. If you need anything, just let me know. I'm here to help you. This is my brother, Uncle Dirk." He turned and pointed to the man who had promised to buy me the *Santa Maria* in Palenberg. Dirk waved at me, a thoughtless gesture, which to me felt more like a five-fingered salute, as if he was proud of the fact that he'd been able to lure me away so easily.

I felt a growing revulsion for the exuberant crowd and went to the only two people who hadn't greeted me yet: my father and Mimousse. My father laughed sheepishly, muttered something that was supposed to be an expression of joy, and gave me a hug. When he noticed that I didn't return his embrace, he stepped back, took a sip of champagne, and lit a cigarette. Mimousse, on the other hand, seemed overcome with deep emotion. She looked at me, her warm, dark eyes full of love, and took a deep breath. "I am so happy to have you with us now, Bully," she said. "The three of us are going to be a happy family. I'll do my absolute best." She looked around at all the family and friends who were listening, each one with a freshly filled glass in hand, and went on. "With all these people as my witness, Bully, I promise to care for you as a mother."

Everyone fell silent for a moment, and before Mimousse could finish, I blurted out: "You're not my mother, and you never will be." I looked her straight in the eye, and, shaken, turned around and walked back toward the sunroom.

My departure gave way to murmurs of confusion. Through my tears, I could just make out the white jacket of the heavy Surinamese woman. She was waiting for me with a kind smile. I let her take me back to my room. All of a sudden, I felt exhausted. I took off my beautiful new shoes and fell into a deep, dreamless sleep.

TWENTY-NINE

Children are opportunists, and I was no exception. My attitude toward Mimousse lasted a few weeks at most, and that's including the rare moments of melancholic confusion and urges to push her away that came later on. But after a month, my new reality had sunk in, and I eventually started adapting to the situation. I understood that from then on, there would be two women in my life with a claim on my heart and soul: Wera, my real mother, and Mimousse, who'd assumed the role of mother and, as far as I could tell, had no intention of giving it up. Never in a million years would I have thought of renouncing my real mother, but it was made very easy for me to at least give my new mother a chance.

I hadn't heard from Wera, and meanwhile Mimousse was patiently caring for my every need. On the way back to The Hague the day after the kidnapping, she'd sat facing me and never took her sparkling brown eyes off me. In her soft Flemish accent, she relayed the circumstances that had led to my return. The judge had decided that I belonged with her and my father—they had gotten married—but Wera didn't want me to live with them, and *she* had kidnapped me by taking me to Germany. She explained that the Old Boss had decided to just bring me back where I belonged. Otherwise, they'd have to waste a lot of time on court cases, even though the ruling had already been made. Time was of the essence to the Old Boss, because he was sick and wanted to make sure that everything was settled before he died.

She told me it was she who'd enlisted Dirk and Louise to pick me up. Why Dirk and Louise? He was bold; she was calm under pressure. Moreover, they didn't have children, so Mimousse thought they'd be less sentimental about it—but Mimousse didn't mention that. There was also the fact that the Marggraff family estate was in Vught, less than an hour and a half from the border, and Louise's brother, the eccentric Ewald Marggraff, had no objections to the plan.

I listened to what she was saying, with a lump in my throat. I stared out the window and gave no reaction. It was still all so new that I must've been in shock. My father was driving silently. He just smoked his beloved Lucky Strikes with his black cigarette holder. He might as well have been a robot, I thought, if not for that sweet-smelling tobacco. I stared at his square shoulders and the back of his angular head; his eyes were fixed on the road the whole time. I wondered whether he was listening to anything Mimousse said.

Only when we drove into The Hague did I muster up enough courage to ask the question weighing on my mind: "Does Wera . . . Does my mother know?" My father shot me an irritated look in the rearview mirror and opened his mouth, undoubtedly to say that Mimousse was my mother from now on, but she was one step ahead of him. I didn't need to worry about that, she said. After we had crossed the border, Dirk and Louise had sent Wera a telegram that read: "Bully safe in the Netherlands, more information to follow."

I found this reassuring. But what I didn't know, nor did Mimousse at the time, was that although the message had been sent at a quarter past four on Saturday, it didn't make it to Aachenerstrasse in Palenberg until Monday morning.

That was the first thing my mother told me when I was reunited with her again eighteen years later. At first, she was panicked, and once she realized what had happened, desperate. She was filled with self-reproach, and, when the telegram finally arrived on Monday morning, confirming her suspicions, there was nothing left but powerless rage. The Saturday I disappeared, she was brought home in a Jeep at midnight by Peter, her jolly American date. As soon as the headlights appeared in the yard, Nadia ran out in tears. Wera understood at once and sent Peter away. As soon as he was gone, she burst into tears as well.

The next morning, she went down to the police station to report a missing child and meekly filled out the paperwork handed to her by the cold, disinterested German officers. Her eyes were red from a sleepless night, and she realized that any effort to get her son back would be in vain. The irremediable reality of the situation, that she had lost her son forever, had started to sink in. She had no legal defense to speak of, nor did she have a powerful network to help her take matters into her own hands via illegal means.

Since resistance seemed futile, she gave up—that was just the kind of person she was. Fighting back was not an option. She didn't try to contact anyone in The Hague, not even when she received a formal confirmation on behalf of the Old Boss. She absorbed all her suffering, buried her grief, and tried to carry on with the people she had left: her mother, Nadia, and her daughter, Tatiana. And, in her heart alone, with me.

I was unaware of her undying love for me. As time wore on, I all but forgot that I had another mother out there somewhere, let alone a "real" one, and gradually became closer to Mimousse, or Mousse, as I called her. She did a good job with me. The Zionsburg incident was never mentioned again, and, as promised, Mimousse did her best to be my mother. And really, she did more than that, which I only realized later: she started to see me as her own personal project. After her third miscarriage in 1953, doctors strongly advised her to stop trying to have children, and she began to view raising me as her life-fulfilling task.

At first, we lived on the *Juno,* but before the start of the new school year, we moved from the creaky old barge into an upstairs apartment on Boreelstraat, one of the minor streets in the wealthy Statenkwartier district in The Hague. Naturally, this was all arranged by my grandfather. Now that things had been settled according to his liking, and he'd regained control of the situation, he did everything he could to make sure that my new life was relatively comfortable—with emphasis on *relatively.* Although he could have certainly afforded better accommodations for Frans and Mimousse, he didn't approve of their frivolous lifestyle, and so chose a more modest row house apartment.

My father and Mimousse lived a fairly loose lifestyle there until the end of January 1954, when the Old Boss died, and the squabbling over the family estate began. And at least twice a week, they went out dancing at the Savoy, a somewhat seedy nightclub on the Plein—the city's central square—right across from the Dutch parliament in The Hague. This meant that there was no one to make me dinner, so they sent me down to Chai Yen, a greasy Chinese restaurant on the corner. I didn't mind, and even felt pretty grown up sitting by myself in front of the window and being served by Chai himself. The Asian restaurateur would exit the steamy kitchen in his dirty apron, dripping with sweat, and whenever I asked for anything, he'd respond with a giggle.

Of course, I hoped that my classmates might walk by and see me in this decadent position. I even practiced raising one eyebrow in the mirror at home and imagined gazing back at them through the window with a look of utter ennui. While waiting for my food at Chai Yen, which always seemed to take forever, I read comic books, *Tintin* and *Donald Duck*, the latter being quite new in the Netherlands. There was also a magazine full of pictures of women in bathing suits and all kinds of jokes that I didn't understand but still found intriguing. The few times that I tried to get my father to explain them to me, he'd shoo me away and tell me I was too young for those kinds of things.

I was allowed to return to the Duinoord School, which was at least familiar. I listened to my classmates' bland summer vacation stories and was secretly proud that while they were camping in Callantsoog or northern France, I had been at the center of a real adventure. I got along well with some of my peers, but I didn't feel close enough to any of them to share the details of my wild summer. As far as anyone knew, I had been away "due to family circumstances," as Headmaster Van Westering had announced to class after my sudden departure in April. Once I was back, he cited the same reason for my absence and said that he hoped I'd be able to finish grade school without any further disruptions. No one knew that I'd been kidnapped, twice as a matter of fact.

So, I grew up to be a boy with secrets: about my father in the war, about my impoverished mother and illegitimate sister in Germany, about my devoutly Catholic grandfather and his dubious activities that I learned more about over time, about my abductions, about the fact that we still preferred to speak German at Briva Latvija. All of this impeded developing normal friendships with my Dutch peers and led to a lonely, withdrawn existence. I was well aware that my family wasn't like the other Dutch families around us, and that was enough to keep me from inviting friends over.

The one friend I could count on was my dog, Bobby, a clever black mutt with four white paws and a white tip on his bushy tail. Mimousse had brought him home right before I arrived in The Hague—it turned out that she loved dogs as much as I did. Like Freddy had been before him, Bobby became my number one confidant during those long evenings home alone. We didn't have a television, so I entertained myself with my own hybrid of table tennis and squash. I'd dribble the Ping-Pong ball up and down the hallway, then whack it against the doors on either end and award myself points based on how far it bounced back. The fact that I had to play both sides of the court didn't bother me; I was on one side, and on the other was Cor du Buy, the undisputed table tennis champion of the Netherlands. I learned it was more exciting when you played by the rules, so I'd always hit the ball as hard as I could, and—except in the very rare cases where I actually managed to return it with the help of Bobby—I'd carefully measure the distance down to the last centimeter. If there was any doubt, I'd let Bobby make the call.

My dog's devotion made me the envy of all my classmates. In the morning, he'd grab the belt I'd attached to my scooter and pull me down the street to school. At twelve o'clock, he'd be outside the school wagging his tail, waiting to take me home for lunch, and when lunch was over, he'd pull me back to class. I often took him on walks in the former antitank zone, where he became a lightning-fast retriever, and we worked together to fix up my headquarters, which were still there when I got back to The Hague.

Bobby was the type of dog that could be left to wander around on his own. One day I followed him around town and discovered that he did all the things typical street dogs do: mark his territory, scrounge for things to eat, and chase female dogs. He was a fighter, too—sometimes he'd turn up with a bloody ear or a puncture in his leg. And we never had to wait for him to come home at night; he'd bark twice when he was ready to come inside, and I could always hear him from three stories up. No one else had a dog like Bobby.

THIRTY

As Mimousse devoted more attention to my upbringing, my father drifted further and further away. In the beginning, before he had any real responsibility at the Poortensdijk factory, he was willing to participate. He taught me how to tie my shoes the Russian way, where you make two bunny ears and tie them together (clumsy, but once you've learned it, you're condemned to using it for the rest of your life). He trimmed my fingernails, taught me to polish my shoes, took me to get my haircut, and accompanied me on my Saturday afternoon horseback riding lessons. His eyes would fill with joy as he watched me practice tricks under the guidance of the riding school's director. The first time I was thrown from the horse, I ran back to him in tears, and he gave me a smack on the side of the head. "Stop whining, you sissy," he said. "The horse sees everything. A man's got to get his ass back in the saddle and show him who's boss, otherwise you can forget about it," he hissed. The director nodded approvingly. She had a sharp tongue herself—the type of woman you'd give a Zippo lighter for her birthday, as my father used to say. That lighter joke was one of my father's many bizarre statements that, although virtually meaningless, somehow mysteriously captured a person's essence. Whenever I think of a Zippo, I see that legendary horsewoman in my mind, either sticking a colossal thermometer up a sick horse's derriere or cracking her riding whip on the side of her boot and urging her students on.

Life lessons weren't generally something I could expect from my father. His three favorite sayings were "The dumbest farmers have the fattest cocks," "You can get anything by force," and "Leave the thinking to the horses—they've got a bigger head than you." None of them you'd expect to hear coming out of a Dutch father's mouth.

Since he'd married Mimousse, my father's Dutch vocabulary had improved significantly in a short period of time, and it got even better when they moved to Brabant in the 1960s, where my father quickly picked up a sort of self-concocted, ultra-rural Brabant accent. After a while, he blended in almost seamlessly. His foreignness only resurfaced when he was at home, bottle in hand, and he'd delve into his endless reserve of memories. He could very quickly become frightening, like the time I came home late to find him alone at the kitchen table with a savage look on his face, shouting orders: "Two degrees left, altitude eighteen, fire! Fire, I said, fire! Where's the fire?! Ivan is already advancing . . ." Deep in his drunken fantasy world, he directed the artillery toward the target.

Over the years, my compassion for my father waned. I had learned it was important that he be able to wear his German soldier's heart on his sleeve without fear of retaliation, like he did on Sunday mornings. Mimousse sometimes told me that my father had woken up in the middle of the night drenched in sweat, shouting because the inexhaustible Russian forces were storming the base, rifles with bayonets pointed right at the German soldiers.

"You can't tell anyone about this," she said gravely. "This is something people in the Netherlands won't understand. They'll call your father a Nazi, but he wasn't a Nazi. Remember that: he wasn't a Nazi. He was a soldier who wanted to fight to get back all that his family had lost to the Bolsheviks. So just listen to his stories, and don't say a word about them to anyone."

I listened to him faithfully, but that didn't prevent me from developing an increasing aversion to Sunday mornings at home. For starters, I'd heard his stories so many times over the years that I knew them in my sleep. Secondly, the hours of sitting and listening were getting harder to fit into my busy schoolboy's schedule. I had other important things to do on Sundays, like play chess or field hockey with the other kids. But more than anything, I became aware that all my father's war stories weren't bringing me any closer to him.

When he first started telling me these stories, about a year after I'd returned to The Hague, I still saw him as a hero in some kind of twisted fairy tale, who after countless exciting adventures had miraculously made it home alive. Comparing him to Hans's father in Palenberg only inspired more awe. Around then, I was fascinated by the few relics he'd brought home from the war, like a cloth from the Caucasus that, although it looked deceptively conventional on the table in our living room, had once served as a Mingrelian horse blanket, and the grenade shrapnel removed from his leg that he used as a paperweight. The shrapnel that couldn't be surgically removed was still floating around in his body, or so he said. "Look, here are a few pieces," he'd say, pointing to his hand. "They're in my hand now. I can only hope they don't move into my heart because that'll be the end of me."

He was obsessed with death for years after the war. Sometimes on Sunday mornings, he'd lay out the few photos he had of his fallen comrades on the kitchen table like playing cards. And whenever he visited friends or family, he'd pin the Iron Cross on his lapel. All these things were proof that his stories were true. That I wasn't allowed to talk about it with anyone was even a little exciting to me; it was a secret I shared with my father.

But four years later, I'd hit puberty, and by then my father was nothing more than a spiteful Sunday morning obstacle to me. I'd wake to find him sitting in the kitchen in his bathrobe and pajamas, chain-smoking from his black Bakelite cigarette holder, a bottle of jenever within reach, ready to force me into the weekly ritual of listening to his old, irrelevant communiqués from the front. Stories from a time that was his, but definitely not mine, a time I would just as soon distance myself from as quickly as possible. But nothing else mattered to him. He wasn't the least bit interested in how I was doing in school, my love life, or my hopes and dreams. I was nothing but a sounding board to him, justification for his weekly ritual of diving into the past.

It was around that time that our financial situation started to improve, and we moved to the prestigious Marlot neighborhood on the border with Wassenaar. This move, however, didn't make my life easier. Only now, through writing, am I really able to articulate what I felt: I had a father who wasn't interested in me, who was just obsessed with the idea of becoming richer than the Old Boss; only then would he be happy. I had a stepmother who, frustrated by her three miscarriages, had, for lack of a better option, made my upbringing her life's work and viewed my success as a gauge of her own happiness. But whether she really loved me, I can't say. Her love was for my father—not for the child he had inherited from a failed marriage in a past she wanted to erase.

Frans and Mimousse's bond was impenetrable to me; there was simply no room for a third musketeer, which, as an only child, I was unconsciously striving to be. Thus, throughout my childhood and teenage years, I became increasingly solitary, forced to live with two people who, after dinner, sat at the kitchen table all night talking about their troubles and plans without ever involving me. When I came to say goodnight, all they'd ask was whether or not I'd done my homework. In the morning, I'd bring them tea and coffee in bed and go back to the kitchen to make my own breakfast before leaving for school. We were only ever together at dinnertime, and we usually ate in silence. I didn't share any details about my day because I knew that my father wasn't interested, and my parents—as I had come to see them by then—saved their conversations for after I, the troublesome eavesdropper, had gone up to my room.

Even Christmas went by without any real care for each other; presents were methodically purchased from our jointly drawn-up lists, placed under the tree, unwrapped, and examined (my father excelled at this—with a look of distrust on his face, he'd carefully inspect the quality of the gift), after which the giver was thanked with a dutiful kiss. Thank God for alcohol, which softened the sharp edges of togetherness and brought my father to tears during the annual singing of *Silent Night*: *Christ der Retter ist da* . . . Christ the savior is born . . .

I imagined him sitting in his foxhole, looking out at the damnation in front of him, hoping that Christ the savior would appear on the battlefield and wipe out the swiftly approaching Reds. And although I suspected that the song took him back to the delirious Christmas of 1943, when everyone knew that Germany was going to lose the war, I couldn't stand to watch him wallow in his melancholy and began to take a cruel pleasure in drowning him out with *Sleep in heavenly peace* . . . in Dutch. This made him so angry that Mimousse would have to intervene. She'd look at me reproachfully and then proceed to calm him down.

The only person who could have given me the warmth I longed for had faded from my memory. Over the years, I began to forget what she looked like, and could hardly recall the sound of her voice.

THIRTY-ONE

The Old Boss only believed it when he received confirmation from his brother-in-law. Uncle Walter, a German oncologist, studied the pages of my grandfather's medical report with a grave look on his face. It was conclusive: "You've got two months at most, Joan. It's time to start making arrangements." That was in December 1953. I was nine years old, and Mimousse had just confirmed what I'd already suspected for a while: Santa Claus wasn't real. She couldn't believe that I hadn't already figured this out for myself.

I didn't fully realize that my grandfather was dying until the eve of January 23, 1954, the day he closed his eyes forever. He died surrounded by his wife, children, Uncle Walter, and Father Kolfschoten, who came by every day in the weeks leading up to his death to anoint him with oil. "Farewell, dear brother, great friend, until we meet again. *In coelo quies*," I heard the Jesuit priest say, stifling his tears. He had been with the family since Riga and played an instrumental role in countless decisions in the smoking room. I stood with Mimousse and Trees in the doorway to the Old Boss's bedroom, shortly before he passed. He called me over to him, stroked my head, and said nothing. I took in a final impression of him in silence. His face was pale, with hints of light yellow and purple, devoid of all emotion. My grandfather had stiffened into a neat gentleman with distinguished features. When his hand dropped down powerlessly on the sheet, the only life left in him was in his dark eyes, which were locked on me as I slowly moved toward the back of the room. He blinked a few times, as if he'd suddenly remembered something he needed to say, and his eyes closed.

When Dr. Van Tilburg announced it—*Dear Friends, he is dead*— my grandmother, being the good Russian woman she was, collapsed into convulsive sobs at the Old Boss's bedside. That much I expected; what surprised me was that my father immediately walked over to the window overlooking the backyard and opened the curtains that had been drawn all week. Xeno followed him and, in one swift motion, pulled them shut again. The two brothers looked at each other in silence for a few seconds and returned to my grandfather's bedside, Xeno at the head and my father at the foot, as far from each other as possible.

That image perfectly encapsulates the conflict between my father and my uncle, which would characterize their relationship after my grandfather's death. It was also indicative of Xeno's determination to become the undisputed custodian of the Old Boss's estate—the way he sat there, hands folded, head bowed over the dead man's lips, it was as if he were hoping to catch one last breath with a message just for him. The little spat with the curtains was a sign, at least in my eyes, that Xeno had something to hide, and he wanted to keep it that way. It was something that my father talked about a lot in the weeks that followed: "He'll screw us all over if we're not careful."

Naturally, these words were rooted in jealousy and mistrust, which turned out to be well warranted. In the weeks leading up to my grandfather's death, Xeno had taken matters into his own hands. He picked his father up at the hospital and brought him back to Briva Latvija so he could die at home. Meanwhile, he arranged a procession of notaries, lawyers, and the Old Boss's directors and advisers to come say their goodbyes. They arrived carrying briefcases and stacks of paperwork under their arms, ready to record the Old Boss's dying wishes and receive his final instructions. My grandfather spent his final days on oxygen, propped up with three cushions, breathlessly issuing orders from the big mahogany bed, where Frau Kochmann and I used to bring him his breakfast on Sunday mornings. There was even a "conference" in that room the day before he died, as a nurse would testify under oath five years later as part of a lawsuit that Titty and Guus filed against the rest of the family. The main question was whether the Old Boss had been fully accountable for his actions when he drew up his final will and testament. The nurse's statement left little room for interpretation: the patient was "deathly ill, but still able to have a conversation [. . .]. While some patients become dazed, he did not. He most certainly didn't fall into a coma [. . .]. I was able to talk with him the entire time."

It was partly because of this testimony that Titty and Guus lost their case, and shortly afterward, they got divorced. Convinced that the Münninghoff family was no longer of any use to him, Guus van Blaem left the mother of his five children, the youngest of whom was only three months old, and started a new life very much like the previous one—based on appearances, fantasies, and various forms of deceit.

"Don't forget Switzerland." According to the adults present when he died, these were my grandfather's last words. This statement, trivial as it may seem, sent the Old Boss's sons on a frantic search through various banking institutions. Forever the lone wolf, my father carried out his investigations alone. I have a handful of postcards from him, most of them from Zurich, but a few from Vaduz, the financial capital of Liechtenstein, and other Swiss cities like Fribourg, Lausanne, and Chur. I don't know why he went to these specific places, but one thing is certain: he always came up empty. Xeno's treasure hunts—which Jimmy was forced to endure, since he wasn't about to let his brother travel alone—were equally unsuccessful.

At least, that's what the brothers told each other when they gathered for a rare Sunday afternoon meal at Omi's new apartment. After

Grandpa died, she moved into the luxurious Cats'Heuvel apartment complex in the Statenkwartier. This unique building from the 1920s had an entrance hall entirely covered in mausoleum marble, and in the doorway a beautiful stained-glass window made of thousands of pieces of colored glass. There was a spacious porter's lodge with a separate mailbox for each apartment and a security guard always on duty. We would climb the stately staircase and head down the hall to the right (there was also an identical wing to the left), past the open door to the building manager's office (he'd always pop out to say hello), and through a long gallery of display cases filled with samples from the city's most prominent jewelers, shoe stores, and fashion houses. At the end of the hallway was the elevator to Omi's apartment, right next to the entrance to the elegant restaurant.

Omi, who felt right at home amid this luxury, lived on the second floor. Two floors up, there was a rooftop terrace, where you could call down to the bar via the in-house telephone, and within minutes a waiter in a dark red tailcoat would appear with the desired beverage on a silver tray. All you needed was a signature and apartment number to pay the bill. It was 1956, and I was a student at the Gymnasium Haganum, one of the best high schools in the city. Naturally, I didn't hesitate to treat a carefully selected group of classmates to this unprecedented finery. We'd sit up there—me, Frits, Ernest, and occasionally a girl—reading Homer and Tacitus on lounge chairs in the sun and drinking tonic on the rocks with a slice of lemon as if it were the most normal thing in the world.

Eventually Frans, Jimmy, and Titty all moved to the Statenkwartier. Omi was almost completely deaf by then, which made it difficult for her to manage on her own, and her children living close meant that she had help on a daily basis if necessary.

In practice, however, I was the one who ended up doing my grandmother's daily shopping. I didn't really mind, because Omi was always interested in my life. She liked to joke, and teach me Russian words, and kept right on spoiling me like she used to do at Briva Latvija. By twelve, I'd gained some insight into the family's affairs and was perfectly aware that there was a controversy surrounding the distribution of my grandfather's inheritance.

Whenever Omi had a full house on Sunday afternoon, her small dining area bursting at the seams with her three sons and their spouses (as far as I know, Guus never came to Cats'Heuvel, and Titty only came after they divorced), I'd end up serving the food, pouring the drinks, and clearing the plates. While doing so, I'd try to extract bits of information from the vicious arguments that inevitably broke out between them. Omi, who'd done the cooking, would sit there with a blissful smile on her face, gazing at her offspring, unable to hear a word. She would nod with satisfaction as the family gesticulated in nostalgic delight over her famous Baltic dishes, the first of which was always heavy minced meat crepes called *Komm morgen wieder*. In the meantime, virulent accusations were being flung across the table, causing some to retreat to the living room and stew over a cigarette so as not to disturb Omi's idyllic notion of family time.

The first to withdraw from the situation was Jimmy. Already embittered by the way in which the Old Boss had treated him after his illness (always seeing him as his weak, handicapped son, an effeminate mama's boy, and perhaps even gay), Jimmy had taken on a new identity in Amsterdam. His progressive, artistic social circles were so far removed from the tough, no-nonsense Catholic life at Briva Latvija that he'd become even more disconnected from his family. His marriage in 1952 to Christine Arnold, an attractive girl from The Hague, was the final step in his estrangement from the family. The Old Boss and Omi decided they would rather go on a long-planned business trip to Finland with Xeno and Trees than attend their son's wedding. (Omi later claimed that she hadn't been fully aware of what was going on and was extremely angry with the Old Boss, which I believe.) However, the fact that it had been a shotgun wedding—Jimmy's daughter, Monique, was born just six months later—undoubtedly contributed to the rift between Jimmy and his father. When the Old Boss left him the Stork's ring fan factory after he died, Jimmy had no interest in becoming part of the family empire and let Xeno buy him out as fast as possible.

Later, predictably, the question arose as to whether the arrangement between the brothers had really been fair; this would remain a dispute until the end of their lives. But in 1954 Jimmy was still a carefree, adventurous young man. He and Christine set off with a substantial amount of money to explore the world. They eventually landed in Mallorca, where Jimmy bought a house in Puerto d'Andratx, where over the years, they had neighbors like Gore Vidal and—a little ways away—the Spanish king. Starting in 1956, they spent six months in Mallorca and the other months, usually around the holidays, in The Hague. Their house, where Monique was raised by Christine's mother, became a gathering point for all kinds of artistic types, particularly those who wanted to keep partying after the bars in The Hague had closed. Jimmy and Christine's home was also frequented by former members of the Dutch Resistance, including Kas de Graaf, former head of the secret service agency, Bureau Bijzondere Opdrachten. For me as a teenager, these late-night soirees at Jimmy's house, where the steady flow of vodka and wine facilitated all kinds of stories about his paradise in Mallorca and goings-on behind the scenes of the Cold War (which everyone seemed to know about), were a kind of unexpected entrance into the real world.

Titty was the next to bow out of the disputes over the family inheritance. The Old Boss had decided on his deathbed to liquidate a few of his smaller companies: a food factory in IJmuiden, an office supply factory in Amsterdam, and a trading company in The Hague. The proceeds from these sales went to Titty, who for a long time claimed that she'd had a right to more. However, after she lost the case over the validity of her father's will and her husband left her, she resigned herself to the facts and moved into a house on Viviënstraat, about a half mile away from Cats'Heuvel.

paper. No one ever asked me for my opinion on the matter, and I found the whole idea quite upsetting. One of my classmates had just moved to Australia, and as we bid him farewell on the quay in Rotterdam in a flurry of forced excitement, I couldn't help noticing the despair and uncertainty in his eyes. When the colorful streamers between the wall and steadily moving ship finally snapped, he was standing at the railing with his shoulders trembling and his hands over his face. The thought of moving to New Zealand terrified me, perhaps because after everything I'd been through, all I wanted was stability. Moreover, things were finally going well for me at school; I had friends who I didn't want to leave, and unlike my father, I didn't find life in the Netherlands, and in The Hague in particular, all that bad. But Frans and Mimousse ignored my fuming, and one day we found ourselves having a cup of tea with the New Zealand consul, who informed us that everything was in order for us to move to Auckland. On the way home, we didn't say a word. But as soon as we walked in the door, my father took a bottle of vodka from the fridge, poured us all a glass, and said, "We're not going. We're Europeans. If I can't manage in the Netherlands, I'll go to Germany. No need to run away to the other side of the world. This is our part of the world. We're staying here."

I was thirteen years old at the time and had only ever had a few stealthy sips of vodka in my life. When I threw back the entire glass, just like my parents, I felt like the three of us had made an important pact. For the first time in my life, I felt 100 percent connected to them. The experience gave me goose bumps. I nodded in my father's direction. "Well put!" I said.

But even in his beloved Germany, where he thought he'd find people who shared his mentality, Frans would be bitterly disappointed. The last time he tried to earn money on the oil market in a strictly above-board manner, he was colossally bamboozled by a German man who, by flirting with Mimousse and showering me with presents, managed to gain a position of trust in our family. His name was an ominous one: August Sondergeld, literally August Without-Money.

I remember him as a sweet-talking dandy dressed in a camel over-coat, which was very chic at the time. He had piercing blue eyes and handsome wrinkles in his tanned, weathered face. He and my father spoke German together, which my father clearly enjoyed. Sondergeld told him that there was a major deal with the Americans around the corner. Thanks to the Marshall Plan, the Americans stationed in Germany had gone from being enemies to friends, Sondergeld explained like a true German citizen. There was no better guarantee for business, and with his help Frans Münninghoff could benefit from the opportunity. My father's confession of his history with the SS and the potential issues that could come of that were dismissed. "Uncle Sam doesn't care about that," Sondergeld insisted. "They just want to do business with us."

What the Americans were primarily interested in was used oil. Sondergeld was well aware of my father's knowledge in this field and the monograph he'd written about it. The fact that used oil was so broken-down made it highly suitable as jet fuel. This had only been recently discovered, so now it was just a question of pumping those oil pans empty and selling it to the Americans at an exorbitant price. If my father would agree to handle the supply, Sondergeld would manage the finances, and a settlement would follow each quarter. How Frans wished that he had met August Sondergeld sooner!

The first delivery got off to a slow start; the so-called black gold yielded less than half of what had been promised. *Growing pains* was Sondergeld's soothing magic phrase. That was all my father needed to hear. Three months later, it was the bank's fault (there had been transaction delays due to international financial barriers), and three months after that my father—who hadn't bothered with any interim checks and had blown most of his profits on weekly meetings with Sondergeld at the bar—was out almost half a million guilders. Like so many before him, Sondergeld just disappeared one day without a word, evaporating into thin air.

But this time, my father had been cheated by a *German*, someone who exuded the primal sense of Teutonic ancestry that he'd always believed in, and whose promises had proved to be just as hollow as everyone else's. The whole experience made my father so incredibly angry that from then on, he deliberately sought out opportunities to make money illegally in Germany. He was determined to become richer than his own father, if not by traditional means, then by sinister ones. At the same time, he had to do something to save the Poortensdijk factory, which was on the brink of bankruptcy.

In desperation, Frans turned to his brother Xeno, who received him with skepticism. For Xeno, who'd lived up to his father's every expectation and become a dynamic businessman, any kind of damage to the family reputation would have been disastrous. As the owner of the nationally and internationally renowned paint and varnish factory W. Paulussen, he wasn't interested in seeing his brother go bankrupt.

"Understand that I'm not going to give you any money," Xeno said bluntly. "Even if I wanted to, I don't have it. Everything I earn goes right back into the business; it's the only way to grow. That's what I learned from the Old Boss." He glared at his brother, his eyes full of contempt. "Jesus, Frans, you really let them take you for a ride, didn't you? Well, I can still help you. I told my business partner, Boelie Ommering, about your used oil business. Ommering is prepared to pay off your debts provided that he can take over the daily management of the Poortensdijk factory and have direct supervision over your business dealings in Germany. He wants to bring your product to the Netherlands—apparently there is a need for it in Soesterberg. And of course, he wants more than half the profits, because he's really putting his reputation on the line by associating with you, and the whole project is going to cost him an arm and a leg. But the two of you can arrange things between yourselves."

"So, I'd be placed under some kind of receivership?" my father asked incredulously.

"You could call it that," Xeno replied flatly, "but you got yourself into this mess, and as far as I can see, you don't have a lot of other options."

"What kind of guy is this Ommering?" my father asked.

"Well, he didn't finish high school," Xeno said, "but he can do math—which is something you apparently can't. Actually, he was planning to live off his investments—he owns about seventy streets in The Hague. But he thinks this would be a nice challenge, and he'd also be doing it as a favor to me. The most important thing is that he can be trusted." My father shot him a scornful look, and Xeno added, "And when I say someone can be trusted, they can be trusted."

THIRTY-THREE

The collaboration with Boelie Ommering was successful in that it gave my father ample opportunity to develop his own plans in secrecy. Ommering was a kind man, but when it came to business, he didn't tolerate contradiction and was extremely driven. The first thing he did was pay all my father's creditors, which restored the factory's reputation. Then he made used oil part of the company's standard product line, rather than something that was traded in backroom deals. Poortensdijk started offering a collection service for used motor oil from trucks, which would then be refined at the factory and resold. Clearly, there'd been a gap in the market, and the illustrious businessman was prepared to take full advantage of it. In less than a year, the Poortensdijk factory transformed back into a well-functioning business.

For Frans Münninghoff, this could have been a source of frustration, but he counted his blessings. Not only was he out of debt, Ommering was paying him a monthly salary that afforded him a level of comfort he hadn't had since his youth. Granted, it may have been less than one might expect, given the factory's success under the new management, but it was still enough for him to rent a townhouse on Bezuidenhoutseweg, close to the fancy villas in Marlot. This location suited the tastes of the status-conscious Mimousse and was a major source of pride for my father. Naturally, the fact that the move extended my daily school commute from two and a half miles to twelve was not a consideration.

But most important for my father was the fact that Ommering preferred to keep him out of daily business operations, which meant he had a lot of free time at his disposal—time he needed to start another business in Germany.

It was simple, once you knew how to do it. Due to a government-mandated subsidy scheme, all agricultural diesel, "farmer's diesel," was colored a shade of light pink. This color indicated that no excise duty had been levied on it, and it could be sold at a much lower price than standard, colorless diesel. Now, if you managed to strip farmer's diesel of its pinkish hue, you could sell it at the pump for the price of regular diesel and easily pocket a 60 percent profit. Simple, but highly illegal.

However, the color-stripping process, as Frans Münninghoff had learned from Stubka many years ago, wasn't so easy to carry out. The pink farmer's diesel had to be poured across a bed of sulfur to produce a chemical reaction that would transform the cheap tinted fuel into a colorless and much more expensive product.

How my father, armed with only a basic knowledge of chemistry and on his own (Stubka had passed away), managed to transform the process into an extremely lucrative fraud machine in 1959 is a mystery to me. He never said a word about it, not even to Mimousse, as far as I know. Just across the Dutch border in the German city of Lingen on the banks of the Ems River, he built, undoubtedly with the help of third parties, a kind of factory, which consisted of two buildings: one for receiving the incoming loads of farmer's diesel (up to a hundred tons at a time), and the other for sending out the colorless, sulfur-treated product to be sold for a huge profit.

But once again, my father's naivety got the best of him. Instead of becoming a millionaire in one fell swoop—something he'd always

wanted that now seemed within reach—he let his project be comman-
deered by a number of people who were eager for a share in the profits. It was probably too large an operation, and too many people got
involved. First, diesel shipments had to be "hijacked" in the ports of
Hamburg and Bremen (in other words, taken off the books, smug-
gled out, sometimes even stolen). This could only be carried out by
shady middlemen, all of whom insisted on a piece of the pie. Then the
shipment had to be transported to the color-stripping facility, which
required a captain, and finally, he needed buyers who were willing to
participate in a criminally punishable sale. When my father's activities
were inevitably discovered by the German government, he confessed to
Xeno and one of Titty's children that he'd even gotten a few internationally renowned companies involved in the scheme.

In the end, it didn't make him rich. But I remember the day he
came home in the car that would be in our driveway from then on:
an Armstrong Siddeley, *the expensive little brother of the Rolls-Royce,* he
announced with childlike glee. It was a secondhand, blue-and-silver
monster of a car with hand-finished details, a silver sphinx hood orna-
ment, and an elegantly quiet engine. The whole thing made me laugh.
I was sixteen at the time and found my father's desire to impress me
with the car utterly ridiculous. Mimousse, on the other hand, was crazy
about it, and all too happy to drive it into the city on a regular basis.

My father didn't enjoy the profits of his dirty diesel scheme for long.
The German police raided the factory in 1961 after neighbors complained
about the smell of sulfur. Apparently, local residents hadn't been able to
contact those responsible for the stench—another mistake in the operation. The verdict, four years in prison, was declared in absentia before the
court in Cologne, and once again my father was a wanted man.

Although it wasn't clear if he'd actually be extradited, he considered
The Hague too dangerous. He and Mimousse left for Netersel, a parish
in southern Brabant where he'd been in 1945 on his way to Belgium.
They bought a rundown farm, which they planned to transform into

a veritable mansion with high ceilings, terraces, a giant sitting room, plenty of bedrooms for their future grandchildren, stables for horses, and a separate cottage to be used as a library. The architect's drawings (which cost a fortune) were already finished.

But none of the plans ever came to fruition. Frans and Mimousse would live out the rest of their days in the front half of the house, discussing plans around the kitchen table.

THIRTY-FOUR

It wasn't until the spring of 1969 that I saw my mother again. Eighteen years had passed without any contact from her at all. When I started at Leiden University in 1963, I decided to write to her, mostly to underline the fact that I was old enough to make my own decisions without consulting with my parents.

That summer I moved into a tiny, awful apartment in a small town outside of Leiden. The years leading up to that move had been anything but harmonious. When my parents left Marlot for Netersel, I went to live with Omi at Cats'Heuvel. I slept in her guest room (more of an alcove), where I had a bed, table, and chair at my disposal. During my last year of high school, I was moved into a guesthouse in the other wing of her building, where I had significantly more space and, outside of lunch and dinner, a reprieve from the rather difficult task of talking with my grandmother, who was still as sociable as ever. Despite her deafness, she loved to tell stories, and I had to shout back in reply. The entire ritual was disruptive to my concentration.

I was often alone in that apartment, and could have used it to engage in all kinds of debauched activities, but that hardly happened. Perhaps those were different times, and seventeen-year-olds just didn't do those kinds of things, or perhaps I was a different kind of seventeen-year-old. In any case, I worked hard and focused on my final exams.

Once I'd passed them, I took stock of my family's situation, for the first time in my life, I think.

My father had barely noticed me all those years. Silently, a sense of estrangement had grown between us. Even before he fled to Netersel, the distance became significantly pronounced when I stopped listening to his Sunday morning sermons, saying I had to hurry to the field hockey ground or the tennis court, where I'd find myself waiting in the locker room or hitting balls against the wall for an hour. Mimousse hadn't taken any meaningful interest in me either. She'd kept me on my toes, sent me to rigorous tutors, quizzed me on my studies, and attended parent-teacher conferences, but once it was clear that I was doing well in school and could take care of myself, she left me to follow her Frans to Netersel. No one told me why they were leaving The Hague; I didn't learn about my father's diesel fraud until years later.

At their new home in the forests of Brabant, I was just a framed photo on the sideboard, briefly brought to life during my obligatory visits at Christmas and Easter. They rarely called, and if they did visit The Hague, it was always on business that had nothing to do with me. Frans and Mimousse had their own agenda, and I wasn't part of it. It occurred to me that neither of them had ever come to watch me play hockey or tennis, though there were plenty of other mothers and fathers cheering on the sidelines. Nor did they ever come to my chess tournaments, where I had some success. Neither of them had been present for any significant moment in my high school career, not the plays that I'd been in, not my inauguration as president of the student union, and not my high school graduation. Now that it was over, and I was free of the all-consuming pressure of high school and had a long summer vacation ahead of me before I transitioned into a new phase of life, I realized just how alone I'd been.

I also discovered what a socially isolated life my family had led. While most of my classmates who were planning to study at Leiden University had connections to good fraternity houses on Rapenburg, thanks to their parents' networks, I had no such access. Given my parents' retreat from society and my dear deaf Russian grandmother's detachment from the world, I was forced to settle for that dreadful room far from campus, and wasn't accepted into the top ranks of my fraternity. Though there wasn't a word for it at the time, I felt like a second-generation immigrant in the conservative university town. It didn't matter that I spoke perfect Dutch and my father drove around in an Armstrong Siddeley; things weren't going to be easy for me in Leiden.

I tried to express these feelings in the long letter that I wrote, in Dutch, to my mother. And even though the people I was really angry at were the runaways I'd come to call my parents, I couldn't help but point an accusatory finger at my mother as well. Why hadn't she responded to my kidnapping? Why hadn't she done anything to get me back? But as I wrote those words, I doubted whether I was sincere. Hadn't I been better off in the Netherlands? Shouldn't I have been happy that I hadn't stayed with Wera and become a German citizen? True, Frans and Mimousse hadn't been the epitome of parental love, but who was to say that Wera would have been a perfect mother? "Please understand that I'm only asking you these questions so I can determine my position toward you, my mother. I haven't been able to do this in the last twelve years for many reasons, one of which is that I never heard from you. No one ever talked about you at home; what I do know about you, I heard from Titty and Omi." That was how I concluded the letter.

After six weeks without an answer, I wrote again, this time in German. I noticed how artificial it felt; I had to look up words every now and then and wasn't always sure about cases and conjugations. The letter wasn't in the natural language a child uses with his mother, and I resigned myself to the fact that my alienation had taken this definitive form. But when two months passed without a reply to the second letter, my sadness turned into annoyance. I had the right address, didn't I?

Wera had moved to Würzburg, and Omi had given me her new address. Why didn't she write back? I decided not to press further and to close this chapter in my life. It seemed I was destined to go on without Wera, so that's what I would do.

Six years went by. I started studying law without any real sense of direction, and never finished my classes. Then I switched to Slavic languages and literature, and finally ended up in the army, where I became what's known as a "short-term volunteer" with the Dutch Military Intelligence Service. Wedding plans were on the horizon, even after I was kicked out of the army for being undisciplined. Ellen and I had already sent invitations for the big day: September 20, 1969. The fact that we actually went through with it was a huge relief—I'd told Ellen about everything, and she hadn't been scared off.

Of all the wedding formalities, there was one that especially concerned me: in those years, you needed permission from your biological parents to get married. My father sent me his by mail as soon as I asked for it. Ellen, whose father had died ten years earlier, got her dear mother's signature in Voorschoten. We just needed my mother's in Würzburg.

Since she hadn't answered my letters, and I didn't have her phone number, we decided to go visit her. At first, I was against the idea. My mother had been banished from my emotional world, but my fiancée was eager to meet her. On top of that, in early summer 1969, we were invited to attend the wedding of Prince Leonid von Manssyreff. Manssyreff had been my teacher in the Military Intelligence Service and was getting married to a Dutch woman. Nearly every member of the exiled Russian nobility in Europe was invited, and the reception was set to be held at the castle of Bad Mergentheim, not far from Würzburg. Ellen and I tossed some nice clothes in a bag, walked to the main traffic circle in Voorburg, and stuck out our thumbs; we didn't have any money and hitchhiking was still a fairly common means of travel. And with beautiful Ellen at my side, getting a ride was never a problem.

The sun was setting by the time we stepped into the taxi that would take us to Wera's house. I gazed out the window with mounting horror as we drove out of the center of the old Bavarian town, where our last ride had dropped us off, and headed for the poor neighborhoods on the banks of the Main. The driver had to stop several times to ask for directions; apparently my mother was living in a cluster of dilapidated houses on a dirt road with no streetlights, house numbers, or name plates. The river was barely two hundred yards away, its waters flowing indifferently downstream.

I had to shout her name a few times before any sign of life appeared in the dark, quiet house. A window opened on the second floor, and a man with silvery-white hair stuck his head out. He looked at me for a few moments and then asked me a question that no one has asked me since Palenberg: "Are you Bully?" And just like I did back then, without considering for a moment how strange it was that this person knew my name, I replied with an unsuspecting "Yeah, that's me."

"I'll be right down," the man said. "I'll take you to your mother." Less than ten seconds later, he was in front of us. "She doesn't know you're coming—she'll be scared to death." The man introduced himself as Peter and said that he'd heard a lot about me from Wera—"Frau Bauer, I mean," he said, quickly correcting himself. "She recently got a picture of you in uniform—that's how I recognized you," he explained; I couldn't help but notice how he addressed me in the familiar *du* form, as if I were someone he knew well. He told me that Omi had sent Wera a recent photo of me looking valiant in my military uniform, and I wondered why no one ever told me my mother had remarried, and her last name was now Bauer. I didn't have much time to wonder. A few minutes later we stopped in front of a kind of shed, and Peter signaled for us to wait. He knocked two times on the door and disappeared inside. The last fifty yards of the footpath were sodden, and it was getting dark. The Main, now even closer, shone bleakly in the pallid moonlight. I stood there trying to conjure up the image of my mother that I'd tried to preserve all those years, but it was gone, as was the sound of her voice.

Peter opened the door and invited us inside. "Oh my God! No!" I heard someone cry out behind him. It just then occurred to me that I was about to see a woman who, for whatever reason, had been hiding from me like a wounded animal for years, who I was forcing into a confrontation that was perhaps as unpleasant for her as it was for me.

But *pleasant* isn't a word that carries any real meaning in a mother-son relationship.

THIRTY-FIVE

Poverty distorts a person, physically and mentally. I understood this as soon as I walked into that cold, dark cave where my mother had been living with her monstrously fat husband for years. The walls were moldy from the Main's frequently rising waters, and there were no windows. The remains of their meager supper on the bare Formica table, the smell of resignation hanging in the air, their faded clothes, the miserable clutter, and, above all, the looks on their faces—despondent, empty, passive through and through—all of these things absolved her from any blame in my mind.

Wera, my mother, just sat at the table, frozen. Her hair was flecked with gray, but she'd managed to maintain the full, curly bob she'd always had. Her face had become thicker and worn with age despite her naturally high cheekbones. A lot of time had passed since she skipped out of the house with a sparkle in her eye, saying, "Now, wish me luck!" like an American movie star.

I saw her life after my kidnapping flash before my eyes: long, lonely nights weeping for the child who'd been taken from her, powerless against the Old Boss and his ruthless cronies, cursing heaven and hell for the terrible war that had destroyed her relationship with Frans, a man she'd truly loved, and turned their marriage into a "Lili Marleen"–style affair that could've never lasted, no matter how badly she had wanted it to. *We're destined for each other.* It was the solemn pledge they'd made to each other back in Riga, back when they still had a promising future ahead of them.

Terrified of spending the rest of her life alone and in poverty, she'd married Siegfried Bauer. She chose her words carefully: the man weighed nearly three hundred pounds, so it wasn't like she'd reeled him in, she whispered once the conversation started to find its natural rhythm. After a few uncomfortable minutes, we found ourselves sitting around the table laughing together nervously. I couldn't believe how well she spoke Dutch. Her fat husband, a vacuum salesman and amateur table tennis champion from Bavaria, just sat there like a suspicious dope.

The two had a four-year-old daughter together named Monika, who gazed up at me from under Wera's skirts. She had her father's small, piglike eyes, and her face was covered in snot. It suddenly occurred to me that I had another half sister. And what about Tatiana? Wera closed her eyes and said Tatiana wasn't doing well. She was just eighteen and had already been out of the house for a few years. She lived in Frankfurt—or at least, that's where she was living when she got arrested. Tatiana had gotten into heroin and was forced into dealing. She'd been caught about a month ago and was in jail awaiting trial. It was the first time I saw Wera cry that day, not for me, but for her daughter. I felt nothing.

I suddenly realized that my mother must be nearly fifty years old, which meant that she was forty-five when she gave birth to Monika in this squalid state of poverty. Had she really wanted another child? Had it contributed anything to her relationship with Siegfried Bauer? As I pummeled her with questions, she laid a hand on my arm: "Dear, not so fast. I'm speechless. I need to calm down." Bauer started looking around for four beer glasses. Peter, a friend of theirs as far as I could tell, had disappeared again.

In the meantime, Ellen noticed things I didn't, for example the photo of me in uniform, looking more Dr. Zhivago–like than ever, displayed prominently on the sideboard next to a silly figurine of a dachshund with a red sausage in its mouth that I'd bought for her birthday with my allowance. There was also a box on a shelf labeled BULLY. Inside were drawings I'd made, an essay I'd written, and several trinkets I barely recognized but that my mother had kept with her all those years.

We barely touched each other the whole time, save for a formal kiss on the cheek, both of us powerless to give shape to the moment of reunification. "Did you get my letters?" was the first thing I wanted to know. I hoped she would look surprised and say no and we could blame it all on the German postal service, which would have had trouble finding her in these remote outskirts of the city. But my hopes were in vain. Yes, she had received them.

"Why didn't you write back?" I asked.

She sighed, and her eyes welled up with tears, and she began to sob. Behind my shoulder, Ellen broke into tears as well, but I continued my inquisition.

"Because I didn't dare, love. So many years had gone by. When they took you from me, my first instinct was to do everything I could to get you back. Of course, dear. But I also knew that there was no way I could go up against your grandfather. I had no one, you understand, no one who could help me. Guus, maybe, but he'd been banned from Briva Latvija. And then there was your uncle Jimmy, who I always had a weakness for, but he withdrew from conflict—a real Sunday's child. And Frans was absorbed in his new life with Mimousse."

"All of that may have been true," I said, "but why didn't you answer those two letters I wrote you after I graduated from high school?"

Again, she let out a deep sigh. With tears in her eyes, she laid her trembling hand on my arm. "Everyone was against me. Even if I'd tried to contact you, they kept me out of your life. Answering those letters would've only started something your family would immediately stop.

And then they would've come after me. They were very clear: 'Stay away from Bully!'"

"So, you were blackmailed," I said, and with that I exploded. All the anger I had held inside for years came boiling up. "I'm your goddamn child, aren't I?" I yelled. "We'd been together since Posen, hadn't we? And through all the shit that came after? No one could have come between us! Christ, I didn't want any of this!"

We switched to German, and at that moment, Siegfried Bauer, who had just poured us a round of beer, felt the need to say something: "Prosit! So we can live happily ever after!"

My mother shot me a sad smile. "Understand, this is what my life has become," she whispered.

"I do understand," I said, "but I don't approve." I could tell that this cold response cut her deeply, but I couldn't do anything about it.

In the half day we spent with my mother and her new family in Würzburg, I didn't shed a single tear; Ellen, on the other hand, couldn't stop crying. I felt numb, overwhelmed by the injustice my mother had put me through for years. It was as if I had developed a kind of cold armor to protect me from my own raging emotions.

The next evening as we sat with eighty members of Russian royalty in exile, at a long table at Mergentheim Castle, the wedding singer broke into a melancholy ballad—*The monotonous bell keeps on ringing*—and I felt something stir in my soul. All of a sudden, I thought of my two grandmothers and felt a deep connection to all those present, even though I'd never been to Russia. I felt melancholic about the long road ahead of me. *The way before me is far, far . . .* I wasn't the only one who was moved to tears that evening.

My mother and I agreed to keep in touch. But once again, we didn't. It would be fifteen years before I heard from Wera again.

PART 3

The Guardian Angel

THIRTY-SIX

Karl Reinhard was unhappy with his life. On his fifty-fifth birthday, in 1976, he had to accept the simple fact that he'd made a mess of it. He'd gotten his last job fourteen years ago as a mechanic at the Degenhardt garage in Kiel with the help of his old war buddy Frans Münninghoff. It had ended in fiasco. Degenhardt, a Baltic baron who'd used the garage to escape his SS past and start a new life, had finally fired him because he kept making mistakes. He hadn't kept up with developments in the German auto industry, and years of alcohol abuse left him with a tremor, so he could barely tighten a screw anymore. Old comrades or not, Degenhardt was forced to let Karl Reinhard go in 1972, and he'd been unemployed ever since, almost five years now.

He had only himself to blame, and he knew it. He just couldn't get the war out of his head. After Germany surrendered in 1945, he, like so many others, had wandered around his ruined country for a few years, picking up odd jobs. During the day, he broke his back working to make the streets and squares habitable again, cursing Hitler and the entire Nazi regime, and at night, he drank cheap schnapps in dingy boardinghouses with his so-called comrades, trading war stories and reminiscing about the past, back when they were proud to be fighting for the winning side. How many times had they sat around the table singing old songs that were now officially forbidden? But nobody really cared; it was all part of coming to terms with the past.

Whether Karl Reinhard would ever really be able to close that chapter of his life was doubtful. Still, fate offered him the chance to try when he met his high school sweetheart, Claudia Lüscher, in 1949 in his hometown of Limburg an der Lahn. Call it a rediscovery after ten years. He'd only dared to go after her as a seventeen-year-old, and she, the most sought-after girl in town, only succumbed to his advances thanks to his good looks; he had thick black hair, heavy eyebrows, fiery dark eyes, an athletic build, and a full set of dazzling white teeth. After five years of war, what remained was an intriguing residue of his younger self.

But the extent to which Claudia had managed to preserve her overwhelming beauty throughout the war was almost unbelievable. Karl had no idea what she'd been up to all those years (she'd been in Berlin for most of the war, she said), but it wasn't hard to imagine that with her blonde locks, long legs, and deep blue eyes—the same ones that had looked at him so enchantingly at school dances long ago—Claudia had plenty of wartime suitors, probably high-ranking officers who'd protected her from the miseries of the war. An irresistible Madonna and whore of Babylon in one, Claudia had ridden the runaway carousel of Hitler's Thousand-Year Reich in Berlin—it conjured up all kinds of images in Karl's mind.

And when they ran into each other in their sleepy hometown of Limburg an der Lahn, he didn't ask questions. Overwhelmed by her renewed presence in his life, he confessed in all sincerity that he'd thought of no one but her through the entire war. It was true; in his darkest hours, she had been his beacon, like the Blessed Virgin Mary, but different. Good God almighty, how he'd longed for her in the muddy trenches of Ukraine!

She smiled, and they picked things up again as if nothing had happened. He was her old high school boyfriend, and she didn't have any friends left in Berlin, or at least no one who wanted to be reminded of her. Both Karl and Claudia desperately craved the stability of civilian life, and so, perhaps for lack of a better alternative, perhaps because they were truly fond of each other, they married in 1949. Karl really tried to make something of himself in Limburg an der Lahn. He trained as a carpenter with an old master in the city center and had a growing business with three employees when, in 1951, Frans Münninghoff found him at a gathering of old comrades in Cologne.

Reckless Franz! How could Karl ever forget his wartime friend? From 1943 onward, they'd marched side by side, fighting, cursing, drinking, and dodging death in all its forms during the retreat from Russia. Karl was glad to tag along with Frans. Once the tide of war had turned, you were clearly better off with someone who had a bit of combat experience like Frans, even if he was only a sergeant. Most of the arrogant pricks from the officers' school lost their heads when the Russkies began advancing en masse and chaos rippled through their ranks; those were the moments when you needed someone who could keep calm under pressure and help you navigate the perilous situation. Only when Frans got himself transferred to the punishment battalion—*What the hell got into you, man? Letting a Russian go?*—did Karl lose touch with him.

Finally, the two men had the opportunity to catch up. It was an evening of laughter, clinking glasses, and friendly pats on the shoulder. Frans told him about his parents, his failed marriage, how he'd managed to escape the Dutch justice system and even recover his passport so he could travel freely. He even hinted at the inheritance he would soon receive from his sick wealthy father. Karl gave him an overview of all he'd been through, showed him a photo of Claudia, and invited his old friend to visit him.

Twelve months later, my father showed up on the Reinhards' doorstep. Many years later, my father and I were driving down the Autobahn and we passed Limburg an der Lahn, and he told me the story. "The woman who opened the door took my breath away. I think I stood there speechless for a whole minute just staring at her, and she at me. I swear, I thought my heart was going to pound out of my throat. We both knew right away what was going to happen—I felt it."

Despite their efforts, Karl and Claudia couldn't conceive. Claudia was just about to turn to doctors when they discovered, to their delight, that she was expecting. She wasn't yet thirty years old. On March 5, 1953, their daughter Andrea was born; when Frans received the birth announcement, he immediately announced he wanted to be godfather. A week later, he was standing beside the parents at her christening ceremony in the beautiful cathedral of Limburg an der Lahn, without Mimousse. His wife had given him a questioning look when he left for Germany under the guise of "comrade service."

THIRTY-SEVEN

Karl Reinhard was quick to pick up on Frans and Claudia's relationship. It was hard to miss; until his color-stripping operation in Lingen was shut down, my father traveled to Limburg an der Lahn dozens of times, initially as a family friend, and eventually as a member of a recurring *ménage à trois*. Karl accepted the situation quickly when he came home from work early one day and found his wife and former comrade in the act. The lovers just looked up at him with ruthless confidence in their eyes.

Karl had one condition: no more children. From then on, precautions were taken. He also didn't want to hear any allusions to who Andrea's real father was. They agreed. From then on, Karl Reinhard was mostly just tolerated, forced to bridge the gaps between the high points of their extramarital affair.

And Mimousse? Frans's absences were always short, usually no more than a week, and they were usually explained by his endless search for the Old Boss's secret bank accounts in Switzerland. Later, the story was that he had to go to Germany on business and eventually that he was planning to set up a factory near Lingen. My father, the entrepreneur. Most of the time he was home with us in The Hague. But still, she must have known. Mimousse had always been a sensual woman, the kind of woman who sees and smells and feels. Cheat on a woman like that, and you'll be the one who will end up begging for mercy.

When Germany became unsafe for my father after the Cologne court ruling in 1961, life changed dramatically in Limburg an der Lahn. Karl Reinhard took the reins—or at least he tried. Andrea was eight by then and had become attached to her Uncle Franz; he was her favorite, with all his jokes and presents—much more fun than her father. Her uncle would be back, Claudia promised. His absence was only temporary. For Karl, that was by no means certain. "Am I her father, or not?!" he'd shouted more than once after having a drink too many, as if he didn't already know the answer to the question. At first, Claudia would put a finger to her lips and point at Andrea, but after a while Karl started dealing out blows.

Claudia began sleeping alone and refused to speak to him. To make matters worse, his carpentry shop went up in flames due to the negligence of one of his employees. The building had been full of dry wood. "The fire of the century," one of the firemen reverently called it. A short paragraph in the newspaper report stated that Karl had failed to take out adequate insurance, and the incident had thus left him destitute.

Frans heard about all of this. Going to Germany was out of the question—he would be immediately arrested, but he still had some old friends who could help Karl out. *Meine Ehre heißt Treue*—and, of course, he was concerned about Claudia and Andrea's well-being as well. He quickly rekindled his friendship with his old Baltic riding mentor, Baron Degenhardt, in 1962, and after two telephone conversations, he arranged a job for Karl as a mechanic at the Degenhardt garage in Kiel. Would Claudia go with him? When Frans got her on the phone, she began sobbing uncontrollably. She didn't want to go to Kiel; she wanted to go to *him*—with Andrea, who asked about him constantly. "Are you my father?" came a mousy, girlish voice on the other end of the line.

"I'm your guardian angel, Andrea," he answered, intuitively adding a mystic aura to their relationship. It worked like a charm. Everyone had a father, but how many people could say they had a guardian angel to protect them?

In the end, Claudia went with Karl to Kiel, but it was a complete disaster. As a carpenter, Karl was totally out of place at the garage and proved to be a clumsy mechanic. His frustration eventually gave way to domestic violence, destroying any hope of a tolerable future. A year later Claudia left—no one knew where she went—leaving Andrea behind with Karl. The little girl had a portrait of my father hidden in her wardrobe, and at night she'd take it out and stare at it longingly.

In 1976, this was the situation my father found Karl Reinhard in when he was able to travel back to Germany after the statute of limitations on his 1961 sentence expired. It was also the year that Mimousse—entirely against her nature—told Frans he could no longer live with her on the farm in Netersel. For years, she'd tolerated his longing for Germany, a country she deeply despised, and when he expressed his desire to go back to doing business there, she even gave him her blessing. But she couldn't tolerate his behavior when her mother died in 's-Hertogenbosch in 1973.

The baroness had been imprisoned in a Japanese POW camp in the Dutch East Indies with her daughters Jacquot, Yvonne, Edith, and Dieuwke, the daughter she'd had with her second husband. After the war was over, she learned that her husband had died of exhaustion two years earlier while working as a forced laborer on the Burma railway. She was more broken by this news than by the misery she'd endured in the camp herself. She and her younger daughters moved in with Yvonne, who'd since married a Czech by the name of Jozka Komzak, the Southeast Asia representative for the world-famous shoe brand Bata. They had a large, colonial-style house near Jakarta, but once the so-called police actions broke out, Jozka was recalled to Europe. This meant repatriation for the entire family.

Granny, who was soon bedridden, was able to keep a close eye on everything at her beloved Ridderborn Castle from her mansion in 's-Hertogenbosch. When her parents died within a month of each other at an extremely old age in the 1950s, she had Frans, with whom she got along quite well, take her directly to Belgium so she could personally oversee the distribution of their considerable inheritance. Although both the castle and the surrounding estates had fallen into a state of disrepair, as the elderly couple's only child, she became a millionaire in her old age.

Or, at least on paper. The castle had an estimated value of over one and a half million guilders, but Granny refused to sell it. This irked Frans, who repeatedly asked her for financial support to carry out his business plans, and he had trouble hiding his irritation.

He finally succeeded in persuading Granny to sell a sizeable piece of land, and the profits were equally distributed among her five daughters. Mimousse's share was just enough to finance Frans's first overseas oil deal in Aleppo. When it became clear that Frans had been cheated, Mimousse's sisters turned against him completely. Why had he forced Granny into the sale? Nobody had needed that money, and the whole thing jeopardized the unity of the Ridderborn Estate. He'd taken their sister's money and flushed it down the drain! They warned Mimousse that she would be wise to trust less in her husband.

The sisters' suspicions toward my father were tempered by the fact that their husbands didn't share in them. Both thought my father was a bit naive, but by no means a bad person. Twenty years later, Jozka would admit that he'd severely misjudged Frans Münninghoff.

THIRTY-EIGHT

Ellen and I had entered a confusing phase of our lives. In the five years after our visit to Würzburg, we were busy trying to finish university—or at least Ellen was—and looking for jobs. At first, we worked as tour guides for Americans traveling through Europe. This meant that we were apart most of the summer and spent the winter months together hibernating in Leiden. In 1974, our lives got a bit more structure when we moved to The Hague. Ellen got a job teaching French, and I got a permanent position as a traveling journalist at the *Haagsche Courant* newspaper.

A year later our first son, Michiel, was born. I couldn't help but dance a little sirtaki when I came home the night after Ellen had given birth at the hospital. It was a feeling of total happiness: Michali, Misja, our sweet little Michiel. We didn't hear anything from Würzburg, but we did receive word from Netersel. My father declared he would never recognize a grandson with a name like Michiel—could it be any more Dutch? What on earth were we thinking?

We were baffled, angry, and crestfallen. How dare he! In the end, we gave in to his demands for the sake of keeping the peace and changed our son's name from Michiel to Michael, which sounded less Dutch and would work better internationally anyway. My father was satisfied. He said he would reimburse us for the administrative costs—four hundred guilders—but he never did.

What my father was up to in the '70s is, for the most part, a mystery to me. He wanted us to believe that he and Mimousse were leading a wealthy landowner's life in Netersel, where the local peasants would remove their caps whenever he spoke to them. Everything from his silvery-white hair to his walking stick with the silver head, his friendly affect, and proper manners, which he made a point to exhibit everywhere he went, was a show to ensure he was considered a highly respected man, a prominent figure. Not just in Netersel, but in the surrounding areas as well, he wanted people to see him as a kind of emissary from another world. The great exodus of wealthy city dwellers to countryside farmhouses had not yet begun. There was still a striking difference in lifestyle between the rich western Netherlands and the deep, dark south, especially in the towns along the old smuggling routes near the Belgian border, where he and Mimousse were living.

And in fact, things weren't going badly for my father. He'd leased two gas stations in Limburg from smaller companies that were primarily active on the German and Belgian borders. Occasionally, when one of the farm boys he'd hired to pump gas had to stay home to help out in the fields or stables, he'd stand behind the cash register or pump the gas himself; he didn't consider himself too good for that. And the customers loved having their tanks filled and windows cleaned by the gentleman who'd make all kinds of jokes in his bizarre, self-invented accent. Business was going quite well, and he was even able to set aside some money every month for their renovation plans.

But he was far from satisfied, let alone happy. His existence was much too marginal for that. His main goal in life was to get rich, and managing two gas stations in the countryside was definitely not the way to go about it. At their farmhouse in the evenings, he'd drown his troubles with alcohol, which only fed his spiteful contemplations. As the situation worsened, Mimousse fell into a state of silent despair.

After Granny's death in the fall of 1973, however, things changed. She left more than a million guilders to be distributed among her children, which amounted to a tidy two hundred thousand per child after taxes. Only, it would take a while to liquidate her assets. First, the family needed to sell the land and find a buyer for Ridderborn. They gladly left the job to their sister Jacquot.

The plucky widow from Bloemendaal was wary of Frans from the start. She stubbornly rejected his offers to help her avoid various inheritance taxes. Frans argued that he'd been to Belgium with Granny many times and had a good sense of the situation, but this just reinforced Jacquot's suspicions. With his drinking problem and megalomaniacal scheming, she considered him a far-from-reliable partner when it came to managing the family's estate. She preferred to consult Koos Wijkers, Dieuwke's husband, who lived less than a mile from her. Koos, a pragmatic chemist, took decisive action. He told Frans that he wouldn't be involved, and he'd have to wait and see how much Mimousse received.

Mimousse had no problem with this, but it really made my father's blood boil. The mood in Netersel became tenser by the month. When Ellen and I visited for Christmas and then for Easter, it was clear that my parents weren't communicating with each other the way they used to. There were—even in our presence—harsh accusations of betrayal (Frans to Mimousse: *Your whole family is against me, and you like it*) and petulant remarks (Mimousse to Frans: *You're drunk—I can't understand a word you're saying*). The distribution of Granny's inheritance had become a divisive element in their marriage.

There was nothing Ellen and I could do, and since I'd never played an active role in their relationship, they didn't expect anything from me, anyway. Looking back, I think they suppressed their heated arguments when Ellen was around, out of shame. Ellen came from a proper, intellectual family, and for the first time she saw firsthand the kind of domestic fighting that belonged on a talk show.

Things came to a head in 1976, when everyone had signed the notarial deeds and the settlement had been distributed. According to the Bloemendaal bastion, Mimousse was to receive a little more than two hundred thousand guilders, as were each of the other sisters. Koos informed the family that, as anticipated, the Belgian authorities had indeed taken a large percentage of the final sum. My father scoffed, "You see? You should have let me in on it. No Belgian official is going to make concessions to a bullheaded Calvinist like Koos. You know, I feel like I'm the one being cheated here."

In the end, life on the farm in Netersel became unbearable. "Why don't you go to Germany if you love it so much?" Mimousse shouted at him at the end of a long summer. Omi had been staying with them for two months, and with her deafness and all her reminiscing about Riga, she hadn't provided the distraction Mimousse had been hoping for; in her mother-in-law's eyes, Frans was still the war hero of thirty years ago, and no matter how often Mimousse shouted in her ear or wrote down her objections to Frans on a notepad, the old countess didn't respond. All she did was look at her daughter-in-law thoughtfully.

It was during this maelstrom of suspicion and icy contempt, compounded by the pain of lost love and downright greed, that my father received a telegram from Germany on September 16, 1976: "Birthday tomorrow. Must speak to you. Problems with Andrea. Cologne central station, 2pm OK? Karl."

The message came as a calling. Frans Münninghoff didn't hesitate; he packed his suitcase and left.

THIRTY-NINE

When he saw Karl Reinhard in the main hall of the central train station in Cologne, he hardly recognized him. It had been fifteen years since Frans had been forced by the German justice system to end his relationship with Claudia, and during that time Karl had seen little joy or prosperity—that much was visible. The cheerful face of the former ski instructor had grown tired and bitter; his clothes and shoes were clearly worn, which gave him a shabby appearance.

Naturally, Frans had heard about the departure of their shared femme fatale, just as he knew that she'd ended up in Stuttgart. One day my father had come home a bit earlier than usual—Mimousse was out walking with the spaniels on the heath—and found a letter in the mailbox. He immediately recognized Claudia's loopy schoolgirl handwriting on the envelope, which set off all kinds of alarms in his head. What did this woman want from him after all these years? He read through the calamitous litany, noted the address, and burned the letter.

That was five years ago. Andrea, who was nineteen, had gotten pregnant, Claudia wrote. Her daughter had had it with Karl and started dabbling in the Cologne art world. She'd gotten involved with a forty-five-year-old gallery owner, and that's how it happened.

"Understand that Andrea is a very attractive girl," Claudia wrote, "and she has no trouble attracting attention." At that, my father grinned. He didn't have a photo of her, but he had no trouble imagining it. It didn't matter whether he or Karl was her real father (he wasn't 100 percent sure); Claudia was the incarnation of beauty, and he and Karl weren't too bad themselves. But the fact that Andrea had gotten pregnant at such a young age made his self-appointed role as her guardian angel, which Claudia mentioned in her letter, more demanding. Nevertheless, he didn't have the money or means to help her.

He wrote back to Claudia and told her never to send another letter to his home address. He said if she or Andrea ever wished to contact him, they could address their letter to a PO box in The Hague; however, there was little he could do to help. Contrary to his expectations, the PO box remained empty. He never even learned the name of Andrea's child.

All of a sudden, my father found himself face-to-face with his old friend. He was struck by the lifeless look in Karl's eyes, but even after fifteen years, the man briefly lit up at the sight of his old friend. It was as if he momentarily forgot about all the misery with Claudia—of which Frans was very much aware—to make room for what they'd once shared: true, honest camaraderie. They went to a bar near the station and took a table in the corner. Frans ordered a round of beers. Karl laid his hand on his friend's forearm, a gesture of trust that Frans had no longer thought possible.

"I won't burden you with everything I've been through," Karl began. "You stole my wife, but she and I aren't innocent either. Apparently, we couldn't resist you, and I've learned to accept that. To be honest, I don't know what Claudia's situation is—we're not in touch anymore. But now we're facing the consequences."

His dark eyes became sharp and tense. Frans remembered that it was Karl's birthday, and insisted on making a toast, if only to ease the tension. But Karl was more focused than he'd ever seen him before. He ignored the gesture and continued. "You once said that you were Andrea's guardian angel. Believe it or not, Andrea clung to those words throughout her childhood. Now she's twenty-three. She lives in a hippie commune here in Cologne and has a child. The father is a gallery owner, a degenerate chump, if you ask me—the guy couldn't care less about the child he's brought into the world. That little girl is lucky if she sees her father twice a year. Andrea's daughter's name is Daniela—she's five now. I've seen her all of four times."

Karl suddenly let out such a deep, woeful sigh that Frans got nervous and ordered two more beers.

"But Andrea needs help," Karl continued. "She has no income and lives off of whatever those hippies she lives with can give her. It's the bare minimum, you understand? My beautiful, intelligent, artistic daughter is barely hanging on by a thread, living with her child in some squat in Cologne with a bunch of degenerates. I went there once, and I'm telling you, when you walk in the door, the smell of weed practically knocks you on the floor. Andrea wasn't there, so I asked where I might find her, but all I got were stupid, hostile answers. Nobody would help me. They all looked at me as if I were Hitler himself. I left and never went back. What little contact I have with her is by phone and postcards, but I'm not the one she wants to talk to. She wants you."

Karl took a breath, and my father interjected. "Listen, Karl," he said in a somewhat dramatic tone. "What I said about being Andrea's guardian angel still stands. I am going to do everything I can to protect her. This is a sacred matter to me, you know that. My financial options are pretty limited at the moment, but I'm expecting some money from my wife's inheritance pretty soon. Tell Andrea to contact me and everything will be fine—for Daniela too."

For a moment, Karl was silent, then he said: "I think you should go see her yourself. She's totally apathetic from all the drugs." Frans gave him a quizzical look, and Karl continued. "You know how things are nowadays. They start with marijuana and hash, and soon enough try something else, because, y'know, they can't think of anything more interesting to do with their time, and before you know it, they're doing lines of coke and spreading their legs for cash."

"Are you telling me that Andrea is a whore?" Frans cried in horror.

"No, not yet," Karl replied, struggling to hold back tears, "but she needs someone to help her get back on the right path. She can't do it on her own, and she won't let me help, and apparently I'll never mean anything to her anyway, neither as a father nor as some kind of rich uncle." For the first time in the conversation, Karl let out a chuckle, and his friend laughed awkwardly along with him. My father knew what he was getting at: that he ought to become Andrea's benefactor *and fast*.

Frans thought about how he should go about this. Although he hadn't made any explicit promises during that telephone conversation fifteen years ago, he knew what he'd said and that he'd meant it. And Andrea, who had been listening in on her mother and Frans's conversation, knew he meant it too. His soldier's honor prevented him from haggling over the terms, which meant that he'd have to take Andrea and Daniela under his wing at any cost. He thought of the two hundred thousand guilders on their way to Mimousse's bank account, and he believed that there was even more hidden in the murky financial swamp of Ridderborn. Mimousse declared that the money would all go to Michiel and any other children that we might have in the future. Michiel—he could barely get the ultra-Dutch-sounding name off his tongue. In a stubborn denial of the fact that our son was, in fact, Dutch, he'd started calling him Timofey. He liked the little guy, but if he had to choose . . .

Suddenly, my father was overwhelmed by the feeling that had always been latent in him, but which, in that particular moment, pulsed through his veins with unequivocal force: he was *not* a Dutchman, *god damn it*. He'd fought and risked his life for Germany. Karl was his comrade, one of many, and it didn't matter that he'd stolen his wife; these things happened, even among best friends. The point was that these were *his* people, these *German* people in this *German* city of Cologne, and they needed him. They had problems that he, *Franz* Münninghoff, could solve.

He looked up and into Karl's expectant, tear-filled eyes and declared: "Don't blame yourself. I'll handle everything. Take me to Andrea."

FORTY

It wasn't as bad as Karl had led him to believe. The taxi took the two former SS sergeants to a dilapidated building in Mülheim, halfway down
Berlinerstrasse. Karl said that he'd wait at a bar a bit farther up the road.
It would be better if Frans talked to Andrea alone, Karl said, because his
presence would surely set her off, and those hippies she was living with
wouldn't listen to him either. He was genuinely curious whether Frans,
who was wearing a necktie, could gain admission into their abject little
world. "Don't worry," Frans said, untying his tie and pulling it off. "I'm
good with young people. It's because I'm a rebel, but I don't have to
tell you that. They'll sense it immediately, just watch." And with that,
he walked up to the entrance of the "Meinhofburg" and knocked on
the door. The place was named after Ulrike Meinhof, head of the ter-
rorist Red Army Faction, who'd died in mysterious circumstances in a
Stuttgart prison a few months earlier.

An unshaven young man with wild hair stuck his head out the
window. "Who's there?" he snarled.

"I'm here to see Andrea and Daniela," my father replied. "Tell her
it's her guardian angel."

Those words seemed to do the trick—just as they had fifteen years
ago when he'd spoken to Andrea on the phone. Moments later, the
front door flew open, and the twenty-three-year-old girl flung her arms

around his neck. "You came!" Andrea whispered in his ear. "Please get us out of here."

"That's exactly what I came here to do," Frans said.

She led him up a bare staircase, and he couldn't help but compare her to her mother, Claudia. She had the same long legs and the same long blonde hair. But echoed in her eyes and mouth, he couldn't help but notice, were his own features, especially her big, dark brown eyes. They weren't pitch black and sparkling, like Karl's in his prime, nor were they radiant blue like Claudia's, but a velvety brown like his.

At the top of the stairs he saw Daniela, a frail five-year-old girl with braids, puttering around with four other kids in the squalor. The squatters had turned the once-beautiful turn-of-the-century house into a total dump—unmade cots, clothes scattered all over the place, piles of dirty dishes, and in the middle of it all were three men sitting at a table. They eyed Frans suspiciously. Andrea told him to wait there and rushed over to the oldest of the three, a somber-looking man of about forty with a gray beard and wool hat, and whispered something into his ear.

Frans wondered whether whispering into ears was her chosen method of communication—an absurd thought, but it made him smile.

"What's funny?" the man barked at him irritably. Without waiting for the uninvited guest to reply, the man turned to the other two and said in an accusatory tone, "Comrades, Andrea says that she wants to leave us. This man"—he made a disparaging gesture toward Frans—"is her uncle, and she wants to go with him."

"Do whatever you want, bitch," said the one who'd stuck his head out the window earlier. He looked at Andrea with hostility, which Frans immediately interpreted as the look of a man rejected; naturally he hadn't gotten her into bed, though probably every man in that house had wanted to, and maybe the women too. How had she managed to keep these good-for-nothing creeps off her? He wondered what had gone on in that house, and in front of little Daniela.

The third man, a burly thirtysomething wearing a headband with some kind of Chinese characters on it, a sleeveless denim jacket, camouflage pants, and black combat boots, let out a loud burp and started rolling a cigarette. "She can't just leave," he said after a while. "Andrea and her kid have been living here at our expense—or at least, I've never seen her pay for anything."

"But I did all the housework," Andrea said indignantly. "That's what we agreed three months ago?"

"Yeah, and look what a good job you've done," the guy with the headband retorted, gesturing at the chaos around them. "No way, missy. You've been living here on our dime, and now you want to run off with your sugar daddy because you think things will be better with him. What a worthless comrade you've turned out to be. What do you think, Herbert?" he asked the guy in the wool hat.

My father decided it was time to intervene. "I understand your predicament here," he started, but Herbert cut him off.

"Three hundred marks," he said curtly, staring at the ceiling.

"Excuse me?" my father asked in dismay.

Herbert looked at him as if he'd just given him a good idea. "You know, you're right. That's not very much for three months," he said with a malicious grin. "On second thought, we're going to need four hundred for our welfare fund. And if I were you, I'd say yes pretty quickly, old man, or this party's over."

Andrea, who'd just been downgraded from an activist to a commodity on the squatters' market, had something to say, but Frans silenced her with a determined gesture. "Get your clothes," he said, reaching for his wallet. Ten minutes later the three of them were out on the street; everything Andrea and Daniela owned fit into two duffel bags. In the chilly autumn light on that barren street, the mother and daughter's poverty was harrowing.

"Your father is waiting at a bar nearby," Frans began, but Andrea shook her head in defiance.

"I don't ever want to see that drunk again. Did you know that he beat my mother so badly she almost had to go to the hospital? It's that bastard's fault that I lost my mother—she couldn't bear him anymore." Her voice switched effortlessly from vicious to cajoling. "If it's all right with you, I'll go to a guesthouse on Hacketäuerstrasse around the corner. I know the landlady, and it's not expensive. I'll get us two rooms, one for you and one for me and Daniela. If you want to say goodbye to Karl, I'll wait for you there, and then we can discuss the situation. OK?"

Karl nodded approvingly when Frans walked in the bar and reported that the mission was accomplished. "It's a lot of money," he said, "and there's no way I can ever pay you back. Thanks a lot."

"Don't mention it," my father replied. "I see it as my duty—to you, to Claudia, and above all to Andrea and Daniela. I'm going to stay with them for a little while and make sure things get sorted out. I'm not rich, as you know, but I'm not poor either, and I've got some savings. Plus, I've got that inheritance coming. We'll see how that all works out. You know, Karl, you've got to take life as it comes. Things didn't work out between us the way they should have, damn women! But we don't have to let it come between us. Let me help in this phase of your lives. Come on, one more round."

After two more glasses of Doornkaat they said their goodbyes and even embraced before parting ways. Frans headed for the Salm guesthouse, where he collected the keys to his small single room. He picked up Andrea and Daniela in their cozy room and took them out to eat at a nearby Italian restaurant.

Karl took the tram back to his apartment on the other side of the city, staring out the window the entire trip, lost in his thoughts.

Andrea. He knew his daughter inside out—in the eight years since Claudia had left him, that little bitch had ruined his life with her endless whining and lying. She couldn't be trusted; he knew that from his own bitter experience. And she was a kleptomaniac. She was constantly stealing money, not just from him, but also at school. She stole from stores, from her friends' houses, and even a few times from the old Degenhardt garage on the pretense of coming to ask her father a question.

Of course, he understood this was because she'd been abruptly abandoned by her mother; no child can stand that kind of rejection. Claudia's departure had come as a shock to him as well, though he knew his violent drunken outbursts were most likely to blame. But still! What kind of mother walks out on her child like that?

He'd done the best he could with Andrea on his own, but the child had rejected him. She certainly had talents, drawing and painting, for example, and she was extremely bright. He'd even had her intelligence measured—an IQ of 132. Now that's something you don't see every day! But she never finished high school. Instead, she started hanging out with moronic lowlifes in one of Kiel's youth gangs.

She was a conniving little vixen, that he knew. Even when she was a child, he'd been surprised by how effortlessly she could turn on a flattering voice when she wanted something, and then explode into burning rage when she didn't get it. In recent years, she had grown increasingly bitter and provocative, and at times she was so challenging that he thought she wanted him to hit her, like he'd hit her mother. Fortunately, he'd always managed to restrain himself. But her accusations had become almost unbearable for him, particularly when she went after him in his weaker moments. In the evenings, he'd be sitting at the kitchen table brooding over the past with a drink in hand, and she'd start harassing him about his history with the SS. (*The way you hit my mother, you learned that while working in the camps, didn't you?*) As she got older, she raged against him more fiercely. He'd destroyed both her and her mother's life, and she would never forgive him. That was something he had to accept.

And Andrea was right—sort of. His drinking was most certainly to blame, but there was also the resentment. Justified resentment. And Frans Münninghoff was the source of that. Daring Frans, who'd turned out to be nothing but a dirty adulterer. He was an old comrade. He'd saved his life twice during the retreat from Russia, and Karl realized that these were the determining factors in their relationship, even now that the war was over.

The first time Frans saved his life was during a reconnaissance mission, when he chose a different observation point from the one their commander ordered; the two men watched with horror and relief as their assigned post was pummeled by a Russian howitzer. The second time was in the woods when, after a partisan attack, Karl found himself face-to-face with a young Russian blonde. Suddenly she had him pinned, her strong thighs wrapped around him, and she was just raising her bayonet to deliver the fatal blow when Frans shot her down. These are things you don't forget, but it didn't mean Frans Münninghoff could just have his wife! Or did it? The thought made him desperately unhappy.

All things considered, it came as a relief when Andrea turned eighteen and took off. But when he heard she'd gotten mixed up with a gang of drug addicts in Cologne and was pregnant by some wacky art dealer—which came as no surprise to him whatsoever—he was overwhelmed with fatherly instinct. Shortly after Degenhardt fired him, he went to try to find her. With his savings and severance bonus, he had just enough to rent a gloomy apartment in Cologne. All he really wanted was to not lose his only child forever.

But that, too, was a disaster. The first time he contacted her, she fought with him on the street in front of twenty of those lice-infested delinquents in combat suits—her new so-called friends—screaming at the top of her lungs that he was a motherfucking Nazi pig. She refused to let him visit her in the hospital after she gave birth, and in the years that followed, as he managed to scrape by doing odd jobs in Cologne, he saw his granddaughter, Daniela, all of four times. Each visit cost him two hundred marks, an amount that took him weeks to pull together.

On those occasions, he noticed that his feelings of paternal affection no longer existed. Andrea was a harsh, calculating, secretive, and malicious person. *It's no wonder she'd been born on Stalin's death day,* Karl thought. And she would be equally horrible to Frans Münninghoff. She would get him wrapped around her finger and use Daniela—in whom he already noticed some of the same ugly traits—as bait to squeeze out every last pfennig she could. He was their prey, and only after they'd completely sucked him dry would they let him go.

Was this revenge for losing Claudia? He didn't know. Maybe.

But what did it matter? He had handed over Andrea and Daniela, his last millstone, to Frans Münninghoff, the man he both hated and tolerated for so many years. He wondered why he hadn't just murdered him on the spot when he came home to find him with his wife. But that didn't matter anymore either. He savored the feeling of freedom that washed over him. No more responsibilities.

When he got home, he headed straight for the wardrobe and took his old Luger from the top shelf. The gun was wrapped in cotton rags and oilpaper; he unwrapped it and set it on the table. He stared at his trusted weapon with a tender gaze. After thirty years of faithful maintenance, the 9-mm pistol wouldn't fail him now. He tried to imagine what the kitchen would look like when the police, alerted by the neighbors, forced their way through the door. As he slid the smooth, cold barrel into his mouth, one final question ran through his mind: Was there anyone, maybe someone he had forgotten, to whom he mattered on his fifty-fifth birthday?

He shook his head, closed his eyes, and calmly squeezed the trigger.

FORTY-ONE

The man sitting beside me that morning in March 1979 in the front row of the St. Anthony and Brigid church in Netersel didn't look anything like the father I'd once known. He was wearing a morning jacket, unusual attire for a cremation ceremony at the time, especially in the Brabant countryside. He'd lost a tremendous amount of weight and dyed his hair a strange, orangey shade of blonde. He slid over silently when Ellen and I sat down. Only after the village priest began the service did he lean over to me and ask: "Are you going to say something?" His empty brown eyes looked indifferent. I could tell he'd been drinking.

Between us and the altar was a plain wooden casket with a few flowers on top. Inside lay Mimousse.

Behind us in the small sanctuary were thirty people at most, primarily farmers from Netersel and one family member, who'd come to pay their final respects to Marie-Louise Amédée Huberte Ghislaine Münninghoff-van Blaem, my stepmother, Mimousse. She'd passed away three days before, after one last miserable year living in a rented house in the village of Bladel. She'd sold the farm, which was in her name, after the doctor had given her the diagnosis: lung cancer—the result of all those years puffing away with Frans.

During the final months of her life, Frans had moved back in with her. To help her, he said. Mimousse was initially reluctant, but she gave in. Though the tension between them hadn't disappeared, she was happy to have someone to help with her daily tasks. And at first, he did. No one—Mimousse included—had any idea what he'd been up to for the last year and a half, and on the day of her funeral, no one cared. Ellen and I were already grieving: on March 4, two days before Mimousse passed away, our third child, Valentijn, had died. At twenty-eight weeks, he'd been born too early to survive, the doctors said. He lived twelve hours. This, after our second son, Sebastian, had succumbed to meningitis at one month old, was more than we could take.

We didn't receive condolences from any of my parents for the deaths of our two children, and we saw this as symptomatic of the family's current state: nobody really cared about each other. We attended Mimousse's funeral purely out of duty; beyond that, we were completely depleted.

My speech was no more than a few platitudes, sniffed out in a voice trembling with my own unrelated emotions. After the service was over, we filed into the parish hall, where we accepted the hesitant condolences of those in attendance before they retreated with my father to commemorate the deceased over jenever and beers. The sounds from that side of the room soon became increasingly cheerful as my father talked loudly in his fake Brabant accent. Two days later, on Sunday, my aunt Jacquot came to visit us in The Hague with one of her sons, who'd driven her down from Bloemendaal. We could tell by the look on her face that she had unpleasant news to deliver.

"I didn't say anything at the ceremony out of respect for Mimousse," she began, "but now I have to tell you something that I would've preferred not to. But you need to know for your future dealings with Frans."

Her blue eyes—she was the only one of the sisters to inherit father's blue eyes—were cold as she told us the story. Frans actually lifted a finger to help his wife after she could no longer take care of herself, and when Mimousse finally called her sister Jacquot, she was at her wit's end. Yvonne had died the year before, and Edith lived in New Zealand, so Jacquot was her only option. "She didn't want to burden you with it, Ellen being pregnant and all," she added. Jacquot went to stay with her sister in Bladel, so she could take care of her.

"Your father was getting letters from a woman," my aunt continued. "I could tell by the handwriting. I always got the mail because he spent most of the day at his gas stations, or God knows where. To avoid making things worse, I hid the letters from Mimousse. But after she'd gone upstairs to bed, I was alone with Frans, so one night I said something. That he shouldn't leave those letters lying around, which made him laugh. Mimousse didn't suspect anything, she was too sick, and moreover, she couldn't care less, she already despised him. He didn't care—he was so terribly cold and cynical."

Jacquot paused for a moment, letting the memory of those evenings sink in. They always ended in arguments, she said, and in the end, she would retreat to the guest room, and he would plop down in his new recliner in front of the television—invariably set to one of the German channels—and fall asleep.

"Well," she continued, "after a while, I started reading those letters. I mean, he left them lying around all over the place, and I was constantly trying to hide them from Mimousse. I even found a folder full of letters that had fallen behind the sideboard. They had all been sent to a PO box in Eindhoven, addressed to Herr Franz von Schumacher Münninghoff. They were from a woman in Cologne by the name of Andrea Reinhard. She wrote to him almost every week, usually to ask for money for her daughter, Daniela, who always needed something. That Andrea is a vulture, I'm telling you, Bully. She's got your father wrapped around her finger."

She took out a large envelope from her purse and passed it across to us. "I took a few of them. He won't even notice they're gone, he's so drunk. I think you should read them so that you can understand what's going on with your father."

Jacquot leaned back. Ellen got up to go make tea, a clear sign she didn't want anything to do with this. I opened the envelope, which contained about twenty letters, and started reading. With growing indignation, I saw how my father had been pulled into Andrea's web. All she had to do was say the word, and my father would send her cash. At first, this money was to help her pay for her apartment and to subsidize her daily expenses. But soon, Andrea got involved with an Englishman by the name of Richard Powell, whom she'd met at a party. Even after she unabashedly shared the details of her drug use, he kept sending her money. Two thousand marks for a clinical rehab program, five hundred for a painting course that Andrea absolutely had to take because it brought her "enlightenment"—*Now I know what kinds of images I need to paint to be happy*—one hundred marks a month for Daniela's ballet lessons, a six-week vacation in Florence where she, Daniela, and Richard (who was clearly benefiting from my father's generosity as well) could find their "calm." My father just kept on paying. My head was spinning. I didn't understand. Who is this Andrea—besides some artist–drug addict? His girlfriend?

I skimmed through some of the opening lines: *Bel Ami, Dear Angel Franciscus!, Dear, Dear Franz.* It had all the signs of a secret love affair. But I also saw lines like *Your "daughter" and friend. I hope your wife gets well soon, my dear father, Franz!*, and *Your crazy adopted daughter Andy*—she'd been going by Andy since she met Powell. The two of them seemed to have some kind of father-daughter relationship, though clearly a strange one. Was he being blackmailed? But how?

I looked up from the letters at Jacquot. "I don't understand," I said. "Besides the fact that my father is an idiot for sending money to her, I can't make heads or tails of it."

With a sad smile, my aunt took a school notebook out of her bag. "Andrea is not just an aspiring artist, apparently she has literary ambitions as well. She wrote a short story that explains the details of their relationship. You can read it later, it's all in there. But the short version is this," Jacquot continued. "Frans had a long-term affair with her mother in Limburg an der Lahn. She was married to one of his old war buddies, who eventually committed suicide. According to Andrea, this was mainly because Frans is her real father. Out of devotion to his comrade, whose life was destroyed by his adultery, he has taken Andrea under his wing. And I mean that literally—he calls himself her guardian angel, which is also the title of her story. If you ask me, your father has gotten caught up in a cruel psychological game with a woman who is exploiting his sense of guilt and need to be appreciated. Since he wasn't appreciated by you or Mimousse, he has taken on this glorious new role as father to Andrea and grandfather to her daughter."

I nodded and said, "I get it. But it's unbelievable. Andrea is my third half sister after Tatiana and Monika, only this time on my father's side. What do you call a half sibling out of wedlock? Never mind, it doesn't matter. But surely Frans can't go on like this forever? As far as I know, he doesn't earn very much, and it says here"—I riffled through the stack of letters—"that they need £38,000 to buy a house in Wimbledon, and they're counting on him to help them. I mean, that's not realistic, is it?"

Jacquot sighed again, this time with a tormented look. I had a feeling she wasn't telling me everything.

"Is there something else you'd like to tell me?" I asked.

She shook her head. "First try to come to terms with this," she said.

FORTY-TWO

The letters I found in my father's house in Bladel after his death in January 1990 show that he spent tens of thousands of guilders on Andrea over roughly four years. Although she led a reckless life, my father never stopped sending her money or tried to use the flow of funds as a motivation to get her back on the right path: "One thousand marks arrived just in time for my birthday," she wrote. "I'm completely euphoric!"

She did, in fact, move to Wimbledon, Richard's hometown. Daniela, who was ten by then, was dropped off at her great-grandparents' house in Odenthal near Cologne; the two kindhearted octogenarians never understood why their son committed suicide. They lovingly took Daniela into their home, no questions asked, and cared for her for many years to come. The £38,000 apartment was purchased, though Richard had to take out a loan for it. This was the first note of discord in their strange game: Andrea blamed my father for not having kept his promise. Whether or not he'd ever made such a promise, and on what terms, is uncertain.

In any case, my father made up for it—or tried to—by taking fifteen paintings from his private collection to England to be auctioned at Sotheby's. The customs forms also indicate that he took his old Renault 4, presumably so he could be more mobile in England. He checked into a hotel in Haslemere, a rustic town southwest of the capital. The auction in London was a flop: in the end, Frans made less than four thousand pounds, which he promptly gave to Andrea and Richard. They weren't happy. They'd taken out a considerable mortgage because Frans had promised, or at least given them the impression, that he would be making a substantial contribution. A bleak, miserable, desolate image emerges. Despite the fact that my father had kept his distance from us, my eyes filled with tears as I read the customs clearance papers for the paintings.

It turned out that Frans Münninghoff had another reason for not financing the flat in Wimbledon: he was planning to use Mimousse's money to start a pub in London and thought that his lovely Andrea could work there as a bartender, allowing him to keep a closer eye on her. I know exactly what he would have named the place: *Arshin*, an old Russian unit of measurement. How many times had he told me about this idea? It would be a bar where you could order vodka by the arshin, in other words, a yard stick with nine holes cut into it for shots of vodka. All you had to do was call for "an arshin of vodka," and the glasses would be topped off and you'd be on your way. Preferably, you'd have two friends with you because as the Russians say, *God loves a trinity!* Three men drinking together was my father's idea of a perfect evening; in his eyes, there was no better recipe for success.

And of course, he would make sure there were plenty of *zakuski*, traditional Russian appetizers like mushrooms, herring, caviar, or salmon on buckwheat pancakes with sour cream—Omi had taught him how to make all of them. And for hungrier guests, he'd whip up some beef stroganoff, chicken Kiev, borscht—like it was nothing! The way he talked you'd think there was no better chef on earth, but surely I already knew, having tasted his cooking myself over the years, he said.

In these moments I couldn't help but remember those Christmas Eves when he tried to roast a pheasant in the oven for twelve hours. He'd hover in the kitchen, basting constantly—"because that meat goes tough before you know it, and once it does, there's nothing you can do about it," he'd say to me pedantically. And sure enough, we'd find ourselves at the table gnawing on a sinewy piece of pheasant breast while the rest of the carcass remained in the kitchen because it was inedible. My father's naive sense of optimism had even obscured his image of himself in the kitchen.

I'm not sure whether Andrea knew any of this, but she made it clear that she would not, under any circumstances, be working behind a bar. Disillusioned after less than a month in London, Frans returned to Bladel. After that, however, the financial losses continued to pile up. Andrea began calling him things like Sir Francis, Francesi, and *old agony uncle*. Nevertheless, she managed to get more money to rent a painting studio. When he asked to see some of the fruits of her labor, she sent back a drawing of a cup and saucer—beginner's work—with the caption "Happy now?" She also needed an additional 250 guilders a month to pay for her theatre classes, which she said helped her fight her morning depression.

She doesn't seem to have stopped using drugs either. Her sentences rambled from one subject to another, and her demands became increasingly more explicit. When Richard broke his leg in a traffic accident at the Strand in London and ended up in the hospital for quite some time, she complained about how little help she got from British social security and demanded help from "Sir Francis." "You should send me something, after all those promises you made us. What is it with you, dear Francis? You wanted to buy me a car!" The letters only become pricklier from there.

The end finally came in the spring of 1983, when she called him drunk and high and went on for an hour about how he was nothing but a dirty Nazi and how he'd murdered her father. That crossed the line; she must've known that she'd passed the point of no return.

The next day my father wrote her a letter, the only one of his letters to her that I have a copy of. He states that he will no longer allow himself to be manipulated and dominated by her. Although he could accept that she had been under the influence when she called, he told her that, as long as she continued using, the Reinhard chapter of his life was closed. He added: "I want you to know that our friendship and closeness are sacred to me, and nothing will ever change that. But I am very sad."

A few more letters follow, the first of which is telling. Andrea invites Frans to come to Wimbledon and says, "Let's say one week. I'd start making plans soon if I were you. Write back with your answer. I give you 2 (two) weeks. Your Andrea." This was her ultimatum, but my father stood firm: he wouldn't go to Wimbledon, and he wouldn't send any more money. The last two letters that my father received from Andrea both arrived in 1985, and in a surreal way, both shed light on the situation.

In the first, she writes that Richard sold the apartment they bought for £38,000 for £82,000. The second is dated December 29, 1985, and written in English on Powell stationery. "Dear Sir Münninghoff! I will remind you that you still owe me the sum of thirty-eight thousand pounds. Best wishes, Andrea Reinhard."

This was the last time Frans ever heard from her.

FORTY-THREE

"You won't believe it, but I still have a mother living here," I said to my friend and travel partner Hendrik de Jong, editor of the *Volkskrant*. We were on our way home from an exciting three-week reporting trip through Hungary, Romania, and Yugoslavia, and had stopped at a rest stop near Würzburg for lunch. It was early December 1984, the Germans were getting ready for Christmas, and the hills of Lower Franconia were covered in snow.

Halfway through the trip, my mother-in-law had passed away, not unexpectedly, in a nursing home in Leiderdorp. I had managed to get a call through to Ellen from the Romanian countryside, and she relayed the sad news over the crackly phone line. "She'll be cremated the day after tomorrow. Your father said he'd come," my wife said. We agreed that there was no need for me to go to extreme lengths to get back in time. That day, I lit a candle for my mother-in-law at the cathedral of Tîrgu Mureş in Transylvania and talked about her at length with my colleague. Her life was characterized by tremendous love, care, and sacrifice as a mother, which she later extended to her grandson, Michiel, and Tessa, the daughter we adopted from Sri Lanka in 1981 when she was one month old. Hendrik had picked up on the pseudo-casualness of my remark and listened attentively for the next hour as I told him about Wera.

"So, you've only seen her once in the last thirty-three years," he summarized in a slightly bewildered tone. "Can you even still call her your mother?"

His question made me think. It goes without saying that being physically separated from your mother becomes more normal after adolescence. It's more important how the memory of a person settles in your mind. In that sense, my relationship with Wera was not good. Every time I thought about her—and I did often—I thought of all the things I blamed her for. Was that fair? Did I have to go on being angry at her for letting me go without a fight? Perhaps I was being melodramatic, but there was more to it than that, I noted bitterly. After we met fifteen years ago, my mother slipped back into her habitual silence. Even the death of two of her grandsons hadn't been enough to elicit a response. What kind of mother did that?

Hendrik saw it differently. "But there could be reasons why she simply couldn't bring herself to write to you. Perhaps she thought she'd become worthless? A human being is a human being, after all. She was dirt poor, you told me yourself; she knew she didn't have the money to come visit you. She had no means to give substance to her motherhood, and maybe she was ashamed of that. That's understandable, isn't it? She felt completely sidelined, and fifteen years ago, in this very city, you confirmed that for her with your distant behavior."

As usual, Hendrik didn't mince words, a quality I appreciated in him. But it didn't solve my problem. What was my mother to me, then? Would she forever be this inaccessible icon, silently watching me from a dark corner? Hendrik and I paid the bill and headed home to our families.

When I came home that evening, Ellen was waiting for me, her blue eyes wide as saucers. "You'll never guess who called today. Your mother! Wera! For the first time in fifteen years!" She burst into tears, and I did too. It was a hair-raising coincidence. We both had goose bumps. Wera had called our house at around one o'clock in the afternoon, exactly when Hendrik and I were talking about her over lunch near Würzburg.

What had she said after all the years of silence? Not much at first. Ellen immediately told her that her mother had just been cremated, and Wera responded dutifully—well, *dutifully* is perhaps too strong a word . . . The news made an impression on her, and she struggled to find the words. "We spoke Dutch. It was all completely unreal—she calls here after all this time, and suddenly finds herself right in the middle of a family tragedy."

But had Wera said anything else? How was she doing?

Better than ever, Ellen said. She was living in a decent apartment in a good neighborhood in Würzburg that the father of Tatiana's daughter, Dorothea, had bought for her. It sounded almost too good to be true. After Tatiana had finished her two-year prison sentence for drug trafficking, she managed, with tremendous discipline, to stay out of the criminal world she'd fallen into before. She got a job at an office supply store, where she met Hans Rakemann, who was blonde and German, through and through. Pretty soon, Tatiana was pregnant with his child.

Rakemann, a successful businessman who lived in a beautiful villa on the Main, had no problem with her having his child, but he didn't want to get married. He was a man who liked his freedom, who sailed the oceans, rode horses in the Argentinian pampas, and climbed mountains in the Himalayas. He wasn't interested in being stuck at home and chained to domestic life. At first, he did what many men in that situation do: he refused all responsibility. When Dorothea was born, in 1973, Hans Rakemann was nowhere to be found. Soon enough, Tatiana found herself in a situation as hopeless as her mother's. But Rakemann turned out to be from nobler stock. After ten years of remorse, he went looking for his child and found her in the dreary shed on the banks of the Main, where Tatiana had moved in with her mother. Rakemann decided to put an end to their misery once and for all. He bought a respectable apartment for his daughter Dorothea in Höchberg, a quiet middle-class suburb of Würzburg where many civil servants lived with their families. Her mother, Tatiana, could live there as well, and so could Wera and Monika, who'd since been abandoned by Siegfried Bauer. The four-room apartment was big enough for the four women, and on top of that, Rakemann provided them with a monthly allowance.

"She has a telephone now. We're going to restore contact, and in a few weeks, after we're back from our ski trip, we can go visit her," Ellen said excitedly.

She then told me how my father had behaved at her mother's cremation ceremony. "I have to say, he was a perfect gentleman. He wore his tailcoat the entire day. During the service he offered me his arm, and of course he made a big impression on all of Mama's old lady friends—you know how those women from the volunteer committee are. And when we got home and people started coming by to pay their respects, he went into the kitchen—still wearing that coat—and made sandwiches and served drinks. He didn't mingle much; he seemed happy helping in the kitchen, so I didn't interfere."

I thought back to the last time I had experienced my father up close. It was in 1982, when Omi died at ninety at the Red Cross hospital in The Hague. The last time the family was together, we were standing at her grave in St. John's churchyard in Laren: Xeno and Trees, Jimmy and Ellen Vogel (who Jimmy had married after Christine's early death), Titty, my father, and Ellen and me. There, too, my father had been the only person in tails, just as he had been at Mimousse's funeral and our wedding. He loved the ceremoniousness of it.

There was a time when all men wore morning coats for such occasions, but that had changed dramatically in the last fifteen years. Nevertheless, he'd stood in the kitchen, in 1984, making sandwiches in his formalwear and speaking to no one. The way I saw it, that jacket was his armor, and this was a silent display of his self-imposed Baltic loneliness and detachment from Dutch society.

FORTY-FOUR

It's strange how quickly we developed a normal relationship with Wera. In January 1985, we visited her for the first time in Würzburg after two weeks skiing in Switzerland. We had a lot of catching up to do, but our conversations remained focused on the future. I was being sent to Moscow to work as a correspondent for the Dutch broadcasting association AVRO, which meant our lives were about to change dramatically. "What does your father think of this?" Wera asked. I gave her a somber look and said that my father's opinion was not my concern. My mother just smiled and looked away.

Naturally we asked her to come visit us in The Hague. "The Hague has very bad memories of me, and I of it," she said. "But I'll definitely pay a visit some time and bring Dorothea," she said, tousling the blonde curls of her lovely twelve-year-old granddaughter.

What struck me about the renewed bond between my mother and me was the ease with which we became part of each other's lives. All the drama of our past, the war, the poverty, my abduction, the fact that we hadn't spoken for decades—after a few conversations all was forgiven and forgotten, swallowed, swept away. By what? Time, apparently. And our desire to move forward. My father also played a role in this. We saw Wera about four times before my father died. And in the late '80s, she made a confession.

"Oh, you know"—she usually spoke in Dutch, but for some reason she switched to German—"after Mimousse died, I asked your father if he wanted to continue his life with me."

"Jesus, Wera. It actually sounds like a great idea," I said. "What did he say?"

My mother gave me a look I'll never forget. In her eyes was all the love, insecurity, and despair that characterized her life with my father, the man she thought she'd been destined for. "He just laughed," she said, "and hung up the phone."

When my father finally died, on the morning of January 9, 1990, at home in Bladel, hardly anyone cared. He didn't want anyone to care. He died alone in his recliner, surrounded by twenty empty liquor bottles, the TV on the German channel with the volume turned all the way up so his deaf ears could hear it. The last person to see him was the manager of the local Asian takeout restaurant, who'd delivered his usual order of nasi goreng the night before.

I got a call from two local welfare cases, who'd been drinking with my father and listening to his stories for months. "He drank himself to death"—this was their honest opinion.

His church funeral was perhaps even soberer than Mimousse's had been twelve years prior. The only difference was that no one from Bladel or Netersel showed up at all. Even Wera didn't come, and I understood why.

It turned out that the music I'd requested, the *Grosser Zapfenstreich* march of the Prussian army, wasn't available in Bladel. I began my speech with the words "A difficult life has come to an end." I saw my aunt Ellen, next to Jimmy, nod in agreement, as did Xeno, Trees, and Titty's children (Titty had passed away in 1986). Contrary to habit, I hadn't put my thoughts on paper beforehand; I preferred to let my emotions direct the speech, though I don't know why anymore. Maybe

I felt I'd drifted too far away from him to say anything that would do him justice. I didn't get much further than a choked-up acknowledgment of how I could understand why, from his perspective, he'd joined the Waffen-SS, in 1940. After the ceremony, Jacquot approached me with a worried look on her face. She offered her condolences—which I accepted stoically, knowing full well that she and my father had been at odds over Granny's estate and Mimousse's care—and tucked an envelope into my jacket pocket.

"There was something I didn't tell you when Mimousse died," she said. "I think you noticed, but the moment passed, and sometimes it's better not to reveal everything at once."

Jacquot looked at me intently with her blue eyes. "The news would have made you rebellious, I think," she continued.

I stared in confusion. Rebellious? What did she mean?

She gave me a summary explanation and told me that all the details were in the envelope, along with corresponding documentation. In short, her mother had left one hundred thousand guilders to each of her children—money that had slipped under the radar of the Belgian tax authorities. Mimousse had requested that Jacquot place the money in an account where Frans couldn't touch it. The money, she said, was for her grandson, Michiel. Frans learned about it when, in one of their frequent disputes, Mimousse let it slip that she had stashed away a secret trust for her grandson. "*My* grandson," she screamed, a provocation that, much to her dismay, my father didn't even bother to correct. "My grandson isn't going to waste that money on hopeless projects like you do. My grandson isn't going to blow it all on trips to Germany, on whores and God knows what—I don't even care."

To which he replied: "You don't know what you're talking about. Why don't you go walk your dogs? But let me tell you something: that money is not Timofey's, it's ours. We're married, with community property, in case you've forgotten."

After that it was war. The fact that he would so bluntly torpedo her intentions came as a major eye-opener for Mimousse. Frans, her husband, whom she had always defended, had deteriorated into a money-lusting scam artist. She might be able to understand his behavior, in light of all of his deep-seated frustrations with his father and constant need to outdo him, but she couldn't accept it. With the help of Jacquot, who had witnessed many of these scenes, she went to extreme lengths to make sure that Frans wouldn't get a dime.

But in the end, my father still went after it. "Frans came to see me in Bloemendaal immediately after Mimousse died," Jacquot said. All of a sudden, her voice began to shake. "Your father blackmailed me. He threatened to report me to the Belgian tax authorities if I didn't hand over the money. There was nothing I could do, Bully. I had my own affairs to think about. So, I signed over authorization to him. The next day he went to Zurich to get the money."

I told Wera all this when she came to stay with us for a month after my father's cremation. As someone who'd loved him and longed to reunite with him, she deserved to know the truth.

She threw her hands over her eyes.

"Is it true?"

"I don't have any reason to believe that it isn't, Mom."

Wera took a deep breath and looked at me in a way that only she can.

"And even still, I loved him like no one else. That's true too."

I nodded. "Well, what do we do now? Forget everything?"

She nodded back. "Yes," she said. "We forget everything." I heard how adrift and utterly exhausted she was.

I put my arm around her, stroked her sweet, wet cheeks, and kissed her forehead. We sat next to each other on the couch like that for a long time, both lost in our own thoughts but our hearts beating together.

Wera Bauer, actually Wera Lemcke—but to me just Wera, my mother—died of cancer on July 11, 1999, at the age of seventy-eight. According to the humanist minister who led the funeral ceremony, she didn't want to be cremated because during the Second World War she'd been forced into a bomb shelter moments after giving birth, and nearly buried alive and caught in a fire. After this, the thought of being burned after death was a nightmare to her.

Her grave has become so overgrown with wild roses that you can barely read her name.

ABOUT THE AUTHOR

Photo © 2014 Willy Slingerland

Alexander Münninghoff was born in Posen, Poland, in 1944. A journalist and expert on Russia, he won the prize for newspaper journalism (a
Dutch Pulitzer), and is the author of *Tropical Years in Moscow*, about his
time as a correspondent in the Soviet Union. A passionate chess player,
Münninghoff wrote the biographies of Dutch chess grand master Jan
Hein Donner, and the chess master he dethroned, former world champion Max Euwe. In the anti-German postwar years and throughout
his career, Münninghoff never told his friends or colleagues about his
family, the complex chronology of which he reveals in his memoir, *The
Son and Heir*. The book went on to win the prestigious Libris History
Prize in 2015 and the Littéraire Witte Award in 2016.

ABOUT THE TRANSLATOR

Photo © 2018 Friso Gouwetor

Kristen Gehrman earned a master's in language science and communication with a specialization in literary translation from the University
of Lausanne, Switzerland. Originally from the United States, she now
lives in The Hague, where she works as a freelance translator, editor,
and teacher. In addition to Alexander Münninghoff's *The Son and Heir*,
her many translation credits include the Dutch-to-English translation
of Annejet van der Zijl's bestselling novel, *The Boy Between Worlds*. For
more information, visit www.kristengehrman.com.